1KBW on Enforcement in Financial Remedy Proceedings

1KBW on Enforcement in Financial Remedy Proceedings

Richard Harrison KC
Harry Oliver KC
Laura Moys
Charlotte Hartley
Thomas Dance
Max Turnell
Elle Tait

Bloomsbury Professional
LONDON • DUBLIN • EDINBURGH • NEW YORK • NEW DELHI • SYDNEY

BLOOMSBURY PROFESSIONAL
Bloomsbury Publishing Plc
50 Bedford Square, London, WC1B 3DP, UK
1385 Broadway, New York, NY 10018, USA
29 Earlsfort Terrace, Dublin 2, Ireland

British Library Cataloguing-in-Publication Data

A catalogue record for this book is available from the British Library.

ISBN: PB: 978 1 52652 254 2
Epdf: 978 1 52652 256 6
Epub: 978 1 52652 255 9

Typeset by Evolution Design and Digital (Kent)
Printed and bound by CPI Group (UK) Ltd, Croydon, CR0 4YY

To find out more about our authors and books visit www.bloomsburyprofessional.com. Here you will find extracts, author information, details of forthcoming events and the option to sign up for our newsletters

Preface

This book is intended to be a practical guide to the enforcement of orders made in financial remedy proceedings in England and Wales. The book is written from our perspective as specialist family law barristers and we have endeavoured to focus on practice and procedure wherever possible.

Few journeys begin without a clear destination in mind, and sound litigation strategy likewise requires anticipation of the final objective. We hope this book will serve as a useful and accessible guide to solicitors, barristers and judges engaged in all forms of financial remedy proceedings, not just after they have reached the enforcement stage, but perhaps from before they even begin.

We are indebted to many people who have supported us, individually and collectively, and who have shared with us the benefit of their own knowledge and experience over time. We would like in particular to recognise the contributions of Barry Singleton KC, James Turner KC and Charles Howard KC to this field of work, and to thank them for the opportunities they have given to many members of 1 King's Bench Walk to learn from their legal acumen and to be part of the law as it developed.

We would also like to thank the publishing team at Bloomsbury for their unfailing professionalism, patience and expertise.

RH, HO, LM, CH, TD, MT and ET
January 2023
1 King's Bench Walk

Contents

Table of Statutes

[All references are to paragraph numbers.]

Table of Statutory Instruments

[*All references are to paragraph numbers.*]

Table of EU and International Legislation

[*All references are to paragraph numbers.*]

Table of Cases

[*All references are to paragraph numbers.*]

CHAPTER 1

Introduction

1.01 In 279 BC, after winning the battle of Asculum, King Pyrrhus of Epirus is famously reported to have proclaimed that 'one such other victory would utterly undo [him]'. The victory had come at the cost of such devastating losses to his forces that its benefits were entirely negated.

1.02 The notion of a Pyrrhic victory is all too familiar to family lawyers. The law reports are littered with tales of litigants who – after incurring enormous legal fees – have obtained substantial awards from their spouses, only to find that the court order is worth little more than the paper on which it is printed.

1.03 As the Matrimonial Causes Act 1973 approaches its 50th anniversary, the enforcement of orders remains a significant problem with which family lawyers must grapple in a sizeable number of cases. It is important – in all cases – to consider questions of enforcement at the outset of the litigation and to devise an overall litigation strategy which pays heed to any problems which may be encountered further down the line.

1.04 Enforcement can present a particular problem in cases with an international dimension. The primary litigation may be proceeding in England and Wales, but if most of the assets are elsewhere the successful party will need to have recourse to the legal systems in other jurisdictions if the loser is determined to frustrate the court's decision.

1.05 Before Brexit, the enforcement of maintenance in intra-EU cases was governed by the Maintenance Regulation[1]. This regulation provided a streamlined and relatively straightforward means of ensuring that decisions about maintenance (which included financial remedy decisions based upon the principle of need[2]) made by a court in England and Wales would be enforced in other EU Member States. The Maintenance Regulation, along with other EU Regulations, ceased to have effect from 1 January 2021; it has not been replaced by any equivalent international instrument. By virtue of Article 67 of the Brexit Withdrawal Agreement[3], the provisions for recognition and enforcement under the Maintenance Regulation continue to apply in respect of orders made in proceedings which commenced on or before 31 December 2020.

1 Council Regulation (EC) No 4/2009 of 18 December 2008 on jurisdiction, applicable law, recognition and enforcement of decisions and cooperation in matters relating to maintenance obligations.

2 *Van den Boogaard v Laumen* (ECJ Case C-220/95) [1997] QB 759, [1997] 3 WLR 284, [1997] 3 FCR 493, [1997] 2 FLR 399.

3 Agreement on the withdrawal of the United Kingdom of Great Britain and Northern Ireland from the European Union and the European Atomic Energy Community.

1.06 The United Kingdom was formerly a contracting party to the 2007 Lugano Convention by virtue of its membership of the EU, the parties to which included all EU member states as well as Switzerland, Norway and Iceland. Since 1 January 2021 this is no longer the case. The mechanism for enforcement under the Convention is no longer available. The United Kingdom has sought to renegotiate becoming a party to the Lugano Convention as an independent state, but at the time of writing its attempt to secure party status has not been accepted.

1.07 For the majority of creditors needing to enforce a financial order, the first port of call is likely to be a general enforcement application under Family Procedure Rules 2010, Part 33. Under this procedure debtors are required to provide disclosure and answer questions about their financial means before the court determines which order, out of a menu of potential enforcement options, to make. We consider general enforcement and the specific orders that can be made under this procedure (attachment of earnings, third party debt orders, charging orders and stop notices) in **Chapter 2**.

1.08 The ability of the court to grant injunctions is an important weapon in the court's enforcement armoury. Where it is feared that a court may take steps to dispose of assets, it may be necessary to seek a freezing order. This jurisdiction is considered in **Chapter 7**. Search orders, obtained in a small minority of cases where there is evidence that a litigant will take steps to destroy relevant evidence, are addressed in **Chapter 8**. The court's ability to make mandatory orders requiring the direction or authorisation of third parties to take certain steps as an aid to enforcement is dealt with in **Chapter 6**.

1.09 Where a debtor refuses to provide disclosure or to comply with injunctions, it may be open to the creditor to seek to commit them to prison for contempt of court; a committal application can also be brought for breach of an undertaking. When a court makes a finding of contempt (which must be made to the criminal standard of proof), the contemnor can be sentenced to a term of imprisonment of up to two years. Committal proceedings are considered in **Chapter 3.** Sequestration, a remedy which enables the court to make orders for the confiscation of the property of the debtor, is also considered in **Chapter 3**. Ordinary committal proceedings cannot be brought to enforce an order for the payment of money. Where a debtor is in breach of a financial order, the judgment creditor may have the option of bringing a judgment summons, under which it is open to the court to commit the debtor to prison for up to six weeks if it is proved to the criminal standard that they have defaulted in an order while having the means to pay. The judgment summons procedure is considered in **Chapter 4**.

1.10 Enforcement issues may arise at an interim stage of proceedings if, for example, a litigant does not comply with an order for maintenance pending suit or for legal funding or otherwise refuses to engage in the process. The ability to restrict a contemnor's participation in proceedings by obtaining a '*Hadkinson*' order (or another related order) is addressed in **Chapter 5**.

1.11 Where a debtor has limited connections with England and Wales and is likely to evade enforcement by refusing to participate in proceedings, it may be necessary to apply for orders to restrict their ability to leave the jurisdiction or to seek assistance from the tipstaff in securing their attendance at court. These issues are considered at the conclusion of **Chapter 2**.

1.12 International cases can present particular enforcement difficulties, especially since post-Brexit the range of potential enforcement options in intra-EU and Lugano cases has now narrowed significantly. In cases where a creditor seeks to enforce an order in an overseas jurisdiction, it will usually be necessary for practitioners to obtain specialist advice in the jurisdiction in question. The enforcement of overseas orders in England and Wales is a complex topic. The means of enforcement will depend on the jurisdiction which made the original order and the nature of the order in question. Issues thrown up by international cases are considered in **Chapters 10** and **11**. The latter of these chapters addresses in detail the legislative minefield relevant to the enforcement of an overseas maintenance order.

1.13 Practitioners will often encounter cases in which recalcitrant litigants take steps to avoid enforcement by placing assets in the names of third parties. Such cases may require the court to set aside transactions. These issues are dealt with in **Chapter 7**. Assets held in trust (whether a genuine trust or a 'sham' trust) give rise to issues which are considered in **Chapter 9**.

1.14 The creation of the general enforcement procedure was a welcome step towards simplifying the enforcement process. Enforcement, however, remains a topic which is blighted by complexity. Financial remedy proceedings can be lengthy and gruelling. Having been through the process and obtained a judgment setting out their entitlement, it can be profoundly disheartening for a litigant to discover that the so-called 'final order' may simply mark the beginning of a new phase of the battle. By anticipating potential enforcement issues at the outset of litigation, it may be possible to take steps which prevent or at least mitigate some of the problems which are likely to arise (eg obtaining orders for the preservation of assets).

1.15 England and Wales is one of the most attractive jurisdictions in the world for economically weaker parties to pursue claims for financial remedies as a result of the perceived generosity of the English court. It must be recognised, however, that in cases where a respondent resides outside the jurisdiction and retains limited (or no) assets here, any orders which the English court makes, may well prove to be unenforceable. Litigants who are aware of this reality at the outset may well be better off accepting a lower settlement which their spouse is willing to pay than pursuing aggressive litigation over many years which ultimately produces no tangible benefit for them.

1.16 At the time of writing, the United Kingdom appears to be heading towards a period of recession involving high levels of inflation and potentially high interest rates. Should this happen, practitioners are likely to encounter an increasing number of cases involving the bankruptcy of one of the parties, company insolvency or steps being taken by creditors such as a mortgagee to recover assets from the parties. Issues of insolvency fall outside the scope of this book. Where such issues feature in a case, it is important that practitioners seek specialist advice as they may well have a significant impact on a party's ability to enforce a financial remedy order.

CHAPTER 2

General Enforcement and Related Remedies

Content at a glance:

A INTRODUCTION

2.01 This chapter addresses the steps most commonly taken when a debtor fails to comply with an order for the payment of money.

2.02 Previously, a creditor faced with such a default was obliged to select a specific enforcement remedy and to an issue an application for that specific form of enforcement. The disadvantage of the old system was that many creditors did not have specific up-to-date information as to the means of a debtor. The remedy they selected might prove to be fruitless if, for example, it later transpired that a targeted bank account had been denuded of funds. It was unfair that creditors in such circumstances should be in a position whereby they had to start again, issuing a further application targeting a different asset.

2.03 The obvious deficiency in the old system has been ameliorated by the creation of a procedure for 'general enforcement' of orders for the payment of money. Under this procedure a creditor has the option of selecting a specific method of enforcement but can also leave open the possibility of enforcement by any method which the court considers appropriate.

B GENERAL ENFORCEMENT OF ORDERS FOR THE PAYMENT OF MONEY

Scope

2.04 Where, in financial remedy proceedings, a respondent fails to comply with **an order for the payment of money**, Family Procedure Rules 2010 ('FPR 2010'), r 33.3 provides that 'except where a rule or practice direction otherwise requires' an application to enforce the order must be made by issuing a notice of application accompanied by a statement, verified by a statement of truth, which states the amount due under the order and shows how that amount is arrived at.

2.05 An order for the payment of money includes:

- An order for maintenance pending suit
- An order for periodical payments
- A lump sum order
- An order for costs: CPR, r 70.1(2)(d) as applied by FPR 2010, r 33.2
- An order requiring money to be paid into court: CPR, r 70.1(2)(d) as modified by FPR, r 33.2(a)
- Orders that have been registered for enforcement: CPR, r 70.1(c)

Application

2.06 The notice of application may either specify the method of enforcement sought or request 'an order for such method of enforcement as the court may consider appropriate' (FPR 2010, r 33(2)(b)). FPR 2010, r 33.2 incorporates (with slight modifications) the Civil Procedure Rules 1998 ('CPR 1998'), Part 70.

2.07 CPR 1998, r 70.2(2) allows a judgment creditor (except where an enactment, rule of practice direction provides otherwise) to use any available method of enforcement, and to use more than one method either at the same time or one after another.

2.08 It has become the usual practice not to specify a particular method of enforcement but to leave all options on the table by making what is called colloquially 'a General Enforcement Application'. It is important, however, for practitioners to note that the ability to make a General Enforcement Application is subject to the limitation in FPR 2010, r 33.3(1) identified above: 'Except where a rule or practice direction otherwise requires'.

2.09 Some enforcement remedies are governed by specific procedural rules which must be complied with. Although it may not always be necessary to issue a separate application for a particular remedy, merely ticking the 'General Enforcement' box on a form will not be sufficient to enable such remedies to be pursued. Practitioners need to ensure that the information required for particular types of remedy is provided to the court. See in particular:

- Applications for Third Party Debt Orders: CPR 1998, Part 72 and FPR 2010, r 2.33.24. The relevant procedure is considered at para 2.48 onwards.
- Applications for Charging Orders: FPR 2010, Part 40. The relevant procedure is considered at para 2.68 onwards.

2.10 An application for a Judgment Summons cannot be issued as part of a General Enforcement Application. The judgment summons procedure is considered in **Chapter 4**.

Procedure after issue

2.11 The issue of a General Enforcement Application will result in an order being made requiring the judgment debtor to attend court for the purposes of being questioned about their means: see FPR 2010, r 33.3(3). This process is – in effect – the same as what used to be known as the procedure for 'Oral Examination' under CPR 1998, Part 71. This is considered further at **2.15** onwards.

2.12 FPR 2010, r 33.3(3) provides that CPR 1998, r 71.2(6) and (7) will apply as though the application had been issued under that rule. CPR 1998, r 71.2(6) requires the debtor served with an order issued under that rule:

(a) to attend court at the specified time and place;

(b) to produce at court documents in his control described in the order; and

(c) to answer on oath such questions as the court may require.

2.13 By virtue of CPR 1998, r 71.2(7) the order issued will be endorsed with a penal notice and thus a failure to comply may result in committal proceedings.

2.14 It is unclear whether, apart from CPR 1998, r 71.2(6) and (7), the remainder of CPR Part 71 applies to General Enforcement Applications under FPR 2010, r 33.3(2)(b). FPR 2010, r 33.23(1) – which incorporates the possibility of making a freestanding application for an Oral Examination into the FPR – applies with a small modification the whole of CPR Part 71 to 'proceedings under this Part'. It is arguable, however, that this does not apply to a situation where a person is summoned to court to answer questions as part of a General Enforcement Applications (as opposed to a freestanding application for Oral Examination) because otherwise FPR 2010, r 33.3(3) would be otiose. This ambiguity is confusing and unhelpful; it is difficult to understand why different rules should govern what are in practice almost identical procedures requiring a person to attend court and be questioned.

C ORAL EXAMINATION

Application

2.15 CPR 1998, Part 71 is headed 'Orders to Obtain Information from Judgment Debtors'; it replaced the procedure under RSC Order 48 which used to be known as 'Oral Examination'. FPR 2010, r 33.23 applies CPR 1998, Part 71 to family proceedings with modifications relating to where proceedings must be issued:

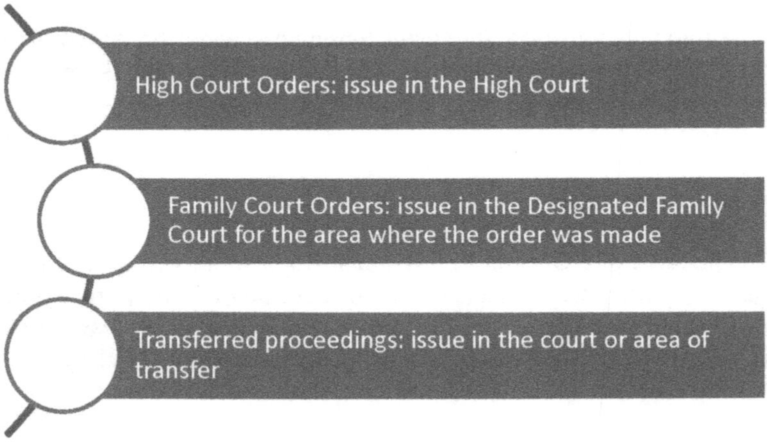

2.16 A Part 71 application may be made without notice (CPR 1998, r 71.2(2)(a)) and must be in the form and contain the information required by CPR 1998, PD71. The order to attend for questioning can be issued by a court officer without a hearing: CPR 1998, r 71.2(4).

2.17 There is no obvious advantage in issuing a freestanding application for an Oral Examination under CPR Part 71 as opposed to a General Enforcement Application under FPR 2010, r 33.3 where the judgment to be enforced is for the payment of money. The advantage of a General Enforcement Application is that the court can, in addition to requiring the debtor to answer questions and provide information, make enforcement orders as part of the same process.

2.18 The procedure under CPR 1998, Part 71 is not confined to orders for the payment of money and applies to the enforcement of any judgment or order. Under CPR 1998, r 71.2 the judgment debtor can be ordered to provide information about their means or 'any other matter about which information is needed to enforce a judgment or order'.

Procedure after issue

2.19 A debtor must produce at court such documents described in the order as are in his 'control': CPR 1998, r 71.2(6)(b). It is open to the court to adjourn the hearing and require the production of further documents at the adjourned hearing: CPR 1998, r 71.1.

2.20 In *Mubarak v Mubarak*[1], Hughes J described the obligation to produce documents in the following terms:

Key citation: *Mubarak v Mubarak*[2]

> 'Whilst the obligation on the judgment debtor to produce books or documents is necessarily ancillary to the process of examination and not independent of it, that does not mean that it is anything other than an important and often vital part of the process. It is a significant tool in the enforcement of the court's order in relation to which, ex hypothesi, the judgment debtor is in default.'

2.21 The expression control is defined in CPR 1998, r 31.8 and encompasses:

(a) Documents in a person's possession;

(b) Documents in relation to which a person has a right to possession;

(c) Documents of which a person has a right to inspect or of which they have a right to take copies.

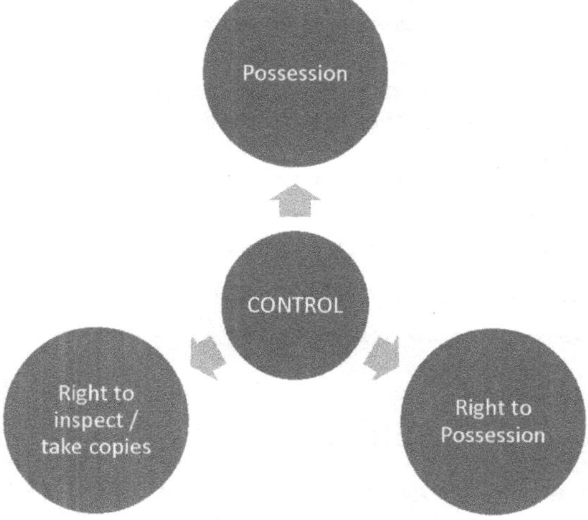

1 [2002] EWHC 2171 (Fam), [2003] 2 FLR 553.
2 [2002] EWHC 2171 (Fam), [2003] 2 FLR 553.

2.22 Where an individual is required to produce documents, the relevant right to inspect must be in his individual capacity, not qua company director or agent[3]. Where a one-person company is merely that person's alter ego, documents in their custody or power qua director may be considered to be in their possession personally[4].

2.23 A holding company does not have the right to inspect the accounts of its subsidiaries[5]. Similarly, a creditor of a company does not have that right[6].

2.24 It has been held that a party cannot be ordered, in this context, to 'use their best endeavours' to produce documents which they cannot otherwise be ordered to produce[7].

Service

2.25 An order to attend court for questioning must, unless the court otherwise directs, be served personally not less than 14 days before the hearing: CPR 1998, r 71.3(1). The judgment creditor is obliged to inform the court not less than seven days before the hearing if they have been unable to serve the order: CPR 1998, r 71.3(2).

2.26 The judgment debtor may, within seven days of service, make a request for reasonable travel expenses which must be paid by the judgment creditor if requested: CPR 1998, r 71.4.

2.27 The judgment creditor must at least two days in advance or at the hearing file an affidavit from the person who served the order providing details of service. The affidavit must[8]:

State that no request has been made for travel expenses

OR

Confirm compliance with a request for travel expenses

AND

State how much of the debt remains unpaid

3 *Mubarak v Mubarak* [2002] EWHC 2171 (Fam), [2003] 2 FLR 553; *B v B (Matrimonial Proceedings: Discovery)* [1978] 3 WLR 624.
4 *Lonrho Ltd and Another v Shell Petroleum Co Ltd* [1980] QB 358, [1980] 2 WLR 367.
5 *Lonrho Ltd and Another v Shell Petroleum Co Ltd* [1980] QB 358, [1980] 2 WLR 367.
6 *Mubarak v Mubarak* [2002] EWHC 2171 (Fam), [2003] 2 FLR 553.
7 *Dubai Bank v Galadari and others* [1990] Ch 98, [1989] 3 WLR 1044; *Mubarak v Mubarak* [2003] 2 FLR 553, [2002] EWHC 2171 (Fam).
8 CPR 1998, r 70.5.

Conduct of the hearing

2.28 CPR 1998, r 70.5 provides that the debtor will be questioned on oath by a court officer unless the court has ordered the hearing to take place before a judge. CPR 1998, PD71, para 2.2 provides that the hearing will only take place before the judge if the judge decides there are compelling reasons for this.

2.29 If the hearing is before a court officer the creditor or his representative *may* attend and ask questions. The court officer will ask a standard series of questions which may be supplemented by questions from the judgment creditor: CPR 1998, PD71, paras 4.1–4.2. If the hearing is before a judge the creditor or his representative *must* attend and conduct the questioning. There are no standard questions for hearing which take place before a judge: CPR 1998, PD71, para 5.1.

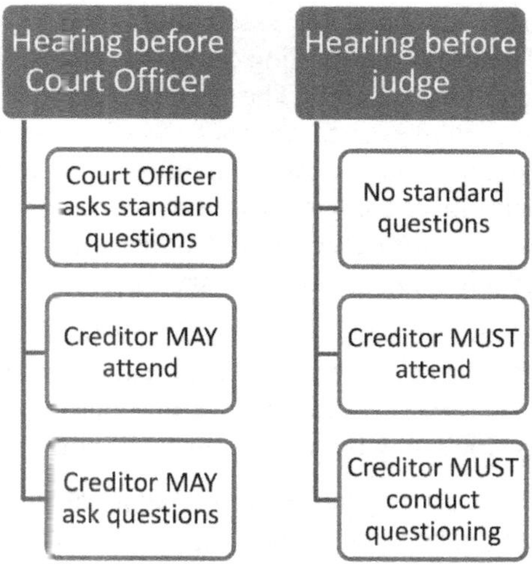

Failure to attend

2.30 If a judgment debtor served with an order under CPR 1998, r 71.2 fails to attend court, or attends but refuses to take the oath or answer questions, or otherwise fails to comply with the order, CPR 1998, r 71.8 provides for the matter to be referred to a judge who may then make a committal order provided that the judgment creditor has complied with the rules requiring conduct money to be provided and affidavits to be filed (CPR 1998, rr 71.4 and 71.5). A committal order made under this rule will be suspended on terms that the debtor attends a further hearing and complies with the original order and any new order made: CPR 1998, r 71.8(4); see *Broomleigh Housing Association Ltd v Okonkwo*[9] for guidance as to the circumstances in which a suspended committal order should be made under this procedure.

9 [2010] EWCA Civ 1113, [2011] C.P. Rep. 4.

Case summary: *Broomleigh Housing Association Ltd v Okonkwo*[10]

Facts:

The appellant was a tenant of the respondent housing association. The respondent had brought three claims for possession against him, each withdrawn on the basis of orders for costs none of which had been paid. The association therefore obtained an order that the appellant attend for questioning. The papers were not served on him. There followed a series of hearings which the appellant did not attend. On 11 December 2006 an order was made committing him to prison, suspended on terms he attended court at the next hearing on 13 March 2007 (which hearing was then adjourned).

After several aborted hearings, the association obtained an order for the appellant to attend court for questioning on 26 November 2007. He attended, but the questioning did not proceed. The appellant asserted that he had given a letter to the officer who was to conduct the questioning stating that he needed more time to complete the financial information required of him. The following day a court officer completed a form recording that he had 'refused' to answer questions. A further committal order was made, suspended on terms that he attend a hearing on 21 February 2008.

The appellant was not served and did not attend that hearing. Further suspended committal orders were made at subsequent hearings which he did not attend, having not been served. He was eventually served and attended a hearing on 5 May 2009, at which the committal orders were discharged.

The appellant brought the appeal as he was concerned about the effect on his reputation of having been made the subject of various committal orders.

Held by the Court of Appeal:

The making of a committal order following a failure to attend court or some other default should not be a matter of routine. The court must be satisfied that any default is intentional. If a case is referred to a judge under CPR 1998, r 71.8 after a debtor fails to attend court for questioning (or fails to answer questions), the court has the following options:

a If there is sufficient evidence to justify a finding to the criminal standard that the default was intentional the judge can make a suspended committal order. Written reasons must be provided.

b If not so satisfied, the judge can adjourn consideration of the making of a suspended committal order and give directions, including for a hearing.

c The judge can decide not to make a committal order and make a further order for the debtor's attendance to provide information to the court.

10 [2010] EWCA Civ 1113, [2011] C.P. Rep. 4.

2.31 A breach of the terms of a suspended order made lead to an immediate warrant of committal being issued: CPR 1998, PD71, paras 8.1 to 8.6.

D ATTACHMENT OF EARNINGS

2.32 The power to make an attachment of earnings order ('AEO') arises under the Attachment of Earnings Act 1971 ('AEA 1971').

Scope

2.33 The High Court can make an AEO to secure payments under a High Court maintenance order: AEA 1971, s 1; FPR 2010, rr 39.1(2) and 39.21. The family court can make one to secure payment under either a High Court or Family Court maintenance order: AEA 1971 s 1; FPR 2010, rr 39.1(1) and 39.4.

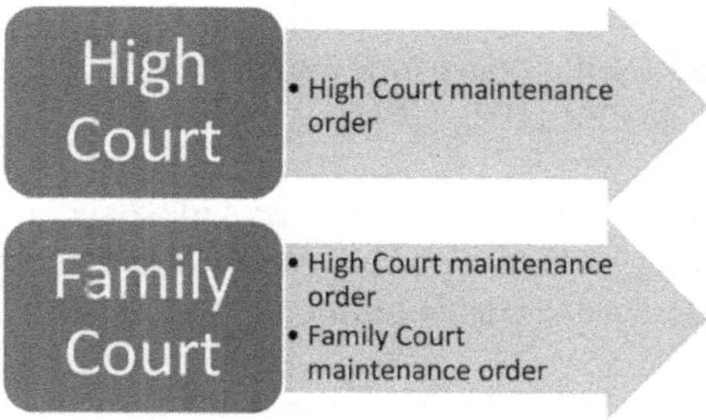

2.34 The types of maintenance order to which AEA 1971 applies are set out in Sch 1 to the Act. The schedule is fairly lengthy. It includes:

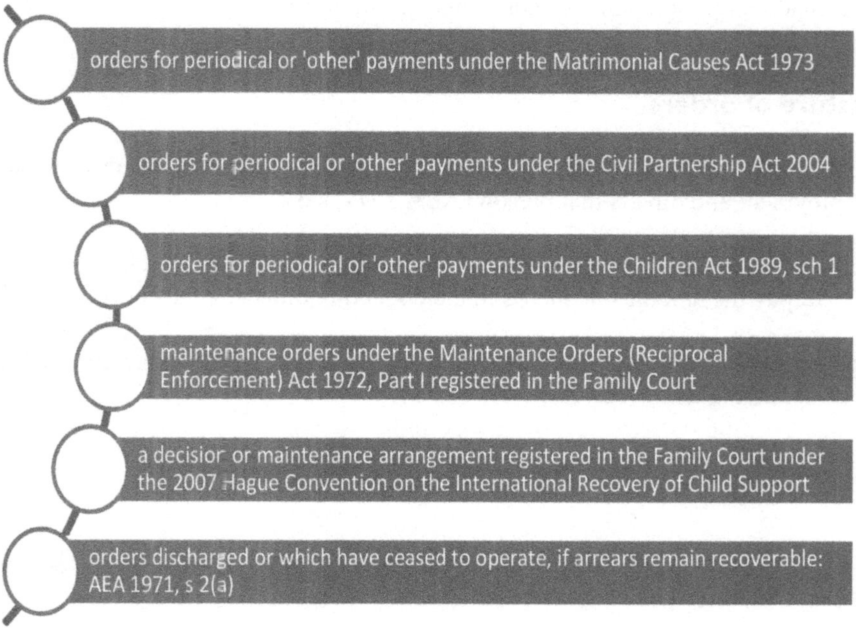

'Other' payments can include lump sum orders and other orders for the payment of money.

Application

2.35 An application for an AEO may be made by the judgment creditor or, in certain circumstances, the debtor or an officer of the court: AEA 1971, s 3.

2.36 Save where an order is sought on the making or variation of a periodical payments order, a creditor must file:

- an enforcement application under FPR 2010, r 33.2;

  together with

- a copy of the sealed maintenance order: FPR 2010, r 39.5.

These must be served by the court in accordance with the rules of service in FPR 2010, Part 6, Ch 3: FPR 2010, r 39.6.

2.37 The court can require the debtor to provide a statement identifying his employer and providing particulars of his earnings and anticipated earnings as well as specified particulars to enable him to be identified by his employer.

2.38 The court can also order a person who appears to be the debtor's employer to provide a statement with particulars of the debtor's earnings and anticipated earnings: see AEA 1971, s 14. Where an AEO is in force the debtor is obliged to notify the court of any change in employment within seven days and to provide relevant details of such a change: AEA 1971, s 15.

Nature of orders

2.39 An AEO is an order directed to a person who has the debtor in their employment and directs that person (AEA 1971, s 6):

(a) To make periodical deductions to the person's earnings; and

(b) To pay the amounts deducted to the collecting officer of the court.

The collecting officer will then forward the payments to the judgment creditor after deducting court fees: AEA 1971, s 24.

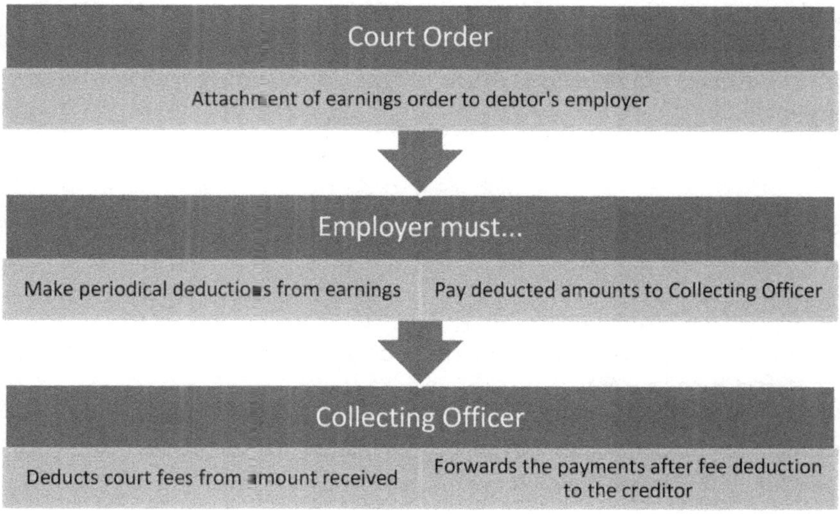

2.40 AEA 1971, s 6(5) requires the order to identify:

(a) The 'normal deduction rate' – the sum considered reasonable for the debtor to pay periodically; and

(b) The 'protected earnings rate' – the level of earnings below which, having regards to the debtor's resources and needs, the court thinks it reasonable that his earnings should not be reduced.

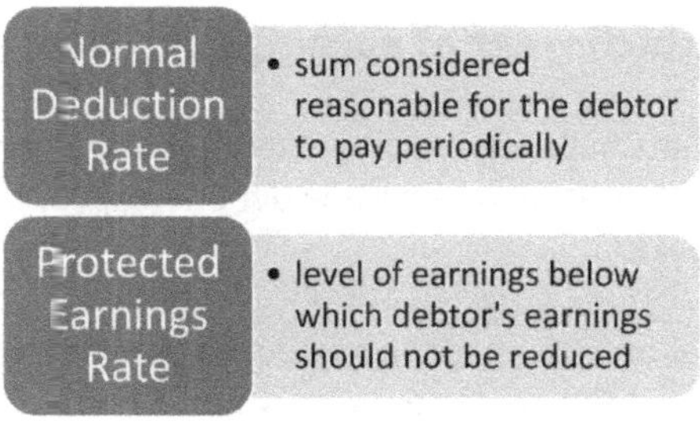

2.41 The scheme of deductions is set out in AEA 1971, Sch 3, Part I. In essence the debtor's net income (gross income after tax, NI and pension contributions) are 'attachable earnings'. The employer must pay to the court officer the 'normal deduction' from the debtor's attachable earnings only to the extent that these exceed 'protected earnings'.

2.42 AEA 1971, Sch 3, Part I contains provisions for cases where more than one AEO has been made in favour of different creditors. The general rule is that AEOs should be satisfied in order of the date upon which they were made: see AEA 1971, Sch 3, para 7 and the exceptions in para 8.

Earnings

2.43 Earnings are defined in AEA 1971, s 24 as sums payable as wages or salary including:

- Fees;
- Bonus;
- Commission;
- Overtime;
- Other emoluments payable under a contact of service (as distinct from a contract for services).

They also include pension payments, payments to compensate for loss of employment or office and statutory sick pay.

2.44 AEA 1971, s 24(2) lists payments that are not treated as earnings. These include the following:

- Payments made to a member of the armed forces (with limited exceptions);
- Tax credits;
- Social security payments including pensions;
- Guaranteed minimum pensions.

Committal and attachment of earnings

2.45 Where the court makes an AEO it cannot make a committal order (eg on a judgment summons[11]) relating to the same debt in respect of proceedings begun before the date of the AEO.

2.46 If a committal order is made in respect of proceedings begun subsequent to the date of AEO, the AEO comes to an end: see AEA 1971, s 8.

2.47 AEA 1971, s 23 contains provisions which allow the court to commit[12] a debtor to prison for up to 14 days in circumstances where, having failed to attend court on an application for an AEO, they then fail to attend an adjourned hearing or do attend but refuse to be sworn or give evidence.

11 For judgment summonses see **Chapter 4**.
12 For committal proceedings generally see **Chapter 3**.

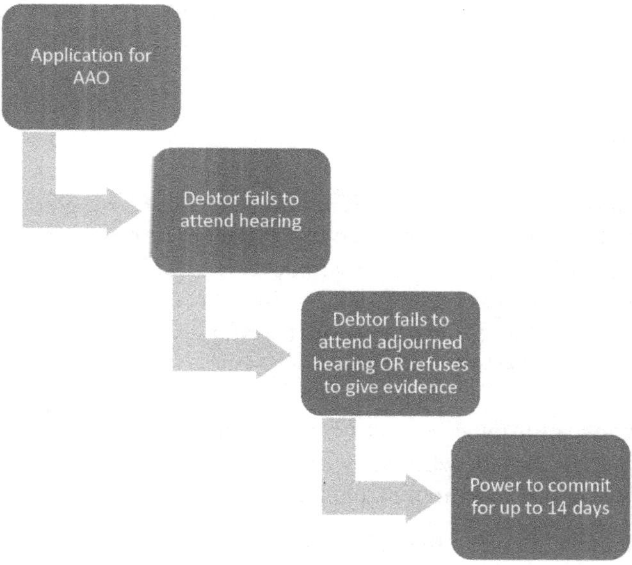

E THIRD PARTY DEBT ORDERS

General

2.48 A third party debt order used to be known as 'a garnishee order'. It is an order for the payment of money to the judgment creditor by a third party who owes money to or holds money for the debtor: CPR 1998, r 72.1(1). FPR 2010, r 33.24 applies (with minor modifications) CPR 1998, Part 72 to applications for a third party debt order made to enforce financial remedy orders.

2.49 Applications under CPR 1998, Part 72 apply to cases involving third parties within the jurisdiction: CPR 1998, r 72.1. A court cannot make an order in respect of a foreign debt unless compliance with the order would be recognised as discharging the debt under the law which governs the debt[13].

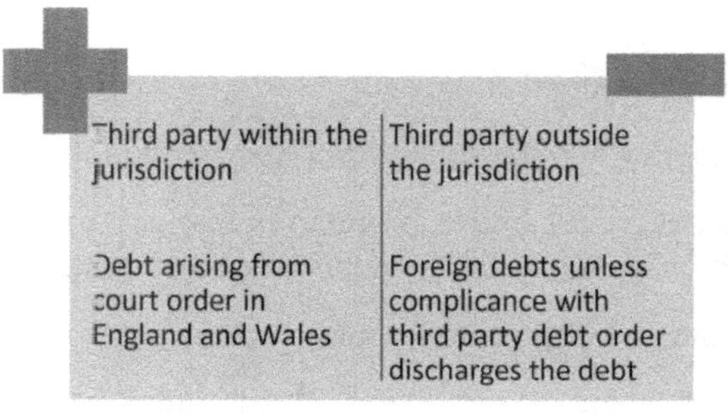

13 *Société Eram Shipping Co Ltd v Compagnie Internationale de Navigation* [2003] UKHL 30, [2004] 1 AC 260, [2003] 3 WLR 21.

2.50 The application must relate to 'a debt' and not, for example, a cause of action.

Application

2.51 An application may be made without notice: CPR 1998, r 72.3(1)(a). It must be made in the court that made the judgment or order being enforced or to the Designated Family Court area within which the judgment or order being enforced was made (unless the proceedings have been transferred, in which case it must be made to the court or area of transfer): CPR 1998, r 72.3(1)(b) as amended by FPR 33.24(1A).

2.52 An application must be in the Form and contain the information prescribed by CPR 1998, PD72 and be verified by a statement of truth: CPR 1998, r 72.3(2). PD 72 para 1.2 requires the application notice to contain specified information:

(1) the name and address of the judgment debtor;

(2) details of the judgment or order sought to be enforced;

(3) the amount of money remaining due under the judgment or order;

(4) if the judgment debt is payable by instalments, the amount of any instalments which have fallen due and remain unpaid;

(5) the name and address of the third party;

(6) if the third party is a bank or building society–

 (a) its name and the address of the branch at which the judgment debtor's account is believed to be held; and

 (b) the account number;

 or, if the judgment creditor does not know all or part of this information, that fact;

(7) confirmation that to the best of the judgment creditor's knowledge or belief the third party–

 (a) is within the jurisdiction; and

 (b) owes money to or holds money to the credit of the judgment debtor;

(8) if the judgment creditor knows or believes that any person other than the judgment debtor has any claim to the money owed by the third party–

 (a) his name and (if known) his address; and

 (b) such information as is known to the judgment creditor about his claim;

(9) details of any other applications for third party debt orders issued by the judgment creditor in respect of the same judgment debt; and

(10) the sources or grounds of the judgment creditor's knowledge or belief of the matters referred to in (7), (8) and (9).

2.53 Practitioners should, within the application form, provide a calculation showing how the amount of money that remains owing is arrived at.

Interim orders

2.54 An application will initially be dealt with by the court without a hearing: CPR 1998, r 72.4(1). The court may at this stage make an interim third party debt order.

2.55 When the court makes an interim third party debt order it must fix a hearing date not less than 28 days after the date of the interim order. The order will direct that pending the hearing the third party must not make any payment which reduces the amount owing to the judgment debtor to less than the amount specified in the order: CPR 1998, r 72.4(2) and (5).

2.56 The amount the third party must retain will be specified in the interim order and comprise the total of:

- the remaining amount owed to the judgment creditor; and
- an amount for the fixed costs of the application: CPR 1998, r 72.4(3). The fixed costs are a maximum of £98.50: see CPR 1998, PD 72, para 2 and the table at CPR 1998, r 45.8.

Service

2.57 An interim third party debt order becomes binding on the third party once served.

2.58 The interim order, application notice and documents filed in support must be served on the third party not less than 21 days before the hearing: CPR 1998, r 72.5(1)(a). They must then be served on the debtor not less than seven days after service on the third party and at least seven days before the hearing: CPR 1998, r 72.5(1)(b). If served by the creditor, they must either file a certificate of service not less than two days before the hearing or produce a certificate at the hearing: CPR 1998, r 72.5(2).

2.59 A bank or building society served with an interim order is obliged to conduct a search and identify all accounts held by the debtor: CPR 1998, r 72.6. This obligation only extends accounts in the debtor's sole name (not joint accounts, save in cases involving joint debtors where the account is in the joint names of the joint debtors): CPR1998, PD 72, paras 3.1 and 3.2.

2.60 Within seven days of service the bank or building society must provide specified particulars to the court and the creditor for each account disclosed including the account number, whether the balance is sufficient to cover the amount specified in the order, and – if it is insufficient – the balance; it must also provide details of any right of set off claimed: CPR 1998, r 72.6. The bank or building society must also inform the court and creditor if it does not hold an account for the debtor or if it is unable to comply with the order for another reason: CPR 1998, r 72.6(3).

2.61 A third party other than a bank or building society must notify the court and creditor within seven days of service if they claim not to owe money to the debtor or to owe less than the amount specified in the order: CPR 1998, r 72.6(4).

Hardship payment order

2.62 A debtor who is an individual and is prevented from withdrawing money from his account with a bank or building society can apply for 'a hardship payment order' if they or their family is suffering hardship in meeting ordinary living expenses as a result: CPR 1998, r 72.7.

2.63 Such an order enables specified payments to be made out of the account. For an example of an application which was refused, see *BM-Bank JSC v Chernyakov*[14].

Return date and final order

2.64 If either the debtor or the third party objects to the order sought they must file and serve evidence setting out the grounds of objection: CPR 1998, r 72.8.

2.65 If it is asserted that another person has a claim to the money this must be set out in evidence: CPR 1998, r 72.8. If the court is notified of such a person it will serve upon them notice of the application and the hearing.

2.66 If the judgment creditor wishes to dispute an assertion that the third party does not owe money to the debtor (or owes less than the amount of the debt) the creditor must file and serve evidence setting out the grounds on which they dispute this: CPR 1998, r 72.8.

2.67 At the return date of an application the court can: (a) make a final order; (b) discharge the interim order; (c) decide issues in dispute; or (d) direct a trial and give directions: CPR 1998, r 72.8(6).

14 [2016] EWHC 3820 (Comm).

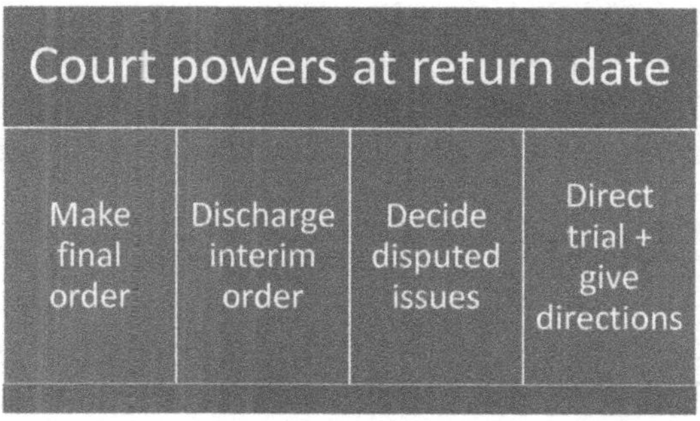

F CHARGING ORDERS

Scope

2.68 The jurisdiction to make a charging order derives from the Charging Orders Act 1979 ('COA 1979'). COA 1979, s 1 provides that where a debtor is required by a court order to pay a sum of money to another person, a court can impose a charge on property of the debtor to secure:

- Money that is due under the order;
- Money that may become due under the order.

2.69 COA 1979, s 1(7) makes it clear that an order can be made when there has been no breach of a requirement to pay by instalments, although the absence of a breach is a matter that the court must take into account in deciding whether to make the order (COA 1979, s 1(8)).

2.70 A charging order can only be made in respect of an order to pay a sum of money, not for example an order to transfer property such as a chattel.

2.71 A charging order can only be made in respect of costs when those costs have been assessed: *Magiera v Magiera*[15].

2.72 The order being enforced must be an order 'to pay money to another person'. Thus, there is no jurisdiction to make a charging order in respect of a settlement of property order which does not fulfil that condition. In *Re N (A Child) (Payments for the Benefit of Child)*[16], Munby J refused for that reason to make a charging order to secure a father's obligation under Children Act 1989, Sch 1 to settle money on the mother for the benefit of a child (for the purposes of buying a home).

15 [2016] EWCA Civ 1292, [2017] Fam 327, [2017] 3 WLR 41, [2017] 1 FLR 1131.
16 [2009] EWHC 11 (Fam), [2009] 1 FCR 606, [2009] 1 FLR 1442.

Property which can be charged

2.73 COA 1979, s 2 sets out the property which may be charged. It includes interests held beneficially by the debtor in the following categories of property:

- Land
- Government stock
- Stock of body incorporated or registered in England and Wales
- Unit trusts where register is in England and Wales
- Funds in court
- Property held in trust

Stock includes shares, debentures and any securities of the body concerned, whether or not constituting a charge on the assets of that body: COA 1979, s 6.

2.74 The debtor must have a beneficial interest in the property held and accordingly this would not extend to cases where a debtor is merely a discretionary beneficiary of a trust.

Application

2.75 COA 1979, s 1(2) and FPR 2010, r 40.4 set out the appropriate court to which an application should be made:

Property to be charged is fund in court	• Court where fund is lodged
Order being enforced is High Court maintenace order or costs order	• High Court, or • Family Court
Order being enforced is Family Court maintenance order or costs order	• Family Court

2.76 It has been held by Mostyn J that, other than in limited circumstances, enforcement applications must be issued in the Family Court: *VS v RE (Family Court: Allocation of Cases)*[17].

2.77 Where more than one order is being enforced, the creditor can apply in respect of all orders to any court that would be the appropriate court for one of them (COA 1979, s 1(5)).

2.78 An application may be made without notice: FPR 2010, r 40.4(1).

2.79 The application must be in the form and contain the information prescribed by PD40: FPR 2010, r 40.4(2).

2.80 The application will be dealt with initially without a hearing: FPR 2010, r 40.5. The court may make an interim charging order and fix a hearing to consider whether to make a final charging order.

2.81 It has twice been held by Mostyn J that the court has jurisdiction to make an immediate final order (in effect bypassing the scheme in the FPR), although the circumstances in which he did so were exceptional[18].

Case summary: *Veluppillai v Veluppillai*[19]

Facts:

Financial proceedings had been affected by H's 'truly abysmal' conduct. There had been 30 hearings including 4 appeals by H. In parallel proceedings, H had made threats to kill W and W's counsel for which he had been committed for contempt. He had been removed from court by security several times and repeatedly warned by judges about his 'unpleasant menacing conduct' in court. He assaulted W and her counsel in court on one occasion and had been convicted of assault, but avoided sentencing by fleeing abroad from where he had 'bombarded the court with abusive emails claiming that he has a fatal illness and demanding that the proceedings be adjourned indefinitely'.

After failing to secure an adjournment of the final hearing, H sent an email to the judge's clerk in the following terms:

> 'ANOTHONY, CAN YOU BLOODY PASS ONTO THIS EMAIL TO MOSTYN WHO HAS BEEN DEALING WITH OTHER PARTY CROOKS ALAGA & CO AND PROSITUTE ANUSHIYA VELUPPILLAI. WHO HAVE GOT HISTORY OF STELING, DISHONEST, COMMITING FRAUD IF YOU HAVE BEEN

17 [2018] EWFC 30, [2018] 1 WLR 3757, [2018] 3 FCR 294, [2018] 2 FLR 1213.
18 *Veluppillai v Veluppillai* [2015] EWHC 3095 (Fam), [2016] 2 FLR 681; see also *Green v Adams* [2017] EWFC 24, [2017] 3 FCR 79, [2017] 2 FLR 1413.
19 [2015] EWHC 3095 (Fam).

RUNNING THE HEARING WITHOUT TELLING ME I WILL F**k YOU ALL MOSTYN I WANT THE FUCKING ANSWER NOW.WHERE IOS MY F**KING ORDER AND YOU HAVE BEEN MY HEALTH WORSE THAN IT IS.WANTS THE RESPONSE AND F***ING UPDATE NOW CROOKS ….'

Mostyn J found the assets to be just short of £1.5 million (including £500,000 of undisclosed assets) of which W sought a total of £733,518.

Held by Mostyn J:

W's proposal was reasonable and was adopted. H was ordered to pay costs. The costs would be charged on a property beneficially owned by H. Under COA 1979, s 3(1) the court had jurisdiction to make an immediate absolute order and would do so.

Procedure after an interim charging order

2.82 Following the making of an interim charging order, the application and documents filed in support must be served not less than 21 days before the hearing on various persons specified in FPR 2010, r 40.6:

(a) the debtor;

(b) if the order relates to an interest in land, any co-owner;

(c) the debtor's spouse or civil partner (if known);

(d) such other creditors as are identified in the application or as the court directs;

(e) if the order relates to an interest under a trust, on such of the trustees as the court directs; and

(f) if the interest charged is securities, then—

- (i) in the case of stock for which the Bank of England keeps the register, the Bank of England;
- (ii) in the case of government stock to which sub-paragraph (f)(i) does not apply, the keeper of the register;
- (iii) in the case of stock of any body incorporated within England and Wales, that body;
- (iv) in the case of stock of any body incorporated outside England and Wales or of any state or territory outside the United Kingdom, which is registered in a register kept in England and Wales, the keeper of that register; and
- (v) in the case of units of any unit trust in respect of which a register of the unit holders is kept in England and Wales, the keeper of that register.

2.83 The creditor must file a certificate of service two days before the hearing or produce a certificate at the hearing: FPR 2010, r 40.6(2).

2.84 A debtor cannot as against the creditor validly dispose of securities subject to an interim charging order: FPR 2010, r 40.7. A person served with an order relating to securities cannot permit their transfer or pay any dividend, interest or redemption payment in respect of them: FPR 2010, r 40.7. Any breach will render the person in breach liable to pay the creditor an amount up to the value of the securities transferred: FPR 2010, r 40.7(3).

2.85 A person who objects to the making of a final charging order must file and serve evidence setting out the objection not less than seven days before the return date hearing: FPR 2010, r 40.8.

2.86 At the return date hearing the court may do one of the following (FPR 2010, r 40.8(2)):

- make a final charging order confirming that the charge imposed by the interim charging order continues, with or without modification;
- discharge the interim charging order and dismiss the application;
- decide any issues in dispute between the parties, or between any of the parties and any other person who objects to the court making a final charging order;
- direct a trial of any such issues, and if necessary give directions; or
- make such other order as the court considers appropriate.

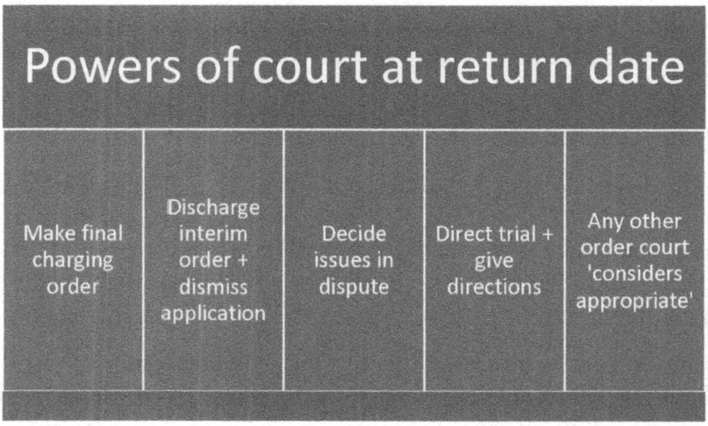

Exercise of discretion

2.87 The court has a discretion whether to make a charging order. In deciding whether to do so it is required by COA 1979, s 1(5) to consider all the circumstances and in particular any evidence as to:

(a) The personal circumstances of the debtor; and

(b) Whether any other creditor would be unduly prejudiced by the making of the order.

2.88 A charging order may be made absolutely or subject to conditions, including as to notifying the debtor the time when it becomes enforceable: COA 1979, s 3(1).

2.89 Although a creditor is not entitled to a charging order as of right, they are justified in expecting that such an order will be made in their favour: see *First National Securities v Hegerty*[20]. A creditor can place before the court evidence of the hardship they would suffer if the order were not made and this can be taken into account as part of the discretion: *Harman v Glencross*[21].

Case summary: *Harman v Glencross*[22]

Facts:

W applied within divorce proceedings for a transfer of the FMH (where she lived with the children). H's former business partner obtained judgment against him for c £9,000 and was granted a charging order nisi against his interest in the property, later made absolute. W applied to vary the charging order absolute.

The registrar varied the order to provide that it was subject to any order made by the court on W's ancillary relief application. He then made an order transferring H's share of the property to W. A judge upheld the order on appeal and the creditor appealed to the Court of Appeal.

Held by the Court of Appeal:

Appeal dismissed. W had locus standi to apply for a discharge or variation of the order under COA 1979, s 3(5). In exercising its discretion to make a charging order, the court had to consider 'all the circumstances of the case'. The judge was entitled to take account of W's interest as well as that of the creditor and there were no grounds for interfering with his discretion.

Where the order nisi has been made after a divorce petition[23], the court should consider whether it is proper to make the order absolute before the hearing of the ancillary relief proceedings. The charging order application

20 [1985] QB 850, [1984] 3 WLR 769.

21 [1986] Fam 81, [1986] 2 WLR 637, [1986] 2 FLR 241.

22 [1986] Fam 81, [1986] 2 WLR 637, [1986] 2 FLR 241.

23 See also *Lloyds Bank plc v Byrne* [1993] 2 FCR 41, [1993] 1 FLR 369 where it was held the circumstances of a resident wife should be considered even if divorce proceedings had not been issued.

should normally be transferred so that both sets of proceedings could be heard together.

2.90 The requirement to take account of other creditors means that a charging order will not be made to give the creditor security where there is to be a liquidation or the court is aware that there are pending or imminent bankruptcy proceedings[24].

Third party applications

2.91 Where a third party seeks a charging order and there are pending divorce proceedings, the court has to balance the interests of the creditor and the interests of the spouse claiming financial remedies against the interests of the debtor.

2.92 Unless it is clear that a charging order should be made, it will usually be appropriate to transfer the application for a charging order to the Family Court so that both applications can be heard together and the position of the claiming spouse can be considered[25]. The interests of any relevant children must be given particular consideration[26]. In *Harman v Glencross*[27] it was suggested that the balance between the interests of a creditor and those of a spouse and children may make it appropriate to make a *Mesher* order[28].

2.93 In *ZH (Tanzania) v Secretary of State for the Home Department*[29] it was emphasised in an immigration context that Art 3(1) of the United Nations Convention on the Rights of the Child requires that in all actions 'concerning' children, the best interests of the child shall be a primary consideration. The principles extend to actions and decisions which affect children indirectly such as where the child's parents are to live: *ZH (Tanzania)* at para [25].

2.94 In *Harman v Glencross*[30] it was held that where a creditor applies for a charging order absolute before a spouse has commenced divorce proceedings there are no other proceedings to which the application could be transferred and it is difficult to see why the creditor's application should be refused. In *Lloyds Bank plc v Byrne*[31], however, the Court of Appeal held that the interests of a debtor's resident family must nevertheless be considered in those circumstances. This is reinforced in cases involving children by the principle articulated in *ZH*

24 *Roberts Petroleum Ltd v Bernard Kenny Ltd* [1983] 2 AC 192, [1983] 2 WLR 305; *Nationwide Building Society v Wright* [2009] EWCA Civ 811, [2020] Ch 318, [2010] 2 WLR 1097.
25 *Harman v Glencross* [1986] Fam 81, [1986] 2 WLR 637, [1986] 2 FLR 241.
26 *Harman v Glencross* [1986] Fam 81, [1986] 2 WLR 637, [1986] 2 FLR 241.
27 [1986] Fam 81, [1986] 2 WLR 637, [1986] 2 FLR 241.
28 *Mesher v Mesher* [1980] 1 All ER 126,
29 [2011] UKSC 4, [2011] 2 AC 166, [2011] 2 WLR 148, [2011] 1 FCR 221, [2011] 1 FLR 2170.
30 [1986] Fam 81, [1986] 2 WLR 637, [1986] 2 FLR 241.
31 [1993] 2 FCR 41, [1993] 1 FLR 369.

(Tanzania)[32]. In such cases, it may be open to the court to make the equivalent of a *Mesher*[33] order, using the power to postpone enforcement of the charging order under COA 1979, s 3(1).

2.95 Where a court has made a charging order and the debt is payable by instalments, the charging order cannot be enforced unless there has been default of any instalment due in respect of the debt. Where there has been default of an instalment the charging order may be enforced in relation to the whole debt (COA 1979, s 3(4A)–(4E)).

2.96 The court may on the application of the debtor or a person interested in any property to which the order relates make an order varying or discharging the charging order (COA 1979, s 3(5)). For these purposes 'a person interested' includes a spouse with a right of occupation in the property; they do not need to demonstrate a beneficial interest in the property[34].

G STOP ORDERS AND NOTICES

2.97 A stop order is an order preventing the taking of steps in relation to securities: COA 1979, s 5.

2.98 The steps which a stop order may prevent are listed in COA 1979, s 5(5) and include:

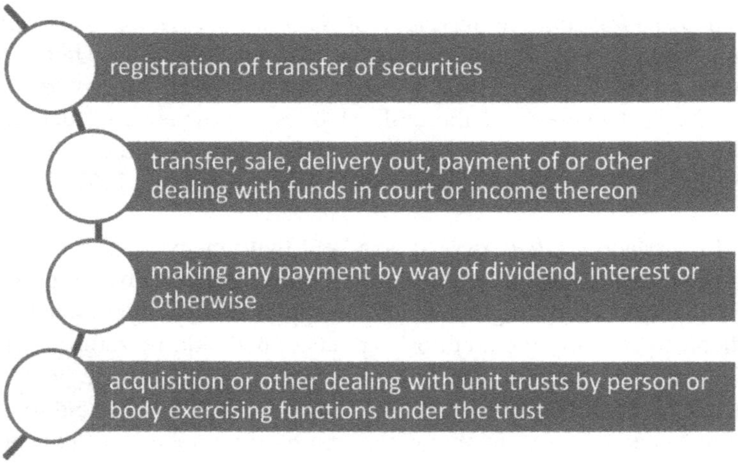

2.99 A 'stop notice' is a notice requiring a person to refrain from taking those steps without first giving notice: COA 1979, s 5.

32 See **2.93**.
33 *Mesher v Mesher* [1980] 1 All ER 126.
34 *Harman v Glencross* [1986] Fam 81, [1986] 2 WLR 637, [1986] 2 FLR 241.

2.100 Where a court makes a final charging order over securities the order must also include a stop notice unless the court orders otherwise: FPR 2010, r 40.8(4).

2.101 For procedural guidance about stop orders and stop notices, see FPR Part 40, Chs 3 and 4 and PD40A.

H PREVENTING A DEBTOR LEAVING THE JURISDICTION

2.102 Particular problems with enforcement can arise where the debtor is based in another jurisdiction, or where significant assets are held in another jurisdiction. Such issues – and possible solutions – are discussed further in **Chapters 10** and **11**. In certain situations, however, the court does have the power to prevent a debtor leaving the jurisdiction.

This is a limited power in that it may only be used as an ancillary aid to enforcement to secure attendance at court, rather than as a free-standing method of enforcement.

2.103 Historically, restraining a debtor from leaving the jurisdiction was done via the issue of writ of *ne exeat regno* (meaning 'that he not depart'). Its availability in the present day is heavily circumscribed: it is only available where a defendant could be arrested and imprisoned under the Debtors Act 1869 and is only available before the final judgment is given, ie where the defendant's absence would prejudice the other party in pursuing their claim[35].

2.104 The writ is therefore not available once a judgment has been given, even if it remains unpaid and unfulfilled. There is, however, another option that derives from the Supreme Court Act 1981 ('SCA 1981'), s 37. As Mostyn J said in *Bhura v Bhura*[36]:

> 'The writ ne exeat regno is a charming historical relic but must be regarded as an anachronism given the availability of the modern form of order.'

SCA 1981, s 37 provides as follows:

> 'The High Court may by order (whether interlocutory or final) grant an injunction … in all cases in which it appears to the court to be just and convenient to do so.'

2.105 The availability of the modern form of order was confirmed by the Court of Appeal in *Bayer AG v Winter*[37].

35 As explained by Wilson J in *B v B (Injunction: Jurisdiction)* [1998] 1 WLR 329, [1997] 3 FCR 262, [1997] 2 FLR 148.

36 [2012] EWHC 3633 (Fam), [2013] 3 FCR 142, [2013] 2 FLR 44 at 51.

37 [1986] 1 WLR 497.

Case summary: *Bayer AG v Winter*[38]

Facts:

The plaintiff pharmaceutical company applied for injunctions against the defendants, whom they alleged were marketing a counterfeit product with a similar mark to the plaintiffs' products. The judge ordered the defendants to disclose a number of documents and deliver them up to the plaintiffs' solicitors, but declined to grant injunctions restraining the defendants from leaving the country and requiring them to deliver up their passports. The plaintiffs appealed, stating that without the injunctions the information might not be disclosed.

Held by the Court of Appeal (allowing the appeal):

The jurisdiction was statutory and expressed in very wide terms. The court should not refuse to grant relief if of the opinion that the injunction was necessary for the proper protection of a party to proceedings, notwithstanding that the terms may be of a novel character.

The Court considered the harm that would be done to the defendant and the harm that would be done to the plaintiffs without the order. The court stated that there was a risk to the plaintiffs that they would not obtain the information without the injunction being granted (noting that if the defendant left the jurisdiction, any order for cross-examination would be frustrated) while the risk of hardship to the defendant was dealt with by the option of applying to a judge for variation or discharge.

As the orders interfere with a party's liberty, they should endure for no longer than is necessary and be of very limited duration.

2.106 The use of such injunctions in family proceedings was considered by Wilson J in *B v B (Injunction: Jurisdiction)*[39]. This helpfully spells out the limits of the jurisdiction, as well as its potential use.

38 [1986] 1 WLR 497.
39 [1998] 1 WLR 329, [1997] 3 FCR 262, [1997] 2 FLR 148.

Case summary: *B v B (Injunction: Jurisdiction)*[40]

Facts:

H and W were, respectively, nationals of Singapore and India. W lived with her parents in London after the breakdown of the marriage. A consent order disposing of an application made by H provided that he should pay £75,000 in respect of W's costs; H failed to comply with that order. When H visited England briefly, W obtained an *ex parte* order that he should attend for oral examination of his means and surrender his passport in the meantime. H was found on examination to have sufficient means, albeit overseas, to satisfy the costs order. W sought an injunction under SCA 1981, s 37 to prohibit H from leaving the jurisdiction until he had paid the amount outstanding.

Held by Wilson J:

There are a number of circumstances in which it is possible under s 37 to restrain a party from leaving the jurisdiction and make a consequential order for surrender of their passport, including after judgment has been given, where it can be invoked to aid the court's procedures for enforcement of the judgment. A judgment summons and oral examination are established procedures for enforcement and they should not be able to be frustrated by the debtor leaving the jurisdiction.

The jurisdiction under s 37 is ancillary to the court's other powers and could not be used to confine a debtor to remaining in the jurisdiction until satisfaction of a judgment.

2.107 An injunction to prevent someone leaving the jurisdiction is therefore ancillary to the court's other powers or mechanisms, rather than a form of coercive enforcement itself.

Some examples of when the injunctive power under SCA 1981, s 37 might be permissibly used are:

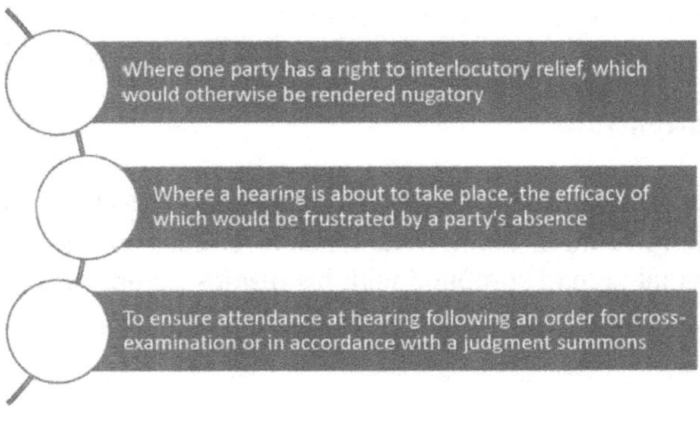

40 [1998] 1 WLR 329, [1997] 3 FCR 262, [1997] 2 FLR 148.

2.108 In *Young v Young*[41], Mostyn J considered the history of both the writ *ne exeat regno* and the injunctive power under SCA 1981. He set out the three points an applicant must fulfil when an injunction under the SCA 1981 is pursued:

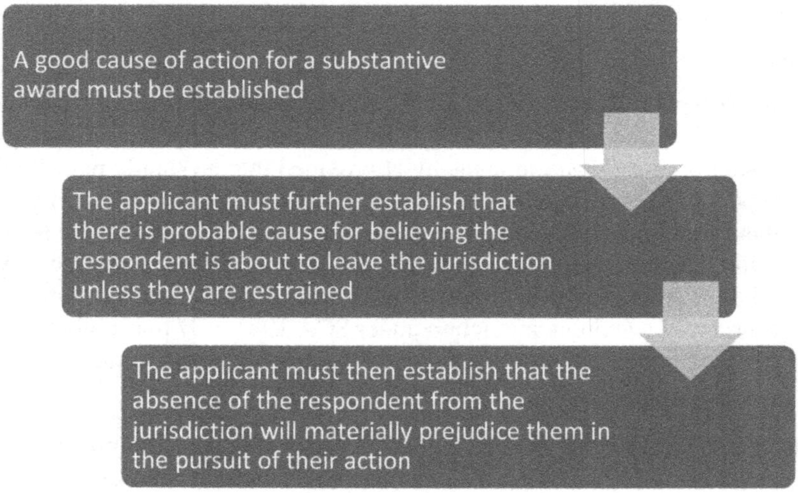

2.109

Case summary: *Young v Young*[42]

Facts:

The underlying financial remedy proceedings were long-running. H had been found to be in contempt for failing to comply with court orders and was sentenced to six months in prison. The committal order was suspended for three months on condition of compliance, but contained a provision requiring the tipstaff to retain H's passport. H continued to fail to comply with court orders and his passport remained impounded. H said he wished to travel to Africa to engage in charitable work and applied for the return of his passport.

Held by Mostyn J:

Applying the principles set out above, it was noted that H remained 'grossly in contempt' in relation to his maintenance obligations. He had failed to demonstrate that he had complied with his disclosure obligations.

41 [2012] EWHC 138 (Fam), [2012] 2 FCR 83, [2012] 2 FLR 470.
42 [2012] EWHC 138 (Fam), [2012] 2 FCR 83, [2012] 2 FLR 470.

W had established a good cause of action for a substantive award. H was about to quit the jurisdiction for reasons that were 'highly implausible' and W would be materially prejudiced in the prosecution of her claim if he did not return.

The final hearing was not listed for some further nine months and Mostyn J considered whether this sat comfortably with the emphasis on the short-term nature of the remedy. It was at the extremities of the court's powers, but was justified on the exceptional facts of the case provided H retained the liberty to apply for a discharge.

2.110 What a court cannot do is use a passport order as a way to apply coercive pressure, regardless of how justified the cause might be and notwithstanding that it might be reasonably considered the only way to secure compliance with an order.

In *B v B (Injunction: Jurisdiction)*[43], Wilson J noted that if he were to make an indefinite order impounding the husband's passport and preventing him leaving the jurisdiction, he believed the husband would likely pay the costs immediately *but* he had no power to do so.

2.111 An application for an injunction is made in accordance with FPR 2010, r 20.4 and PD20A.

43 [1998] 1 WLR 329, [1997] 3 FCR 262, [1997] 2 FLR 148.

CHAPTER 3

Contempt of Court and Committal

Content at a glance:

A INTRODUCTION

3.01 In financial remedy proceedings the breach of a judgment, court order, or undertaking is a contempt of court. That is true whether a person is ordered to do something or not to do something. Where a party is in contempt of court, the other party may make an application for an order committing the defaulting party to prison[1].

3.02 It has long been established that an order for committal should only be used as a remedy of last resort. Indeed in the family court it has been described as a remedy of 'the very last resort'[2]. Thus, before issuing a 'contempt application' (as it is now called under the Family Procedure Rules 2010 ('FPR 2010'), Part 37[3]), it is essential to consider any or all reasonable alternative avenues of enforcement which may be available. That principled point applies with equal force on a practical level: committal proceedings can be cumbersome and fraught with potential procedural pitfalls which, if fallen into, *may* undermine fatally the application itself.

1 Although see **3.43** et seq: an immediate custodial sentence is not the only or the automatic result of a finding that a defendant is in contempt of court.

2 *Ansah v Ansah* [1977] Fam 138, [1977] 2 WLR 760, per Ormrod LJ. Although see the comments of Thorpe LJ in *Zuk v Zuk* [2012] EWCA Civ 1871, [2013] 3 FCR 633, [2013] 2 FLR 1466 at para 16, in which he said that these authorities were more aimed at children proceedings.

3 FPR 2010, rr 37.2 to 37.4.

3.03 As of 1 October 2020[4], FPR 2010, Part 37 and Practice Direction 37A ('PD37A') have been replaced with a 'new' Part 37 and PD37A. In this Chapter, references to Part 37 and PD37A will mean these more recent and current rules unless otherwise indicated. Practitioners and lay parties alike should be careful to ensure that they are using the correct version of Part 37, as the changes made in October 2020 were not inconsiderable[5]; they were intended to create a simplified and self-contained procedural checklist for any person or lawyer making an application for a committal order. Additionally, and as set out again below, there is now a separate and specific **Form FC600**[6] which must be used to make a contempt application. The procedural requirements are discussed at **3.22** et seq.

3.04 The rules in FPR 2010, Part 37 explicitly do not change the underlying substantive law on contempt or the court's jurisdiction to make an order in contempt proceedings[7]. What is crucial to understand (particularly in financial remedy proceedings) is that there remains an important substantive and jurisdictional difference between the following two applications:

APPLICATION FOR COMMITTAL ORDER	- v -	**JUDGMENT SUMMONS**

If the prospective defendant in breach of an order **to pay money**, the debt cannot be enforced under the court's general power to commit an individual for contempt of court, but must be enforced by way of a judgment summons under the Debtors Act 1869 (see **Chapter 4**). If it is not an order or undertaking to pay money, then it may be enforced by way of committal. If the wrong application is made, the application is almost certain to fail[8].

3.05 A whole spectrum of orders or undertakings may be enforced by way of committal. But, as ever, that is subject to the point made in **3.02** that committal is an order of last resort. By way of example, a court is unlikely to enforce an order to transfer property by way of committal, when the court can itself execute the necessary documents and effect the transfer[9]. Similarly, an order to deliver up vacant possession of a property may, more effectively and proportionately, be

4 The Family Procedure (Amendment No.2) Rules 2020, SI 2020/758, Sch 1 para.1. The new Part 37 is modelled on the similarly 'new' Civil Procedure Rules 1998, Part 81.

5 The 38 rules in the earlier incarnation of Part 37 have been reduced to 10 in the current version.

6 From 30 July 2021. Any forms used previously, either N78 (often in error) or D11, should not be used (it should be noted that the Form N78 has not, in fact, been the correct form since 2014 when the original Part 37 was inserted into the FPR 2010).

7 FPR 2010, r 37.1(3) confirms that Part 37 'has effect subject to and to the extent that it is consistent with the substantive law of contempt of court' and r 37.1(4) confirms Part 37 does not 'alter the scope and extent of the jurisdiction of courts determining contempt proceedings.'

8 In *Zuk v Zuk* [2012] EWCA Civ 1871, [2013] 3 FCR 633, [2013] 2 FLR 1466 the Court of Appeal overturned an order committing the husband to prison for failure to pay a lump sum, where the order was made pursuant to the general power to commit for contempt of court, as opposed to under the Debtors Act 1869. See also para 43 of *Olu-Williams v Olu-Williams* [2018] EWHC 2464 (Fam), [2019] 1 FCR 714, per Williams J.

9 Senior Courts Act 1981, s 39 and County Courts Act 1984, s 38.

enforced by seeking a warrant for possession[10]. The following graphic shows an incomplete list of broad categories of orders, the enforcement of which could be the subject of a contempt application:

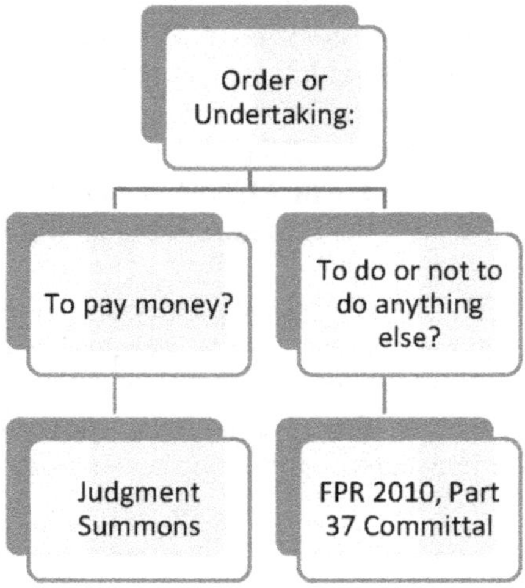

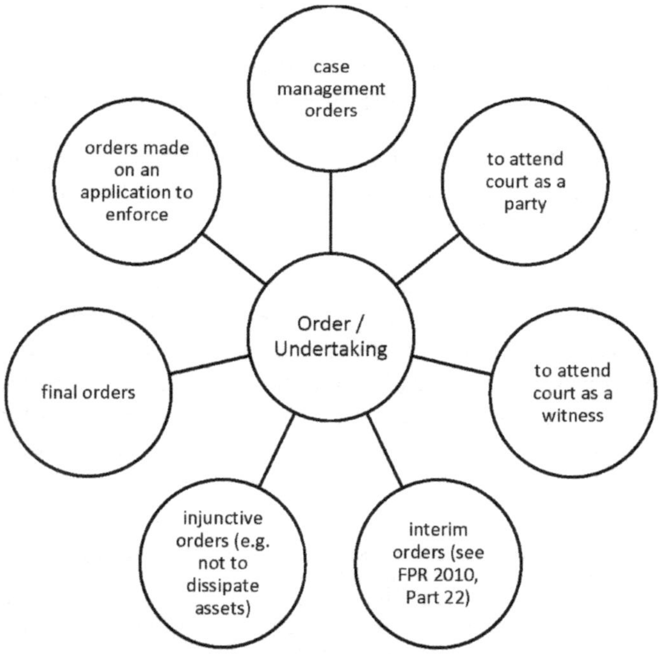

3.06 A contempt application may also be made where it is alleged that a person knowingly made a false statement in an affidavit, affirmation or other document verified by a statement of truth, or a disclosure statement. However,

[10] *Danchevsky v Danchevsky* [1975] Fam. 17, [1974] 3 WLR 709.

in that specific circumstance, the court's permission is needed to make the application[11].

B PRECONDITIONS OF AN APPLICATION FOR COMMITTAL

3.07 Before issuing a contempt application, and assuming that it fulfils the requirement to be a remedy of last resort, there are some important issues to consider:

1
- Order: Is there a penal notice?
- Undertaking: Is there a penal notice? Is there a signed statement confirming that the defendant understood the terms and the consequences of breaching the undertaking?

2
- Is the wording of the order or undertaking in clear, certain and unambiguous language?

3
- Has the defendant been properly served?

Penal notice on an order

3.08 FPR 2010, r 37.2 defines a penal notice as follows:

> 'A prominent notice on the front of an order warning that if the person against whom the order is made (and, in the case of a corporate body, a director or officer of that body) disobeys the court's order, the person (or director or officer) may be held in contempt of court and punished by a fine, imprisonment, confiscation of assets or other punishment under the law.'

3.09 Neither Part 37 nor PD37A contain a prescribed form of words for a penal notice. That is in contrast to the previous PD37A[12] which prescribed the following[13]:

11 FPR 2010, r 37.3(5)(b). Rule 37.3(6) provides for the application for permission to be included in the substantive application.

12 Replaced from 1 October 2020.

13 FPR 2010, PD37A, para 1.1.

> 'If you the within-named ... do not comply with this order you may be held to be in contempt of court and imprisoned or fined, or your assets may be seized.'

Part 37 is clear that an order can be enforced by way of committal *only* if the order was endorsed by a penal notice[14]. FPR 2010, r 37.4(2) provides that contempt application must include[15]:

> '(e) confirmation that any order[16] allegedly breached or disobeyed included a penal notice.'

3.10 It is not *necessarily* fatal to an application if the penal notice is not on the face of an order, as long as it is contained somewhere within the order[17]. Nor is it *essential* to use the precise wording set out above[18]. However, it is good practice (and compliant with the definition of a penal notice under FPR 2010, r 37.2) to include the wording set out above and formerly prescribed by FPR 2010 on the front page of the order in a 'prominent position'.

Case Summary: *Richards v Martin*[19]

Facts:

C made an application to commit D to prison for breach of several orders made at a number of hearings

D's counsel argued that, although each of the orders contained a penal notice, those penal notices were not on the front page of the orders prominently displayed.

Held by HHJ Hughes QC:

> '8. ...I understand that in a lot of cases, where injunctions are obtained, parties may not be present in court, it is very important to draw these matters to their attention.

14 The *former* r 37.9(1) provided that 'a judgment or order to do or not do an act may not be enforced [by committal] unless there is prominently displayed, on the front of the copy of the judgment or order...a warning to the person ... that disobedience to the order would be a contempt of court punishable by imprisonment...'.

15 FPR 2010, r 37.4(2)(e). In *CH v CT* [2018] EWHC 1310 (Fam), [2019] 1 FLR 700 Baker J held that the omission of a penal notice in the order (it had been confused with a more generic warning) was fatal to the committal application and could not simply be ignored.

16 Note. This does not say 'order or undertaking'. It is specific to an order.

17 *Richards v Martin* [2017] EWHC 2187 (Fam), [2018] 1 FCR 256

18 *Iberian Trust Limited v Founders Trust and Investment Company Ltd* [1932] 2 KB 87. The point is that the wording of the notice / memorandum must include the essential elements.

19 [2017] EWHC 2187 (Fam), [2018] 1 FCR 256.

> 9. … I take the view that this case is different, because this is a case where the father has attended the court on all occasions except 7 August; he has been warned about his conduct. The penal notice is so clearly put on all the documents. Whilst it may not be on page one, it is certainly in some cases on page two…[T]his is not a case where the father was unaware of what is required…'

Undertakings

3.11 The *previous* FPR 2010, Part 37 and PD37A (superseded from 1 October 2020, as explained in para **3.03**) provided explicit rules in respect of the enforcement of undertakings by way of committal. In summary:

(a) an undertaking itself had to be endorsed by a penal notice (unless the undertaking was already contained in an order)[20]; and

(b) the court could decline to accept an undertaking unless the party giving it had 'made a signed statement to the effect that that party understands the terms of the undertaking and the consequences of failure to comply with it…'

3.12 The situation is different now. FPR 2010, PD33A is titled 'enforcement of undertakings'. As regards all undertakings (other than those for the payment of money[21]) it says this[22]:

> **'Enforcement of undertaking to do or abstain from doing any act other than the payment of money**
>
> 1. Attention is drawn to the provisions of Part 37 (in particular r 37(2)) about contempt applications for the enforcement of undertakings.'

FPR 2010, r 37(2) does not exist. Rule 37.2 does not refer to undertakings. It is assumed that '37(2)' is a reference to FPR 2010, r 37.4(2), which provides – specific to undertakings – that a contempt application must include [emphasis added]:

> '(f) the **date and terms** of any undertaking allegedly breached
>
> (g) confirmation of **the claimant's belief** that the person who gave any undertaking understood its terms and the consequences of failure to comply with it.'

20 Previous PD37A, para.2.1 and previous rule 37.9(2).

21 Para 2.1 refers to an undertaking for the payment of money, which takes effect as if an order of the court and is, thus, enforceable by way of judgment summons (see **Chapter 4** and the introduction to this Chapter).

22 FPR 2010, PD33A, para 1.1.

3.13 On its face that is a substantial relaxation of the rules in relation to the enforcement of undertakings by way of committal. Although FPR 2010, r 37.4(2)(e) mandates that an 'order' must contain a penal notice, it does not extend that requirement to enforcement of an undertaking. Moreover, FPR 2010, r 37.4(2)(f) and (g) do not explicitly require there to have been a contemporaneous signed 'declaration' confirming that the defendant understood the meaning of the undertaking and the consequences of any breach. All that is explicitly required is confirmation *from the claimant* that, *at the time of making the application*, he/she believes the defendant to have so understood *at the time of giving the undertaking*[23].

What are we to take from this? Can an undertaking be enforced in the absence either of a penal notice or a declaration? Almost certainly, in principle. But in practice, and from the court and claimant's point of view, the best evidence that a defendant understood the terms of his/her undertaking and the consequences of its breach must surely be the existence of a penal notice (wording above) and a signed declaration in the following terms[24]:

> I understand the undertaking that I have given and that if I break any of my promises to the court I may be sent to prison, or fined, or my assets may be seized, for contempt of court.

The wording of the order/undertaking

3.14

Key citation: *Federal Bank of the Middle East v Hadkinson*[25]

Mummery LJ:

> p.404: 'The basic principle in the civil law of contempt is that, although there is an obligation to comply strictly with the terms of an order, the court will only punish a person for contempt of court upon adequate proof that the terms of the order are clear and unambiguous and that he has broken those terms…'

[23] It should be noted that at section 12 of the Form FC600 for a contempt application, the claimant is asked to 'explain the basis' for their belief that the person understood the undertaking and the consequences of non-compliance.

[24] Taken from the previous incarnation of FPR 2010, PD37A, para 2.2.

[25] [2000] 2 All ER 395, [2000] 1 WLR 1695.

3.15 If it is not clear that the defendant has breached the order it is impossible to commit them to prison for not complying with that order. Thus it is essential, when drafting an order or undertaking, to ensure that the wording is as clear and unambiguous as possible. If it is not, then a new order will have to be made, because it is wholly impermissible to imply a term into an order or undertaking for the purposes of contempt proceedings (however reasonable that proposed implied term might be)[26].

3.16 The most obvious example of the importance of drafting is in the case of mandatory orders or undertakings, ie those which require a person to do something. In such cases the order/undertaking must specify clearly and unambiguously:

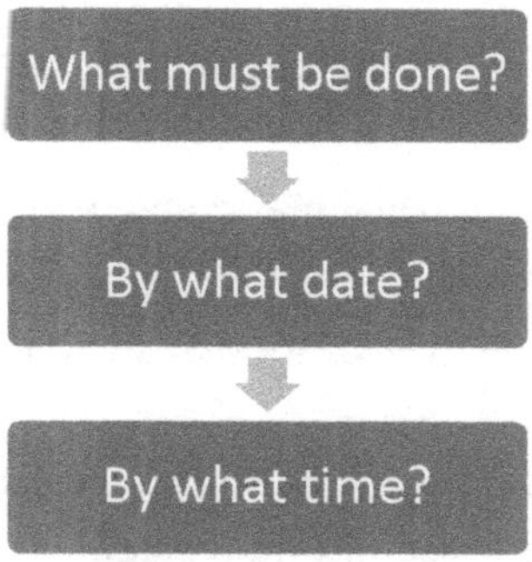

If the order does not so specify, any such omission will be fatal to proving a breach for the purposes of any committal application[27] (see the case summary at **3.17**).

3.17 If a person breaches an order or an undertaking to do a certain act by a certain time, then that is a single freestanding breach on which an application for a committal order can be brought. Until the breach is remedied, that person remains in breach. However, more than one application to commit cannot be brought in respect of the same continuing breach; a further mandatory order must be made, specifying a new, future date and time for compliance, and only a subsequent breach of that 'new' order can found a further committal application[28].

26 *Deodat v Deodat* (9 June 1978); see also *Re Jones* [2013] EWHC 2579 (Fam), [2014] 2 FCR 354, [2014] 1 FLR 852.

27 *Temporal v Temporal* [1990] 2 FLR 98; *Re Jones* [2013] EWHC 2579 (Fam), [2014] 2 FCR 354, [2014] 1 FLR 852, per Sir James Munby P at paras [18] to [21].

28 *Kumari v Jalal* [1997] 1 WLR 97, [1997] 1 FCR 422, [1996] 2 FLR 588; *Re Jones* [2013] EWHC 2579 (Fam), [2014] 2 FCR 354, [2014] 2 FLR 588, per Sir James Munby P at para 23.

Case Summary: *Re Jones, Solicitor General v JMJ*[29]

Facts:

This was an international child abduction case. Hedley J ordered as follows:

(1) The subject children to be returned to Spain from England

(2) The following orders are made to give effect to (1):

> (a) the children to return to Spain accompanied by their father by no later than 12 midnight on 12 October 2012
>
> (b) the mother to deliver up the children into father's care at Cardiff railway station by no later than 4pm on 12 October 2012

The order was endorsed by a penal notice and the mother was present at the hearing.

The children were not delivered to the station by 4pm on 12.10.12. M disappeared with the children.

M argued that it had been impossible for her to deliver up the children on 12 October 2012 by 4pm to Cardiff train station as, on the day, two of the children had run away and by the time she had found them no train would have reached Cardiff on time for 4pm.

An application was made for her committal to prison by the Solicitor General.

Held by Sir James Munby P:

Paragraph (1) of the order:

> '[18] … para.(1) was not addressed to anyone in particular. It directed, in the abstract as it were, that something was to be done. But it did not order the mother, or anybody else for that matter, to do something… Secondly, para.(1) did not specify any time for compliance, and that omission is fatal…'

Paragraph (2)(b) of the order:

The SG argued that M was in continuing breach of the order to deliver up the children by 4pm on 12 October 2012 by virtue of her behaviour subsequent to that date. The President disagreed:

> '[20] There is…simply no basis in law upon which [the SG] can found an allegation of contempt…Para.2(b) was quite specific. It required

[29] [2013] EWHC 2579 (Fam), [2014] 2 FCR 354, [2014] 1 FLR 852.

> the mother to do something by 4pm on 12 October 2012. It did not, as a matter of express language, require her to do anything at any time thereafter, nor did it spell out what was to be done if, for any reason, there had not been compliance by the specified time. In these circumstances there can be no question of any further breach…
>
> [21] A mandatory order is not enforceable by committal unless it specifies the time for compliance… If it is desired to make such an order enforceable in respect of some omission after the specified time, the order must go on to specify another, later, time by which compliance is required…
>
> [23] I do not want to be misunderstood. If someone has been found to be in breach of a mandatory order…then it is perfectly appropriate to talk of the contemnor as remaining in breach thereafter…It does not justify the making of a (further) committal order on the basis of a further breach, because there has in such a case been no further breach…'

The only question was whether M had breached the order to deliver up the children **by 4pm on 12/10/2012**. The judge held that the SG had not proved to the criminal standard that it was within M's power to get the children to Cardiff Railway Station by 4pm on that day and reiterated that:

> '[37]…nothing which happened after 4pm [on 12 October 2012] is capable of being a contempt of court.'

Service

3.18 FPR 2010, r 37.4(2)(c) and (d) provide that a contempt application must include:

> '(c) Confirmation that [the relevant] order was **personally served,** and **the date it was served**, unless the court or the parties dispensed with personal service
>
> (d) if the court dispensed with personal service, **the terms and date of the court's order dispensing with personal service**.'

3.19 The new slim-line FPR 2010, Part 37 omits the previous rule 37.8 which had set out specific circumstances in which the court '*may* dispense' with personal service of an order[30]. As a result, there is nothing in the rules as to how a court

[30] Previous FPR 2010, r 37.8, which distinguished between an order to do an act and an order not to do an act.

should approach this issue. It stands to reason that the order of which a person is alleged to be in breach should be served personally as quickly as possible following the breach unless there is a very good reason to the contrary. A court is likely to want to see evidence of the attempts to serve the defendant personally prior to dispensing with the need for personal service and permitting service by an alternate means, but is unlikely to allow the absence of personal service to prevent the defendant's committal to prison if the defendant can be demonstrated to have been fully aware of the terms of the order and the implications for non-compliance[31].

3.20 The requirement for personal service of the order is not applied to undertakings in the rules. This appears to be a deliberate relaxation of the provisions in the old Part 37[32]. Nevertheless, as discussed above, it is a requirement of an application for a committal order that the claimant believes the defendant to have understood the terms of the undertaking given and the consequences of its breach. It is thus good practice to ensure that:

Either

> The defendant receives on the day of the hearing a hard copy of the undertaking, penal notice and signed declaration and the order records on its face that this has happened

Or

> If that is not possible, or the undertaking is not given at a court hearing, each party and their representatives retain a copy of the undertaking, with a penal notice and signed declaration.

Furthermore, while personal service of an undertaking might not be a formal requirement under FPR 2010, Part 37, it is difficult to see why a claimant would not personally serve on the defendant a further copy of their undertakings, so as to remove any doubt that they are aware of and understand the consequences of the alleged breach, prior to any application being made to commit.

Summary: pre-application checklist

3.21 The following is suggested as a checklist for steps which should be taken both at the stage of drafting an initial order/undertaking and prior to issuing an application for a committal order:

31 See FPR 2010, Part 6 and the cases of *Benson v Richards* [2002] EWCA Civ 1402, and *Serious Organised Crime Agency v Hymans* [2011] EWHC 3599 (QB) on dispensing with personal service.

32 See the previous FPR 2010, r 37.7.

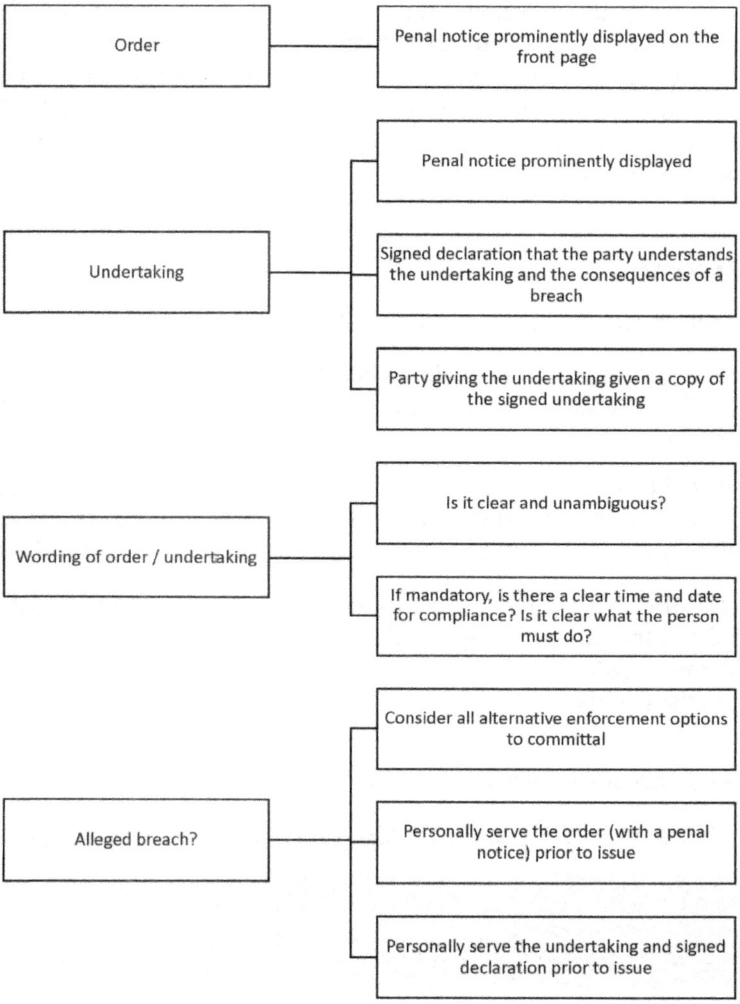

C PROCEDURE

What form?

3.22 The correct procedure to use on issuing an application for a committal order has, until recently, caused practitioners great difficulty. When Part 37 was first inserted into FPR 2010 (April 2014), it made clear that an application for a committal order should be issued under the procedure set out in FPR 2010, Part 18 (ie an application made within existing proceedings). That did not prevent claimants and their representatives seeking to issue applications using the old 'notice to show cause' Form N78 and as recently as November 2021 Poole J was confronted with such a procedural misstep[33].

33 *Borg v El Zubaidy* [2021] EWHC 3227 (Fam), [2022] 2 FCR 46 at para 11. The Form N78 was headed 'Notice to Show Good Reason why an Order for Your Committal to Prison should not be made', itself a mischaracterisation of the burden of proof.

On 30 July 2021, to supplement the revised FPR 2010, Part 37 and PD37A (discussed above), a new **Form FC600**[34] was published, titled 'Contempt Application' under FPR 2010, rr 37.3 and 37.4. This Form has made compliance with the numerous procedural and evidential hurdles provided for in Part 37 much simpler and has addressed many of the issues identified in authorities pre-dating the rule change[35].

Which court?

3.23 FPR 2010, r 37.3(1) and (2) provide that:

(1) A contempt application made in existing High Court of family court proceedings is made by an application under FPR 2010, Part 18 in those proceedings

(2) If the application is made in the High Court, it shall be determined by a High Court judge of the Division in which the case is proceeding. If it is made in the Family Court, it shall be determined by a judge of the Family Court.

3.24 It follows that if the order alleged to have been breached was made in the High Court then any contempt application should be made to the High Court. If the order was made in the Family Court, then any contempt application should be made to the Family Court[36].

Service of the application

3.25 FPR 2010, r 37.5(1) and (2) address service of the contempt application:

(1) A contempt application & evidence must be served on the defendant personally unless:

- The court directs otherwise (see FPR 2010, Part 6),
- See (2) below

(2) If the defendant has a lawyer in the proceedings in which an alleged contempt is committed:

- Application & evidence may be served on the lawyer. Unless the lawyer objects in writing within 7 days of service
- No objection? Lawyer must give the defendant a copy of application & evidence, and take all reasonable steps to ensure he/she understands them
- Objection? Issue of service referred to a judge dealing with contempt application. Determined on papers on written submissions unless court directs a hearing

34 FC600 Contempt application (10.21).

35 See, for example, the procedural guidance of Williams J in *Olu-Williams v Olu-Williams* [2018] EWHC 2464, [2019] 1 FCR 714 at para 36.

36 The Family Court (Composition and Distribution of Business) Rules 2014 make provision for the level of judge in the family court who may determine a contempt application.

Procedural checklist

3.26 The following table shows a simple breakdown of the procedure to make a contempt application:

What Application Form?	• Form FC600
What type of application?	• An application within proceedings (FPR 2010, Part 18)
What court? (37.3(1) and (2))	• Earlier proceedings in High Court? Then issue in High Court • Earlier proceedings in Family Court? Then issue in Family Court
Service of the application (37.5)	• Personal service unless the court directs otherwise OR • Service on defendant's lawyer in the underlying proceedings
What to include in the application (37.4)	• See separate list below (paras 3.27 to 3.29)

Content of the application

3.27 There are several authorities, some of them recent, on the way in which an application for a committal order should be constructed, both as to the specific content and the layout of the application (ie what should be in the application and what should be in the accompanying evidence): see for example the judgment of Williams J in *Olu-Williams v Olu-Williams*[37].

However, the guidance in these authorities has now been superseded by the recently revised FPR 2010, Part 37 and the new Form FC600.

37 [2018] EWHC 2464, [2019] 1 FCR 714, at para 36.

3.28 FPR 2010, r 37.4(1) provides as follows:

> 'Unless and to the extent that the court directs otherwise, every contempt application must be supported by written evidence given by affidavit or affirmation.'

For the avoidance of doubt, a witness statement is not an affidavit. FPR 2010, PD22A sets out the requirements of form and content for an affidavit.

3.29 FPR 2010, r 37.4(2) contains sub-paragraphs (a) to (s). Each one is stated to be mandatory for a contempt application, unless (in the instances of (b) to (g)) they are 'wholly inapplicable'. Good practice must be, therefore, to run through each one of these when completing the application in Form FC600 *and* when compiling a claimant's affidavit evidence. If acting for a defendant, practitioners may wish to cross-check the application and evidence against this list to ensure that all relevant matters have been addressed.

The list is divided into two parts in the graphics below. First, information about the application that must be included within it. Secondly, notifications to the defendant which must be included in the application:

Information About the Application

(a) nature of the alleged contempt. Breach of an order or of an undertaking?

(b) date and terms of any order allegedly breached

(c) confirmation that the order was personally served (including date of service)

(d) if the court dispensed with personal service, the details

(e) confirmation that the order included a penal notice

(f) date and terms of any undertaking allegedly breached

(g) confirmation by the claimant that the person who gave the undertaking understood its terms and the consequences of any breach

(h) a brief summary of the facts alleged to constitute the contempt in numerical and chronological order

Notifications to the Defendant ('D')
(i) D has the right to be legally represented
(j) D is entitled to a reasonable opportunity to obtain legal representation and to apply for legal aid
(k) D may be entitled to an interpreter
(l) D is entitled to a reasonable time to prepare for the hearing
(m) D is entitled but not obliged to give written and oral evidence in their defence
(n) D has the right to remain silent and to decline to answer any question that may incriminate them
(o) the court may proceed in D's absence if they do not attend
(p) if the court finds D in contempt, the court may punish them with fine, imprisonment or confiscation of assets
(q) if D admits the contempt and wishes to apologise to the court, that is likely to reduce the seriousness of any punishment
(r) the court will provide its findings in writing
(s) the court will sit in public, unless and to the extent that the court orders otherwise, and its findings will be made public

3.30 Prior to Form FC600 compliance with each one of these procedural and evidential requirements had somehow to be shoehorned into the appropriate application form for a Part 18 application[38] and/or the affidavit in support.

Form FC600 now includes sections for each of sub-sections (a) to (h) and contains statements complying word-for-word with sub-sections (i) to (s). If that form is completed properly and fully, with an accompanying affidavit consisting only of witness evidence[39] in support of the alleged breach(es) and which exhibits only that evidence which is necessary to prove those breaches to the criminal standard, then there is scant room for a defendant to raise arguments about procedural unfairness or impropriety.

Procedural deficiency/strike out

3.31 Pursuant to FPR 2010, PD37A, para 2(1) the court may strike out a contempt application (on its own initiative or on an application by the defendant) if it appears to the court that:

(a) The application and evidence in support disclose no reasonable ground for alleging that the defendant is guilty of a contempt of court[40]

38 Form D11 in financial remedy.
39 As distinct from legal argument, which should never form part of witness evidence.
40 Necessarily this will depend on the facts of each case.

(b) The application is an abuse of process or, if made in existing proceedings, is otherwise likely to obstruct the just disposal of those proceedings[41]

(c) There has been a failure to comply with a rule, practice direction or order

3.32 While it is advisable to comply with all relevant rules, practice directions and orders when issuing a contempt application, a failure to do so is not necessarily fatal. FPR 2010, PD37A, para 2(2) provides that [emphasis added]:

> The court may waive any procedural defect in the commencement or conduct of a contempt application if satisfied that **no injustice has been caused to the defendant by the defect.**

3.33 Whether the court will waive a procedural defect depends on whether it has caused injustice to the defendant. In the Court of Appeal decision of *Nicholls v Nicholls*[42] Lord Woolf MR said[43]:

> 'While the … requirements of [the procedural rules] are there to be observed, in the absence of authority to the contrary, even though the liberty of the subject is involved, we would not expect the requirements to be mandatory, **in the sense that any non-compliance with the rule means that a committal for contempt is irredeemably invalid.'**

His Lordship then offered the following guidance:[44]

(1) As committal orders involve the liberty of the subject it is particularly important that the relevant rules are duly complied with.

(2) As long as the contemnor has had a fair trial and the order has been made on valid grounds the existence of a defect either in the application to commit or in the committal order served will not result in the order being set aside except insofar as the interests of justice require this to be done.

(3) Interests of justice will not require an order to be set aside where there is no prejudice caused as a result of errors in the application to commit or in the order to commit. When necessary the order can be amended.

(4) When considering whether to set aside the order, the court should have regard to the interests of any other party and the need to uphold the reputation of the justice system

(5) If there has been a procedural irregularity or some other defect in the conduct of the proceedings which has occasioned injustice, the court will consider exercising its powers to order a new trial unless there are circumstances which indicate that it would not be just to do so

41 Same point as made above in relation to (a).
42 [1997] 1 WLR 314, [1997] 1 FLR 649.
43 p 321A, 655D.
44 p 327A, 661E.

3.34 There are some procedural defects which cannot be overlooked and it has more recently been said by Mostyn J that 'it is hard to envisage any circumstances where the terms of Part 37 are waived…'[45].

In *CH v CT*[46] Baker J held that the absence of a penal notice on the order alleged to have been breached rendered it impossible to enforce by way of committal.

In *Andreewitch v Moutreuil*[47] the failure by the judge to explain to the respondent his right not to give evidence was held to be more than a mere technicality:

Case Summary: *Andreewitch v Moutreuil*[48]

Facts:

A freezing order was made in March 2019. In November 2019 company bank statements appeared to show the use of company funds, in breach of the order. W applied to commit H to prison for contempt.

H was a litigant in person at first instance. He was told he had a right to representation and legal aid, but he opted to continue. He was asked to swear a 'note' he had produced at the hearing and was cross-examined for two hours. He was not warned that he was not obliged to give written or oral evidence and to exercise his right to silence. He was found to be in breach. He appealed.

Held by the Court of Appeal, Jackson LJ:

> '[15] Proceedings for contempt of court are unlike ordinary civil or family proceedings in that they may lead to the imposition of a punishment. For that reason special safeguards exist for the benefit of the respondent/defendant. At the same time, the overall objective is fairness, and in seeking to achieve that the court must take into account the interests of all parties and the public interest in the maintenance of the authority of the court. That approach, which is common across all subject jurisdictions, is reflected in FPR 2010, PD37 para 13.2[49] and CPR 1998, PD81 16.2 which permit, but do not require, the court to waive any procedural defect in the commencement or conduct of a committal application if satisfied that no injustice has been caused. Accordingly, while it is of great importance that the procedural rules are complied with, the process will not be invalidated on (to borrow

45 *Re H* [2018] EWHC 3761 (Fam), [2019] 1 FCR 641.
46 [2018] EWHC 1310 (Fam), [2019] 1 FLR 700.
47 [2020] EWCA Civ 382, [2020] 4 WLR 54, [2020] 2 FCR 784, [2020] 2 FLR 213.
48 [2020] EWCA Civ 382, [2020] 4 WLR 54, [2020] 2 FCR 784, [2020] 2 FLR 213.
49 Now reproduced in FPR 2010, PD37A para 2.2.

> from the White Book) purely technical grounds that have nothing to do with the justice of the case. ...**a balance must be struck where the relevant rules have not been followed to the letter**.'

However, in this case, the defect was more than a pure technicality. The 'starting point' when striking the balance was 'the duty upon a court hearing committal proceedings to ensure that the accused person is made aware that they are not obliged to give evidence and also warned that adverse consequences or inferences may arise from exercising the right to silence' [16].

> 'the right to silence is a core element in criminal proceedings and proceedings of a criminal character.' [17]

3.35 In light of the changes to FPR 2010 and the new Form FC600, designed to make procedural and evidential compliance easier, any procedural defects in an application are likely to be more difficult to justify.

D THE HEARING

Directions

3.36 FPR 2010, r 37.7provides that:

> '(1) The court shall give such directions as it thinks fit for the hearing and determination of contempt proceedings, including directions for the attendance of witnesses and oral evidence, as it considers appropriate.
>
> (2) The court may issue a bench warrant to secure the attendance of the defendant at a directions hearing or at the substantive hearing[50].
>
> (3) The court may not give any direction compelling the defendant to give evidence either orally or in writing.'

Rule 37.7(3) upholds the defendant's right to silence[51], but is supplemented by PD37A para 1, which provides that, should the defendant wish to adduce evidence, the court may make directions in that regard.

[50] See *Hanson v Carlino* [2019] EWHC 1366 (Ch) in relation to bench warrants. The issue of a warrant was acknowledged to be an 'extreme step taken in circumstances where the court has made orders and there appears to be 'non-compliance'. It is in essence a power designed to uphold the court's authority 'to secure compliance'. The warrant expires as soon as the defendant has been brought to court.

[51] See FPR 2010, r 37.4(2)(n) above.

Conduct of the hearing

3.37 Proceedings for committal are a criminal charge for the purposes of Article 6 of the European Convention on Human Rights[52]. This has a number of consequences, some of which have already been discussed above, arising from the fact that the liberty of the subject is at stake[53]. Perhaps the most important is this:

> **The burden of proving guilt lies with the person seeking the committal and the contempt must be proved to the criminal standard.**

As to the other principles, in *Andreewitch v Moutreuil*[54], summarised at para 3.33 above, Jackson LJ approved the helpful checklist (set out below) provided by Theis J in the Court of Appeal decision in *Re L*[55]. It was made clear that before a court embarks on hearing a committal application, it should ensure that the following matters are at the forefront of its mind:

(1) There is complete clarity at the start of the proceedings as to precisely what the foundation of the alleged contempt is: contempt in the face of the court, or breach of an order

(2) Prior to the hearing the alleged contempt should be set out clearly in a document or application that complies with FPR 2010, r 37 and which the person accused of contempt has been served with

(3) If the alleged contempt is founded on breach of a previous court order, the person accused had been served with that order, and that it contained a penal notice in the required form and place in the order

(4) Whether the person accused of contempt has been given the opportunity to secure legal representation, as they are entitled to

(5) Whether the judge hearing the committal application should do so, or whether it should be heard by another judge

(6) Whether the person accused of contempt has been advised of the right to remain silent

(7) If the person accused of contempt chooses to give evidence, whether they have been warned about self-incrimination

(8) The need to ensure that in order to find the breach proved the evidence must meet the criminal standard of proof, of being sure that the breach is established

(9) Any committal order made needs to set out what the findings are that establish the contempt of court, which are the foundation of the court's decision regarding any committal order

52 *Re K* [2002] EWCA Civ 1559, [2003] 2 FCR 336, [2003] 1 FLR 277 at para 21.

53 See *Hammerton v Hammerton* [2007] EWCA Civ 248, [2007] 3 FCR 107, [2007] 2 FLR 1133 per Moses LJ.

54 [2020] EWCA Civ 382, [2020] 4 WLR 54, [2020] 2 FCR 784, [2020] 2 FLR 213.

55 *Re L (A child)* [2016] EWCA Civ 173, [2017] 1 FLR 1135, at para 78. See also a similar restatement of the substantive law of contempt by Williams J in *Olu-Williams v Olu-Williams* [2018] EWHC 2464, [2019] 1 FCR 714, at para 33, and by HHJ Wildblood QC in *Hart v Hart* [2018] 2 FCR 625 at para 11.

Public funding and legal aid

3.38 Although committal applications in financial remedy proceedings will take place in the Family Court (or possibly the High Court), they are, in essence, criminal proceedings[56]. FPR 2010, r 37.4(2)(i) and (j) make clear that a defendant has the right to be legally represented, to be provided with a reasonable opportunity to obtain legal representation and to apply for legal aid (which may not be means tested)[57].

3.39 The importance of the right to representation cannot be overstated.

Case Summary: Re O *(Committal: Legal Representation)*[58]

Facts:

At first instance the court had made findings of contempt and made an order of committal in respect of a mother who had been unrepresented at the hearing.

Held by the Court of Appeal, Jackson LJ:

Findings set aside.

> '[2]…respondents to committal proceedings are entitled to be provided with legal representation if they want it and … they will qualify for non-means-tested legal aid. There is an obligation on the court to ensure that this protection is made available. Where this does not happen any resulting order for committal may be procedurally irregular.'

3.40 In practice, however, it may be difficult to obtain non-means tested legal aid for a defendant to a contempt application for two reasons.

(1) Criminal legal aid is *only* available as of right to a person facing *High Court* committal proceedings alleging breach of an order[59].

AND

56 *Hammerton v Hammerton* [2007] EWCA Civ 248, [2007] 3 FCR 107, [2007] 2 FLR 1133.

57 This derives from a decision of Sir James Munby P in *Chelmsford County Court v Ramet* [2014] EWHC 56 (Fam), [2014] 3 FCR 328, [2014] 2 FLR 1081 that committal proceedings are 'criminal proceedings' within the meaning of the Legal Aid, Sentencing and Punishment of Offenders Act 2012.

58 [2019] EWCA Civ 1721, [2019] 4 WLR 140, [2020] 1 FCR 258, [2020] 1 FLR 288.

59 See the explanation in *All England Lawn Tennis Club (Championships) Ltd v McKay* [2019] EWHC 3065 (QB), [2020] 1 WLR 216.

(2) Even though it may be available as of right, there still has to be a 'determination' that an individual qualifies for legal aid by the 'relevant authority'[60] and that relevant authority is not the court, but the Director of the Legal Aid Agency[61].

What is the solution? If a party wishes to apply for legal aid in contempt proceedings in the Family Court and is unsuccessful in such an application, the proceedings will need to be transferred to the High Court. Following the decision of *All England Lawn Tennis Club (Championships) Ltd v McKay*[62], the court does not have the power to grant legal aid; the power lies with the Director of the Legal Aid Agency on an application by the defendant or such legal aid lawyers as they have identified to represent them[63].

Proceeding in the absence of the defendant

3.41 It is possible for a committal hearing to proceed in the absence of a defendant: see FPR 2010, r 37.4(2)(o). In *Sanchez v Oboz*[64] Cobb J provided a 'useful checklist' as to the approach to be taken when a defendant has not engaged or is not present at a hearing. This is summarised in the following graphic:

60 Under the Legal Aid, Sentencing and Punishment of Offenders Act 2012, s 16.

61 *All England Lawn Tennis Club (Championships) Ltd v McKay* [2019] EWHC 3065 (QB), [2020] 1 WLR 216, per Chamberlain J. The judge distinguished the case of *Chelmsford CC v Ramet* [2014] EWHC 56 (Fam), [2014] 3 FCR 328, [2014] 2 FLR 1081, as being an instance of contempt in the face of the court, which is the subject of a different section (s 14) of LASPO 2012.

62 [2019] EWHC 3065 (QB), [2020] 1 WLR 216.

63 It was agreed by all parties in *All England Lawn Tennis Club (Championships) Ltd v McKay* [2019] EWHC 3065 (QB), [2020] 1 WLR 216 that a defendant to civil / family contempt proceedings is *entitled* to legal aid.

64 [2015] EWHC 235 (Fam), [2016] 1 FLR 897 at para 5, The decision was followed by the High Court (Chancery Division) in *Taylor v Van Dutch Marine Holdings Ltd* [2016] EWHC 2201 (Ch), and *Frejek v Frejek* [2020] EWHC 1181 (Ch).

3.42 The approach the court should take will depend upon the facts of the case. The fundamental question is whether the defendant has been served with notice of the hearing and has had sufficient time to prepare and/or to obtain legal representation[65].

E POWERS AND SENTENCING

Powers

3.43 Matrimonial and Family Proceedings Act 1984 ('MFPA 1984'), s 31E provides that:

(1) In any proceedings in the family court, the court may make any order—

[65] *Frejek v Frejek* [2020] EWHC 1181 (Ch), [2020] 5 WLUK 157, per Roth J, applying Cobb J's checklist in *Sanchez* (see **3.40**).

(a) which could be made by the High Court if the proceedings were in the High Court, or

(b) which could be made by the County Court if the proceedings were in the County Court.

3.44 Contempt of Court Act 1981, s 14 provides that in the case of committal by the High Court any sentence of imprisonment for contempt is:

for a fixed term which must **not on any one occasion exceed two years**

However, if the application for committal is being considered by a Lay Justice in the Family Court, the maximum sentence of imprisonment is limited to two months[66].

Sentencing

3.45 The key authority is *Hale v Tanner*[67] in which Hale LJ (as she then was) made ten points about the sentencing for contempt, summarised below.

Principles of sentencing

1 On an application to commit, the court is unsurprisingly thinking about committal. However, 'it does not follow that imprisonment is to be regarded as the automatic consequence of the breach of an order. Clearly it is not. There is, however, no principle that imprisonment is not to be imposed at the first occasion… Nevertheless, it is a common practice, and usually appropriate in the view of the sensitivity of the circumstances of these cases, to take some other course on the first occasion.'

2 The alternatives are limited. But the court has options:

i It can do nothing

ii it can adjourn (possibly where the defendant has not come to court)

iii it has the power to fine

iv it can sequester assets

3 If imprisonment is appropriate, consider the length of the committal without reference to whether it should be suspended.

4 The length of the committal depends on the court's objectives. There are two:

66 The Family Court (Contempt of Court: Powers) Regulations 2014, SI 2014/833, brought into force by the Matrimonial and Family Proceedings Act 1984, s 31H. These Regulations also limit the sentence of imprisonment for contempt in the face of the court to one month (irrespective of the level of judiciary).

67 [2000] 1 WLR 2377, [2000] 3 FCR 62, [2000] 2 FLR 879, CA, per Hale LJ.

i To mark the court's disapproval of disobedience to a court order

ii To secure compliance with that order

Mostyn J has subsequently described these as 'punishment' and 'coercion'[68].

5 The length of the committal has to bear 'some reasonable relationship to the maximum of two years which is available.'

6 Suspension is possible in a much wider range of circumstances than in criminal cases. It *'does not have to be the exceptional case.'* Often it is the first way of attempting to secure compliance.

7 The length of the suspension requires separate consideration, although it is often linked to continued compliance with the underlying order.

8 The court has to bear in mind the context of the breach, including any aggravating and/or mitigating circumstances, such as the existence of dependent children.

9 There may be concurrent proceedings in another court based on the same facts. Court cannot ignore those parallel proceedings. It may have to take into account their outcome and any effect on contempt proceedings. But the contemnor cannot and should not to be punished twice for the same events.

10 The court should usually explain why it has made the choices it has made. A contemnor should know why they are being sentenced to a period of imprisonment, why the length, why not suspended etc. The contemnor must understand the importance of keeping court orders.

3.46 It will be clear from the summary above that each case will turn on its facts. In some of the reported authorities suspended sentences have been imposed; in others, immediate sentences of imprisonment of different lengths up to the maximum of two years.

A contemnor will serve only half of the sentence imposed by the court and is then released unconditionally, removing the possibility of their recall to prison[69]. The Secretary of State may release a contemnor unconditionally *before* the halfway mark, but only in exceptional circumstances which justify the early release on compassionate grounds[70].

Warrant of committal

3.47 If the court decides to impose a period of imprisonment (ie an order of committal), in order to execute that order the court must issue a warrant of committal: see FPR 2010, r 37.9(1) which can be summarised as follows:

68 *Cherwayko v Cherwayko* [2014] EWHC 4252 (Fam) at para 11.
69 Criminal Justice Act 2003, s 258(2).
70 Criminal Justice Act 2003, s 258(4).

They have immediate effect unless and to the extent that the court decides to suspend execution (r 37.9(2))

They must be personally served on the defendant unless the court directs otherwise (r 37.9(3))

The court may attach a power of arrest, subject to the substantive law (r 37.9(4))

They may not be enforced more than 2 years after the date of the order/warrant, unless the court directs otherwise (r 37.9(5))

Fines

3.48 If the court decides to impose a fine for contempt of court, the fine must not exceed level 5 on the 'standard scale'[71]. Prior to 13 March 2015 this was £5,000, but it is now unlimited[72].

F CONFISCATION OF ASSETS/SEQUESTRATION

3.49 Sequestration, or the confiscation of assets, involves an application to the court for orders permitting named sequestrators to take possession of a person's property for a specified purpose. In family proceedings there are two relevant contexts: contempt proceedings and enforcement proceedings. It should be noted that the property is not formally vested in the sequestrators (unlike, for example, a trustee in bankruptcy).

3.50 The first context in which sequestration is used is in proceedings for contempt of court, as a means of procuring compliance with the relevant order. In this context, specified property of the contemnor is confiscated until they have complied with the order (ie purged the contempt). In some cases, further orders have been made permitting the sequestrators to deal with the contemnor's property in some more serious way, whether by means of securing a loan against a property, or even permitting its sale and the use of the proceeds to fund an applicant's legal proceedings abroad[73].

[71] Family Court (Contempt of Court: Powers) Regulations 2014, SI 2014/833, r 5 brought into force by Matrimonial and Family Proceedings Act 1984, s 31H.

[72] Sentencing Act 2020, s 122 continues to set the limit at £5,000, but Legal Aid, Sentencing and Punishment of Offenders Act 2012, s 85 provides that, for all offences taking place after 13 March 2015 (the 'commencement day' under the 2012 Act), the fine may be for 'any amount'. See also the Guide to Fines and Financial Orders on the Sentencing Council Website, Part 9.

[73] *Mir v Mir* [1992] Fam 79, [1992] 2 WLR 255, [1992] 1 FCR 227, [1992] 1 FLR 624; *H v N* [2009] EWHC 640 (Fam), [2009] 1 WLR 2335, [2009] 2 FLR 211. See also *Richardson v Richardson* [1990] Fam Law 176 in which a number of permitted uses of sequestration are listed.

The use of sequestration in this context is governed by FPR 2010, Part 37, following the changes made to that Part in October 2020[74], which mirrored changes to the Civil Procedure Rules 1998 ('CPR 1998'), Part 81[75]. Part 37 now refers to 'confiscation of assets' as opposed to 'sequestration', but they are the same thing. The crucial point to note is that there is no requirement within contempt proceedings to issue a separate application for a writ/warrant of sequestration (as was previously the case). It is enough to issue an application Form FC600 that is compliant with FPR 2010, Part 37[76].

3.51 Sequestration can also be used in family proceedings as a means to enforce a financial order. The procedure is governed by FPR 2010, Part 33 which explicitly incorporates CPR 1998, Part 83[77].

The following procedure applies:

What application?[78]	Either: Application for **permission** to issue a writ of sequestration – if proceedings are in the High Court Or Application for **permission** to issue a warrant of sequestration – if proceedings are in the Family Court[79]
Which judge?	Must be a judge of High Court level, whether sitting in the Family Court or in the High Court[80]
Procedure?	FPR 2010, Part 18[81]
Application notice	Must set out the grounds of the application Must be supported by evidence[82]
Supporting Evidence	Must be in affidavit form unless the court directs otherwise[83] Must comply with the requirements of FPR 2010, Part 18
Service	Must be personally served on the other party unless the court directs otherwise[84]
Once permission is granted	Before the writ/warrant is issued[85]: • The applicant must file a request for its issue • The request must be signed • The applicant must produce alongside the request: the order on which the writ is to issue and the order granting permission to issue the writ

74 See **3.3**.

75 See FPR 2010, r 37.9(1). These changes to the FPR 2010 and CPR 1998 took effect from 1 October 2020.

76 See **3.22–3.34**.

77 FPR 2010, r 33.1.

78 Note that it is possible to issue in the Family Court by way of Form D50K a general application for all forms of enforcement (FPR 2010, r 33.3(2) and (3)). This is discussed in **Chapter 2**.

79 CPR 1998, rr 83.2 and 83.14A.

80 Family Court (Composition and Distribution of Business) Rules 2014, SI 2014/840, Sch 2, Table 3, para 5.

81 CPR 1998, r 83.14A (1)(b) refers to CPR 1998, Part 23, but FPR 2010, r 33.1 modifies the relevant Parts of the CPR 1998 to applications to the Family Court where necessary.

82 CPR 1998, r 83.14A(2).

83 CPR 1998, r 83.14A(3).

84 CPR 1998, r 83.14A(4).

85 CPR 1998, r 83.9 (3), (4) and (5).

3.52 A writ or warrant of sequestration[86], if relating to real property, should be registered against the title to that property. If the property is registered land, it cannot be registered as a notice[87] so should be entered as a restriction. If unregistered land, the writ/warrant can still be registered as a land charge[88].

G PURGING THE CONTEMPT

3.53 A defendant may apply to discharge a committal order made against him (FPR 2010, r 37.10(1)). The application is made by way of an FPR 2010, Part 18 application within the contempt proceedings (FPR 2010, r 37.10(2)). FPR 2010, r 37.10(3) provides that:

> 'The court hearing such an application shall consider all the circumstances and make such an order under the law as it thinks fit.'

There are three possible outcomes to an application to purge contempt[89]:

Immediate release	Deferred release (future date)	Refusal of the application

3.54 A key authority is *Harris v Harris*[90]:

Case Summary: *Harris v Harris*[91]

Facts:

H applied for a third time to purge his contempt, while serving his sentence of imprisonment. He sought an order either for immediate release, or for release and the remaining part of his sentence to be suspended. Munby J granted the latter formulation, akin to a conditional purge of his contempt.

The question for the Court of Appeal was whether a court, releasing a contemnor on his application to purge his contempt, can impose a suspended sentence in respect of the unserved balance of the prison sentence and, if yes, for what period.

86 or an order granting the confiscation of assets, if within contempt proceedings.
87 Land Registration Act 2002, s 87(1)(c).
88 Land Charges Act 1972, s 6(1)(a).
89 *Harris v Harris* [2001] EWCA Civ 1645, [2002] Fam 253, [2002] 2 WLR 747, [2001] 3 FCR 640, [2002] 1 FLR 248, per Thorpe LJ at paras 17 and 21.
90 [2001] EWCA Civ 1645, [2002] Fam 253, [2002] 2 WLR 747, [2001] 3 FCR 640, [2002] 1 FLR 248.
91 [2001] EWCA Civ 1645, [2002] Fam 253, [2002] 2 WLR 747, [2001] 3 FCR 640, [2002] 1 FLR 248.

The Court of Appeal concluded a court could not so do. Its reasons are illuminating in the wider context.

Held by the Court of Appeal:

Thorpe LJ:

> '[21] …the application to purge is rooted in quasi-religious concepts of purification, expiation and atonement. On such an application the judge may only say yes, no or not yet. In family proceedings imprisonment for civil contempt has proved a complex field generating much work in the courts of trial and a significant number of appeals. In my opinion it is of great importance that the powers of the court and the rights of the contemnor should be as clear and as certain as is consistent with the need to design orders that do justice and reflect the infinite variety of fact and circumstance displayed by individual cases…'

Waller LJ:

> '[25] In my view it actually adds very little to the armoury of the court to allow someone to 'conditionally purge' with the remainder of a sentence placed in suspense. Even on an unconditional release, it must be clear to Mr Harris that if he commits a further breach of the orders, the court will in assessing sentence take account of the fact that by his previous promises of good behaviour he was released part way through his ten-month sentence. The court is likely to start from the position that he should at least serve that unserved part plus some further period for the contempts committed in breach of those promises, all subject to the overall limit of two years.'

H. PUBLIC OR PRIVATE?

3.55 There is a presumption that contempt proceedings will be heard in public. FPR 2010, r 37.8(1) provides:

> All hearings of contempt proceedings shall, irrespective of the parties' consent, be listed and heard in public unless the court otherwise directs, applying the provisions of paragraph (4).

3.56 FPR 2010, r 37.8(4) provides that [emphasis added]:

> 'A hearing, or any part of it, **must** be held in private if, and only to the extent that, the court is satisfied of one or more of the matters set out in sub-paragraphs (a) to (g) ***and*** that it is **necessary to sit in private to secure the proper administration of justice**…'

Sub-paragraphs (a) to (g) can be summarised as follows:

3.57 FPR 2010, r 37.8 sets out a number of other rules/considerations relevant to the question of whether contempt proceedings should be heard in private and, if so, the steps to be taken as to the conduct of such a hearing. Some are set out in the graphic below:

In deciding whether to hold a hearing in private, the court must consider any duty to protect or have regard to a right to freedom of expression which may be affected

The court shall take reasonable steps to ensure that all hearings are of an open and public character, save when the hearing is in private

Advocates and the judge shall appear robed, whether or not the court sits in public

The court shall notify the national print and broadcast media, via the Press Association, before deciding to sit in private

The court shall consider any submissions from parties or media organisations before deciding whether to sit in private

If the court decides to sit in private, it shall beforehand give a reasoned public judgment as to why

The court shall ensure judgments in contempt proceedings are transcribed and published on the judiciary website (only where an order for committal is made - PD37A, para.4)

CHAPTER 4

Judgment summons

Content at a glance:

A INTRODUCTION

4.01 This chapter provides an overview of the court's power to enforce orders for the payment of money by way of judgment summons.

4.02 Judgment summonses have existed as a remedy for over 150 years, and prior to the turn of the 21st century were a relatively commonplace tool.

4.03 Historically, the process of application and the manner of its determination were a somewhat informal affair, as described in *Mubarak v Mubarak*[1].

4.04 The seminal judgment of the Court of Appeal in *Mubarak*, however, established that the previous approach to judgment summonses was not compliant with Article 6 of the European Convention for the Protection of Human Rights and Fundamental Freedoms ('ECHR'). Specifically, it was said that because a judgment summons provided for penal sanctions, the same (or similar) safeguards and rights afforded to a defendant in a criminal process had to be afforded to the respondent to a judgment summons.

1 [2001] 1 FCR 193, [2001] 1 FLR 698.

Case Summary: *Mubarak v Mubarak*[2]

Facts:

W had been awarded a lump sum of £4.875 million in the substantive proceedings. H had failed to pay a £3.2 million instalment, so a judgment summons was issued. At first instance that application was determined with no fresh evidence filed, and W relied on findings made in the previous hearings of her substantive claim. The first instance judge imprisoned the husband for six weeks. H appealed arguing the judgment summons procedure was not Human Rights Act 1998 compliant.

Held by the Court of Appeal (allowing the appeal):

Order for imprisonment set aside.

Judgment summons were proceedings of an essentially criminal nature. The procedure then in place made no reference to the criminal standard of proof, the burden of proof or the right against self-incrimination, and muddled the 'means' enquiry stage (ie substantive financial remedy decision) and committal/enforcement proceedings. The prior findings of the court were to the civil standard and had involved compulsion against H to give evidence. They could not be relied upon to found a Human Rights Act compliant application of a subsequent judgment summons.

4.05 Following this decision, a wholly more rights compliant and procedurally and evidentially exacting approach was required. The Family Proceedings Rules 1991, as they then stood, required significant amendment. They were duly amended, albeit too slowly, and not before the Court of Appeal again considered the issue and restated and underlined the importance of a proper approach *in Corbett v Corbett*[3].

Case Summary: *Corbett v Corbett*[4]

Facts:

H was ordered to pay W periodical payments of £22,000 per annum (by consent). He got into arrears following his company's financial difficulties, but did not apply for a downward variation or provide disclosure, despite

2 [2001] 1 FCR 193, [2001] 1 FLR 698.
3 [2003] EWCA Civ 559 [2003] 2 FLR 385.
4 [2003] EWCA Civ 559 [2003] 2 FLR 385.

requests. W applied for a judgment summons to enforce the arrears. Thereafter, but before the hearing, H sold a flat and did not use the money to meet his arrears; instead he paid a debt to his current wife. The judge at first instance found he had wilfully neglected to pay his first wife and ordered him to serve one month in prison, suspended on condition he met the arrears.

Held by the Court of Appeal (allowing the appeal):

Order set aside.

The court had failed to act in a Human Rights Act compliant manner in that the notice of application reversed the burden of proof, did not advise H of his right to silence and purported to compel him to give evidence of his means, and the judge required him at the hearing to provide an explanation rather than requiring W to prove to her case to the criminal standard. The judge also failed to take into account Family Proceedings Rules 1991, r 7.4 which gave the court a discretion to investigate whether an order to pay periodical payments should have been varied or suspended had an application for variation been made, and the variable rather than absolute nature of the payments (including with a potential for remission of arrears) had not been drawn to his attention. The court should ensure that a variation application precedes the determination of a judgment summons as a freestanding process. If and only if that has been done could a judgment summons come into play.

4.06 In the years immediately following *Mubarak* and *Corbett* the judgment summons procedure appeared to fall into desuetude.

4.07 That being said, however, in some cases a judgment summons remains a useful tool in the armoury of a creditor, and a condign power available to the court to extract compliance from and/or visit punishment upon the determined non-payer.

4.08 The potential for a direct sanction against a judgment debtor involving penal consequences may be of particular use in cases where:

- assets are held within trust or corporate structures;
- assets are held by other third parties;
- assets are held in jurisdictions in which enforcement may be complex, costly or time-consuming;
- direct enforcement is difficult for other reasons.

The anecdotal increase in their use in more recent years may not be altogether surprising given the parallel increase in the number of cases with international, corporate and trust dimensions and concomitant enforcement hurdles.

4.09 Whilst more formalities now exist (and/or are expected to be more closely complied with) and thus greater care has to be taken in the preparation and prosecution of a judgment summons, these requirements are far from insuperable. In reality they are no more exacting than (and mirror to a large extent) those which apply to committal for contempt of court. Readers are recommended to consider this chapter alongside **Chapter 3** on committal, as well as **2.102–2.111** which deal with injunctions to prevent a debtor leaving the jurisdiction pending a hearing.

B STATUTORY PROVISIONS

4.10 The source of the power is found in Debtors Act 1869, s 5:

> **'5. Saving of power of committal for small debts**
>
> Subject to the provisions herein-after mentioned, and to the prescribed rules, any court may commit to prison for a term not exceeding six weeks, or until payment of the sum due, any person who makes default in payment of any debt or instalment of any debt due from him in pursuance of any order or judgment of that or any other competent court.
>
> Provided…
>
> (1) ….
>
> (2) That such jurisdiction shall only be exercised where it is proved to the satisfaction of the court that the person making default either has or has had since the date of the order or judgment the means to pay the sum in respect of which he has made default, and has refused or neglected, or refuses or neglects, to pay the same.'

4.11 The general application of this section ('any debt') was curtailed significantly by Administration of Justice Act 1970 ('AJA 1970'), s 11:

> **'Provisions restricting sanction of imprisonment**
>
> **11. Restriction on power of committal under Debtors Act 1869 (c. 62).**
>
> The jurisdiction given by section 5 of the Debtors Act 1869 to commit to prison a person who makes default in payment of a debt, or instalment of a debt, due from him in pursuance of an order or judgment shall be exercisable only—
>
> (a) by the High Court in respect of a High Court maintenance order;
>
> (b) by the county court in respect of a judgment or order which is enforceable by a court in England and Wales and is for the payment of any of the taxes, contributions premiums or liabilities specified in Schedule 4 to this Act.; and
>
> (c) by the family court in respect of a High Court or family court maintenance order.'

4.12 This should not be read so as to preclude the use of a judgment summons in respect of an unpaid lump sum or sums (as opposed to an order for child or spousal periodical payments). The definition of 'maintenance order' is set out at AJA 1970, s 28 and Sch 8 thus:

'28. Other provisions for interpretation of Part II

(1) In this Part of this Act, except where the context otherwise requires—

- 'High Court maintenance order' 'and family court maintenance order' …mean respectively a maintenance order enforceable by the High Court and the family court
- 'maintenance order' means any order, decision, settlement arrangement or instrument specified in Schedule 8 to this Act and includes one which has been discharged or has otherwise ceased to operate, if any arrears are recoverable thereunder;'

'SCHEDULE 8

Maintenance Orders for purposes of 1958 Act and Part II of this Act

1. An order for alimony, maintenance or other payments made, or having effect as if made, under Part II of the Matrimonial Causes Act 1965 (ancillary relief in actions for divorce etc.).
2. An order for payments to or in respect of a child being an order made, or having effect as if made, under Part III of the said Act of 1965 (maintenance of children following divorce, etc.).

2A. An order for periodical or other payments made, or having effect as if made, under Pt. II of the Matrimonial Causes Act 1973.

3. An order for maintenance or other payments to or in respect of a spouse or child being an order made, under Part I of the Domestic Proceedings and Magistrates' Courts Act 1978.
4. An order for periodical or other payments made or having effect as if made under Schedule 1 to the Children Act 1989.

4.13 Lump sums thus clearly fall within the ambit of a judgment summons[5], alongside periodical payment orders for spouses and children.

4.14 A debt arising under an undertaking is susceptible to enforcement by judgment summons providing it is equivalent to a maintenance order (as defined above): *Symmons v Symmons*[6] (which related to an undertaking to pay school fees).

5 See also paras [9]–[12] of the judgment of Thorpe LJ in *Zuk v Zuk* [2012] EWCA Civ 1871, [2013] 3 FCR 633; [2013] 2 FLR 1466.

6 [1993] 2 FCR 247, [1993] 1 FLR 317.

C STANDARD OF PROOF

4.15 The standard of proof is the criminal one. The court has to be 'sure'[7] of the relevant ingredients, not merely satisfied to the usual civil standard (ie 'on the balance of probabilities').

4.16 Thus the court has to be *sure* that each of the following have been established:

- The monies are due;
- They have not been paid; and
- The defaulter has, or has had since the date of the order, the means to pay the sum in respect of which they are in default, and has refused or neglected, or refuses or neglects, to pay that sum.

4.17 The first two of these elements are straightforward to establish in most cases. They usually can be proved by: (a) the production of the relevant order of which the debtor is in default; and (b) a statement from the creditor that the sums have not been received.

4.18 It is in relation to the third requirement – that the debtor has or has had the means to pay and has refused or neglected to do so – that most evidential difficulties arise.

D BURDEN OF PROOF

4.19 This issue is not free from legal debate.

4.20 In *Bhura v Bhura*[8] Mostyn J considered a number of authorities including *Mubarak*, and distilled from these what he considered to be the applicable principles. These are set out in full in the following graphic:

7 This is the modern terminology for 'satisfied beyond a reasonable doubt'; it denotes no lesser level of proof.

8 [2012] EWHC 3633 (Fam), [2013] 3 FCR 142, [2013] 2 FLR 44.

(i) The court to be satisfied to the criminal standard that:

(a) The respondent has had at *any point* since the order the means to pay the sums due; and	(b) has refused or neglected to pay them.

(ii) The use of the present and past tenses in 'either has or has had' and 'and has refused or neglected, or refuses or neglects' means that the section will be satisfied if proof of both ability to pay and refusal or neglect to pay is made at any single point from the date of the order right up to the date of the hearing.

(iii) The use of the alternative verbs 'refuse' and 'neglect' means that the court is not confined to proof of a positive wilful refusal to pay; the section will be equally satisfied if proof is made of a culpable indifference to the obligation to pay.

(iv) It is essential that the applicant adduces sufficient evidence to establish at least a case to answer. Generally speaking, this need not be an elaborate exercise. Proof of the order and of non-payment will likely give rise to an inference which establishes the case to answer.

(v) The respondent is not required to give evidence or to incriminate himself. In the absence of a case to answer being demonstrated the respondent is entitled to have the application dismissed without more.

(vi) If the applicant establishes a case to answer an evidential burden shifts to the respondent to answer it. If he fails to discharge that evidential burden then the terms of s 5 will be found proved against him or her to the requisite standard.

(vii) The applicant does not have to serve evidence prior to the hearing but if he or she fails to do so the court will be astute to ensure that the respondent is not taken by surprise and that the hearing can proceed without unfairness to him or her.

(viii) It is perfectly permissible for *both* the enquiry into the respondent's means at all points since the making of the order *and* the enquiry into whether he or she has been guilty of a refusal or neglect to pay to take place in one conflated hearing.

(ix) Provided that principles (i)–(viii) are carefully observed then the procedure will be Convention compliant.

4.21 Until that case, it had been thought that:

- the burden throughout was placed on the applicant alone;
- the right to silence afforded to the respondent meant that they were entitled to say nothing and put the applicant to proof.

4.22 *Bhura* principles (iv) and (vi) appear to be contrary to those propositions, given that:

- Principle (iv) appears only to require the applicant to provide sufficient evidence to establish a case to answer, being not more than proving a sum was due, and that it was not paid; whilst
- Principle (vi) says that *then* the evidential burden *shifts* to the respondent to 'answer it', and if he fails to do so, then the necessary final ingredient(s) of s 5 (having the means and neglecting to pay) will be proven.

4.23 On Mostyn J's analysis, there would seem to be no requirement on the applicant at all to provide evidence that the respondent had the means and refused or neglected to pay. This is somewhat at odds with the Court of Appeal's decisions in *Mubarak* and *Corbett*.

4.24 This precise concern was taken up by McFarlane LJ in the Court of Appeal in *Prest v Prest*[9]. He cast doubt on the correctness of Mostyn J's principles (iv) and (vi) (taken together).

Key citation: *Prest v Prest*[10]

McFarlane LJ (with whom Gloster LJ and Blake J agreed):

> '55 The collective professional experience of Thorpe LJ[11] and Mostyn J in these matters makes me most hesitant to express a contrary view but my reason for advising caution concerning this set of observations is that they each suggest that, in the course of the criminal process that is the hearing of a judgment summons, it is simply sufficient to rely upon findings as to wealth made on the civil standard of proof in the original proceedings and that those findings, coupled with proof of non-payment, is sufficient to establish a 'burden' on the respondent which can only be discharged if he or she enters the witness box and proffers a credible explanation. The facts of each case will differ, and the aim of Thorpe LJ and Mostyn J in envisaging a process which is straightforward and not onerous to the applicant is laudable, but at the end of the day this is a process which may result in the respondent serving a term of imprisonment and the court must be clear as to the following requirements, namely that:
>
> a. The fact that the respondent has or has had, since the date of the order or judgment, the means to pay the sum due must be proved to the criminal standard of proof;

9 [2015] EWCA Civ 714, [2016] 1 FLR 773.
10 Ibid.
11 This was a reference to the decision of *Mohan v Mohan* [2013] EWCA Civ 586, [2013] CP Rep 36, [2014] 1 FCR 40, [2014] 1 FLR 717, in which Thorpe LJ appeared to endorse *Bhura*.

b. The fact that the respondent has refused or neglected, or refuses or neglects, to pay the sum due must also be proved to the criminal standard;

c. The burden of proof is at all times on the applicant; and

d. The respondent cannot be compelled to give evidence.

. . .

62…It is, indeed, necessary for a judge who is required, at a subsequent stage in proceedings, to make findings on the higher criminal standard of proof, to ensure that earlier findings made on the lower civil standard are not, even inadvertently, relied upon as substantive findings in the subsequent quasi criminal process.'

4.25 In *Mann v Mann*[12], Roberts J followed *Prest* over the *Bhura* approach (noting counsel for the applicant there having accepted in terms that the decision in *Bhura* '*must now be subjected to more rigorous scrutiny in accordance with the guidance given by McFarlane LJ in Prest*').

Key Citation: *Mann v Mann*[13]

Roberts J:

'183… As to the law in relation to the burden and standard of proof, I take the view that the recent guidance given by the Court of Appeal in *Prest v Prest*, whilst not an all-embracing statement of the position, is nevertheless correct and is in any event binding upon me. Thus, I remind myself about the careful guidance given by Mostyn J in *Bhura* in the light of the most recent observations of the Court of Appeal.'

4.26 A rejoinder to *Prest* was subsequently given by Mostyn J in *Migliaccio v Migliaccio*[14], where he doubted whether McFarlane LJ was correct. He observed that McFarlane LJ's comments had been made *obiter dicta* and held that para 57 of the judgment of Richards LJ in *Karoonian v CMEC; Gibbons v CMEC*[15] should have been binding on McFarlane LJ and was thus to be preferred.

12 [2016] EWHC 314 Fam, [2016] Fam 281, [2016] 3 WLR 67, [2017] 1 FLR 559.
13 [2016] EWHC 314 Fam, [2016] Fam 281, [2016] 3 WLR 67, [2017] 1 FLR 559.
14 [2016] EWHC 1055 (Fam); [2016] 4 WLR 90.
15 [2012] EWCA Civ 1379; [2012] 3 FCR 491, [2013] 1 FLR 1121.

Key Citation: *Karoonian v CMEC; Gibbons v CMEC*[16]

Richards LJ:

> '57. It follows that in practice the Commission must adduce sufficient evidence to establish at least a case to answer. In the generality of cases the exercise may not need to be a particularly elaborate one, since there will be a history of default from which inferences can properly be drawn. But the exercise is an essential one: the defendant is not required to give evidence or to incriminate himself, and in the absence of a case to answer he is entitled to have the application against him dismissed without more. If the Commission establishes a case to answer, there will be an *evidential* burden on the defendant to answer it, but that is unobjectionable in article 6 terms. I would add that there is no requirement under article 6 for the Commission to serve evidence in advance of the hearing, but if it chooses to wait for evidence to be given by the presenting officer at the hearing, the court must be astute to ensure that the defendant is not taken by surprise and that the matter can proceed at that hearing without unfairness to him.'

In contrast to Mostyn J's observations in *Miglaccio*, it has been powerfully observed[17] that para [57] could *itself* be considered to be *obiter dicta*. In any event, Richards LJ was concerned with a different issue as was made clear in paras [58]–[62] of his judgment. Moreover, the judgments of Patten LJ and Richards LJ in *Karoonian* in fact provided support for the propositions articulated by McFarlane LJ in *Prest*.

4.27 Thus there remains doubt as to the extent to which the burden remains on the applicant, having established a prima facie case, to prove that the respondent had means to pay and refused or neglected to do so. This has not been resolved conclusively since *Miglaccio*, a case which has not since been considered in detail in any subsequent higher authority.

4.28 In *Iqbal v Iqbal*[18], the Court of Appeal had an opportunity to address the tensions, but did not do so. It did, however, quote paras [55] and [62] of McFarlane LJ's judgment in *Prest* without adverse comment (and, it may be thought, implicit approval). The Court of Appeal went on to say the following about *Bhura*:

16 [2012] EWCA Civ 1379; [2012] 3 FCR 491, [2013] 1 FLR 1121.
17 See Ashley Murray '*The Evidential Burden in Judgment Summons hearings: Migliaccio*' (2016) 46 Family Law 1017.
18 [2017] EWCA Civ 19, [2017] 2 FCR 26.

Key Citation: *Iqbal v Iqbal*[19]

Sir Ernest Ryder, Senior President:

> '[29].....counsel for the wife, urged on us to a limited extent what was said to be a different approach to the law [to that of McFarlane LJ in *Prest*]. He cited the decision of [*Migliaccio*], a first instance decision of Mostyn J which itself relies on an earlier decision of Mostyn J in [*Bhura*]. Aside from the fact that the learned judge's observations and criticisms are not binding on this court, the only principle which it could be said might be relevant to the appeal before this court is whether once a prima facie case on the evidence has been raised against a respondent to a judgment summons, an evidential burden shifts to the respondent which he must discharge if he is not to have the issues found against him to the criminal standard. That question does not arise on the facts of this case and accordingly it would be unwise to develop the point...'

4.29 The Law Commission was alive to this area of debate in its work considering enforcement in family proceedings, which began with an initial consultation published in March 2015. Following responses to that consultation, its report and recommendations were published in Law Com No 370 on 15 December 2016 – '*Enforcement of Family Financial Orders* [2017] EWLC 370'. That report noted the *Bhura* debate and the line of authorities and commentaries in which it has been discussed, and concluded at para [31] that:

> 'We agree with the reasoning of Lord Justice McFarlane [in *Prest*] that proof of the existence of the original order does not necessarily prove that the debtor has the means to pay what is owed on a judgment summons application. The judge hearing the financial proceedings only had to be satisfied as to the debtor's means on the balance of probabilities. In contrast, the judge on the judgment summons application must be satisfied beyond reasonable doubt. However, we do not consider that to *mean that in every case the creditor has to start all over again.*'

4.30 In *Barclay v Barclay*[20], Sir Jonathan Cohen rejected an argument that there was an evidential burden on the debtor to prove his positive defence, namely that he was deprived of funds from his family, and that the burden arose once the debtor accepted, as he did, that he was in breach.

19 [2017] EWCA Civ 19, [2017] 2 FCR 26.
20 [2022] EWHC 2026 (Fam).

Key Citation: *Barclay v Barclay*[21]

Sir Jonathan Cohen:

> '[25]. I have been referred to many authorities on this issue, but in my judgment the burden of proof remains on the applicant. All that the defendant (H) needs to establish is some evidence of the reason that he says explains why payment is not possible. I refer particularly to *Perkier Foods v Halo Foods* [2019] EWHC 3462 (QB), 2019 WL 06878176 at paragraphs 12-14 in which Chamberlain J set out the law as follows:
>
> > '…
> >
> > [13]. Mr Zaman, for his part, submits that, as a matter of principle, the fact that it is possible to comply with the order should be regarded as an essential ingredient of contempt. That being so, the position is similar to that which applies in criminal law: the respondent bears an evidential burden; but once this is satisfied the burden of proving that compliance was possible passes to the applicant and the standard of proof is the criminal standard: …
> >
> > [14]. In my judgment, Mr Zaman is correct on this point. Contempt of court, whether criminal or civil, was at common law a misdemeanour: see *Dean v Dean* [1987] 1 FLR 517, per Neill LJ, cited in Arlidge, Eady & Smith on Contempt (5th ed.), §12-51. That, together with the fact that its potential consequences include imprisonment and other penal sanctions, is why its elements must be proved to the criminal standard. …'

In the light of the above, the approach of Roberts J in *Mann* and that of Moor J in *Haskell v Haskell*[22], it is suggested that practitioners are likely to encounter difficulties if they conduct a judgment summons application on the basis that the applicant can rely upon the fact of the original order as proof that the debtor had the means to pay without providing any other evidence in relation to this issue. A successful judgment summons pursued on that basis may be vulnerable to challenge on appeal.

E EVIDENCE

4.31 The balance of the authorities discussed above suggests that it is likely to fall to the applicant to establish their case on all Debtors Act 1869, s 5 elements to the criminal standard.

21 [2022] EWHC 2026 (Fam).

22 [2021] EWHC 1867 (Fam), [2021] 3 FCR 727 at para 5.

4.32 It is important to be aware, however, that in some cases it may well be sufficient to rely on the terms of the original order as proof that the debtor had the means to pay. As the Law Commission 2016 report put it [emphasis added]:

> '32. The circumstances that were prevailing at the time the original order was made, and the evidence that was adduced in the original proceedings, will fall somewhere on a spectrum from unequivocally establishing a case to answer to not greatly assisting doing so. **In cases where the debtor has admitted to having certain assets or consented to certain orders, we are of the view that those facts, in addition to establishing that the debtor has not paid what is owed, may, without any more, establish a case to answer[23]. For example, if the order is for a lump sum and was made with consent three months prior to the judgment summons application, then we suggest it is very likely that would establish a case to answer. However if, for example, the order had been made two years ago and was based on the judge making findings that the debtor had assets that the debtor denied, then we suggest that order would not, without more, establish a case to answer.**
>
> 33. It is a matter for the judge in each case to determine what evidence is necessary to establish a case to answer. We do not think there is any debate that the burden of proof rests on the creditor on every judgment summons application, but that does not prohibit the creditor relying on the original order or evidence from the original proceedings to discharge that burden in certain circumstances…'

4.33 In addition, whilst bearing firmly in mind that the respondent cannot be compelled to give evidence either orally or in writing (FPR 2010, r 33.14(4)), and enjoys a privilege against self-incrimination, the court may be entitled to draw adverse inferences from silence – see *Khwaja v Popat*[24], *Inplayer Ltd. v Thorogood*[25] and *Dhillon v Sampuran*[26] (this latter case dealt expressly with a judgment summons, and applied *R v Chohan*[27]). The court, however, declined to draw adverse inferences in *Barclay v Barclay*[28] where the debtor was aged 87 and had a cognitive impairment, and evidence was given by his solicitor to whom conduct of the proceedings had been delegated.

4.34 In *Masri v Consolidated Contractors International Company SAL & Oths*[29], a case about committal proceedings, Clarke J endorsed the following submissions[30]:

23 If the defaulted upon final financial remedy order was one that was reached by consent this fact may be of particular weight – see *Rundell v Rundell* [2005] EWCA Civ 1764.
24 [2016] EWCA Civ 362.
25 [2014] EWCA Civ 1511.
26 [2020] EWFC B70.
27 [2005] EWCA Crim 1813, [2006] 1 Cr App R 3 (31).
28 [2022] EWHC 2026 (Fam) at paras [29] and [37].
29 [2011] EWHC 1024 (Comm).
30 See also *R v Chohan* [2005] EWCA Crim 1813, [2006] 1 CrAppR 3 (31) as cited and relied upon in *Dhillon v Sampuran* (ibid).

> '…although (i) an application for contempt is criminal in character, (ii) an alleged contemnor may claim a right to silence, and (iii) the provisions of sections 34 and 39 of the Criminal Justice Act 2003 do not apply, it was open to the Court to draw adverse inferences against the judgment debtors to the extent that it would be open it to do so in comparable circumstances in a criminal case. Thus it may be legitimate to take into account against the judgement debtors the fact (if it be such) that, when charged with contempt, as they have been in these proceedings, they have given no evidence or explanation of something of which they would have had knowledge and of which they could be expected to give evidence if it was true.
>
> …. the court should adopt by analogy the approach summarised in Archbold 4 – 398 in relation to an accused's failure to testify namely that (i) an inference from failure to give evidence cannot on its own prove guilt; (ii) the court must be satisfied that the judgment creditor has established a case sufficiently compelling to call for an answer before drawing any inference from silence and if it concluded that the silence could only sensibly be attributed to the defendant's having no answer, or none that could stand up to cross examination, the court could then draw an adverse inference.'

4.35 In reaching its conclusions it is open to the court to make findings to the criminal standard on the basis of inferences drawn from primary facts which it finds established by evidence. A court may not, however, infer the existence of some fact which constitutes an essential element of the case unless the inference is compelling, ie such that no reasonable man would fail to draw it: *Kwan Ping Bong v R*[31].

4.36 Practitioners seeking to rely on evidence provided in previous proceedings between the parties should take particular care before adducing evidence which was provided by the respondent by compulsion. It is important to delineate between evidence created by the defendant by compulsion and evidence which was disclosed by compulsion but which that had an independent existence. This stems from the application of the privilege against self-incrimination.

4.37 This is of particular concern when considering the interrelation between a judgment summons and an application for general enforcement under the Family Procedure Rules 2010 ('FPR 2010'), Part 33[32]. The latter can trigger requirements for the debtor to provide evidence as to their means. That evidence can include or consist of the provision of financial documentation that exists in any event (eg bank statements or accounting records). Equally it can include giving oral or written statements and answers which by their nature entail evidence being created by the debtor (eg the annotation of bank statements or answers to a questionnaire).

31 [1979] AC 609, [1979] 2 WLR 433.
32 For general enforcement see **Chapter 2**.

4.38 This issue was addressed by the Court of Appeal in *Mohan v Mohan*[33]:

Case Summary: *Mohan v Mohan*[34]

Facts:

H was in breach of a financial remedy order. W issued a general application for enforcement and H was ordered to file and serve a Form E, a sworn statement and provide certain documents. H complied.

W then issued a judgment summons. The same day she issued a committal application. These two applications were listed for hearing. The circuit judge ruled as inadmissible statements from H provided under a compulsion *and* documents produced by him that had an independent existence (ie the Form E itself and the attachments to it). He thus excluded from evidence all information and documents provided by H in accordance with the Order made within W's general enforcement application proceedings.

W appealed, seeking to rely on such documentation and statements. H did not attend nor was he represented at the appeal. Accordingly, an advocate to the court was appointed.

Held:

The original documents (eg bank records) provided had been wrongly excluded from evidence, but the statements *made* by the debtor under the order (eg a witness statement or narrative completions of his Form E itself) had been correctly excluded, as these came into existence at the hand of the debtor in response to a compulsion by order, and a debtor in those circumstances was no longer a compellable witness (FPR 2010, r 33.14) and he was not warned of the danger of self-incrimination on the disclosure order.

Any statements made by a debtor under compulsion in enforcement proceedings are inadmissible, and this includes any statement made by the debtor in response to orders made in prior or contemporaneous proceedings resulting from a general enforcement application.

4.39 Thus, in considering the ambit of any disclosure sought in general enforcement proceedings, should it be ever intended that this could be used in judgment summons proceedings following it, practitioners must pay close attention to the form of the order sought, and what it requires of the debtor (eg to

33 [2013] EWCA Civ 586, [2013] CP Rep 36, [2014] 1 FCR 40, [2014] 1 FLR 717.
34 [2013] EWCA Civ 586, [2013] CP Rep 36, [2014] 1 FCR 40, [2014] 1 FLR 717.

frame such an order in separate parts: (i) listing independently existing documents required to be produced; and separately to that: (ii) setting out requirements to provide a narrative statement or other bespoke form of document to be created in satisfaction of the order).

4.40 An applicant can adduce evidence from their own knowledge or investigations. Such evidence should focus upon the debtor's means subsequent to the original order being enforced and, in particular, their means at and after the time the payment was due. Evidence might include:

- A statement setting what they have observed or learned of the debtor's spending or lifestyle from which inferences as to the debtor's access to funding can be drawn;
- Publicly available evidence such as information from Companies House, a company website, a company announcement or the Land Registry;
- Matters to which the debtor has referred in correspondence with solicitors as to their means;
- Information gained from separate third-party disclosure orders or similar routes to obtain information from other sources (eg banks, accountants, businesses and colleagues).

F PENALTIES AND SENTENCE

4.41 The maximum penalty is six weeks imprisonment: Debtors Act 1869, s 5. Of this only three weeks is likely to be served. This is the effect of Criminal Justice Act 2003, s 258 which provides for automatic unconditional release of a contemnor after half the sentence has been served.

4.42 The aims of the court's sentence are twofold[35]:

- To mark the gravity of the offence (punitive element); and
- To secure future compliance (coercive/inducement element).

4.43 In *Thorpe v Thorpe*[36] it was held by the Court of Appeal in relation to an ordinary contempt (of which a judgment summons is species) that:

> 'there is no principle that a first breach cannot result in a sentence of imprisonment'.

35 See inter alia *Hammerton v Hammerton* [2007] EWCA Civ 248, [2007] 3 FCR 107, [2007] 2 FLR 1133 at para 9(v); and *Thursfield v Thursfield* [2013] EWCA Civ 840, [2013] CP Rep 44, [2013] 3 FCR 469, [2014] 1 FLR 389.

36 [1998] 2 FCR 384, [1998] 2 FLR 127.

Nevertheless, the court must also consider whether a suspended order of imprisonment is appropriate or sufficient: see *Slade v Slade*[37].

4.44 Whether or not the court imposes a sentence of imprisonment is thus a matter of discretion and committal is not the necessary consequence of a contempt: *Hale v Tanner*[38]. Equally so as to whether any custodial sentence is suspended. The suspension may be on terms as to the future payment of any re-timetabled sums due: FPR 2010, r 33.16(2).

4.45 It is not appropriate to argue for a 'tariff' by making reference to other sentences in other cases: see *Thursfield v Thursfield*[39] at para [33]:

> 'Mr Maguire referred in his skeleton argument, by way of contrast, to a wide variety of other cases including some in the *JSC BTA Bank v Solodchenko* saga. I derive no assistance from any of them and I deprecate the citation of cases which are really said to be precedents or guidance on the facts. Each case, particularly of committal, depends on its own facts, and a comparison with the facts of other cases, unless they are so closely related as to be in effect the same case, where there might conceivably be arguments as to inconsistency between different contemnors in relation to the same contempt, seems to me to be altogether unhelpful.'

4.46 It is nevertheless instructive to note, by way of example of the ranges of outcome, that:

- In *Bhura* a suspended sentence was given notwithstanding a finding of a wilful refusal to pay (rather than culpable inadvertence) and the fact that the respondent had given false evidence;
- In *Prest* a failure to pay £360,000 resulted in a four-week sentence of imprisonment suspended on terms that the debt was satisfied by a certain date (three months later);
- In *Rogan v Rogan*[40] no order was made at all, but the proceedings were twice adjourned to allow time for the debtor to pay over £140,933 (it had been agreed that he should have such time to pay, but the wife argued for a suspended committal order on those terms, which the court declined to make in circumstances where he had issued an application for downward variation of the maintenance).

4.47 Unlike in relation to committals for contempt simpliciter, the debtor's general conduct unrelated to the specific default under consideration is not

37 [2009] EWCA Civ 748, [2010] 1 WLR 1262, [2010] 1 FCR 227, [2010] 1 FLR 160 per Wilson LJ at para 25 where he stated 'It would in my view be good practice for the court which imposes a sentence of imprisonment for contempt always expressly to ask itself in judgment whether the sentence might properly be suspended'.

38 [2000] 1 WLR 2377, [2000] 2 FLR 879.

39 [2013] EWCA Civ 840, [2013] CP Rep 44, [2013] 3 FCR 469, [2014] 1 FLR 389.

40 [2018] EWHC 2512(Fam), [2019] 1 FCR 97; [2019] EWHC 814 (Fam); [2021] EWHC 2587 (Fam).

relevant to the sentence to be imposed: *Abecasis v Brandon*[41]. Nor by extension is the debtor's conduct of the judgment summons proceedings a relevant factor.

4.48 The court may also make an order for an attachment of earnings or, as an alternative to an order for immediate committal, a new order for the payment of the amount together with the costs of the summons: FPR 2010, r 33.16(1).

G PROCEDURAL REQUIREMENTS AND FORMALITIES

4.49 The procedural rules governing a judgment summons are set out at FPR 2010, Part 33, rr 9–17 and FPR 2010, Part 37 also applies '*as appropriate*' (per FPR 2010, r 33.5). The application, a '*request for issue of judgment summons*', is made using Form D62.

4.50 As with committals for contempt, the procedural rules must be scrupulously followed: per Holman J in *Quan v Bray*[42] at para [11]:

> 'It is very well-established that all the procedural steps specified by the Debtors Act 1869 and the rules of court must be strictly followed, and there cannot be short cuts.'

4.51 A judgment summons will usually be issued in the Family Court pursuant to FPR 2010, r 33.10, and be allocated in accordance with Family Court (Composition and Distribution of Business) Rules 2014, r 17. This provides for it to be dealt with by the same level of judge who made the original order defaulted upon (subject to any application for re-allocation within the terms of the Rules).

4.52 The summons must be accompanied by a statement which contains all the evidence on which the creditor intends to rely (FPR 2010, rr 33.10(2)(b), 33.11(2)) which must state how much is due, how that is calculated and be accompanied by a statement of truth (FPR 2010, r 33.3(1)).

4.53 As to service, this must be not less than 14 days prior to the hearing (FPR 2010, r 33.11(5)). The rules provide for either personal service (FPR 2010, r 33.11(3)(a)) *or* service by first class post (FPR 2010, r 33.11(3)(b)). If served by post, then there must be filed at court a certificate for postal service (FPR 2010, r 33.11(4)).

4.54 If the hearing is adjourned without the attendance of the debtor then the notice of adjourned hearing and the original summons and evidence must be served personally, rather than by post (FPR 2010, r 33.13). Equally, by virtue of FPR 2010, r 33.14(2) a debtor cannot be committed to prison where the summons

41 [1947] LJR 325.

42 [2019] EWFC 46. See for instance *Morris v Morris* [2016] EWCA Civ 812, [2017] 1 WLR 554, [2016] 3 FCR 224 where a committal order was set aside where it had been subject to fundamental procedural errors.

was served by post, unless he attends the hearing. Given these restrictions, it would be advisable for practitioners to seek to serve the proceedings personally, or seek an order for deemed or substitute service should circumstances require or permit it.

4.55 There is no longer any requirement for the summons to be served with 'conduct money' (ie sums for travel expenses to court of the debtor) *but* the corollary is that if it was served without such sums, then in the event that the debtor fails to attend the hearing, he cannot be committed for contempt for such a failure (FPR 2010, r 33.14A).

H SUCCESSIVE JUDGMENT SUMMONSES

4.56 Where a debtor has been committed in respect of a judgment summons the judgment creditor may issue a further judgment summons in respect of the same order with the leave of the court (FPR 2010, r 33.12). This rule appears to overrule the decision of the Court of Appeal in *Kumari v Jamal*[43], which although not specifically a judgment summons case, was to contrary effect.

4.57 This is a potentially useful tool in the court's armoury to deal with particularly recalcitrant debtors. Although the maximum sentence of imprisonment on a judgment summons is six weeks, the possibility of successive summonses means that an unrepentant debtor may have to face more than one jail term.

4.58 Although this is not dealt with in the rules, presumably any further judgment summons would have to be based upon evidence that since the first order for committal the debtor has had the means to pay; otherwise he would face double jeopardy (or more) for the same offence.

43 [1997] 1 WLR 97, [1997] 1 FCR 422, [1996] 2 FLR 588.

CHAPTER 5

Hadkinson and related orders

Content at a glance:

A INTRODUCTION

5.01 When a party has breached orders in the course of proceedings, it is not always desirable to wait until the conclusion of the case to obtain a remedy, nor to issue freestanding enforcement proceedings. In some circumstances, it will be preferable to pursue an interim remedy as a means of securing compliance with the order before the proceedings have concluded.

Situations where one party's contempt may warrant an *interim* remedy:

- Breach of an order for payment of maintenance pending suit
- Breach of a legal services payment order
- Breach of a case management order
- Failure to provide disclosure
- Pursuit of appeals/ variation applications while in breach of existing orders

5.02 The focus of this chapter is on a particular remedy known as a '*Hadkinson* order', named after the case of *Hadkinson v Hadkinson*[1]. A *Hadkinson* order is one which prevents a respondent from participating in proceedings or otherwise limits that party's ability to do so. These are discussed below in **5.04** et seq A *Mubarak* order, named after the case of *Mubarak v Mubarik (No 2)*[2], is a species

1 [1952] P 285.

2 [2006] EWHC 1260 (Fam), [2007] 1 WLR 271, sub nom *Mubarak v Mubarik (Contempt in Failure to Pay Lump sum: Standard of Proof)* [2007] 1 FLR 722.

of *Hadkinson* order which makes a respondent's participation in proceedings conditional upon the payment of the applicant's legal fees in an amount equal (or proportionate) to the fees paid towards the respondent's own solicitors. These are discussed in **5.32** et seq.

5.03 More generally, where a respondent has breached an interim order, practitioners may also wish to pursue one of the other enforcement remedies discussed elsewhere in this book. See in particular:

- General enforcement: **Chapter 2**.
- Committal: **Chapter 3**.
- Judgment summons: **Chapter 4**.

B *HADKINSON* ORDERS

Definition

5.04 The court has a discretionary power to refuse to hear a party who appears before the court while in contempt. A debarring order of this nature is habitually termed a '*Hadkinson* order'.

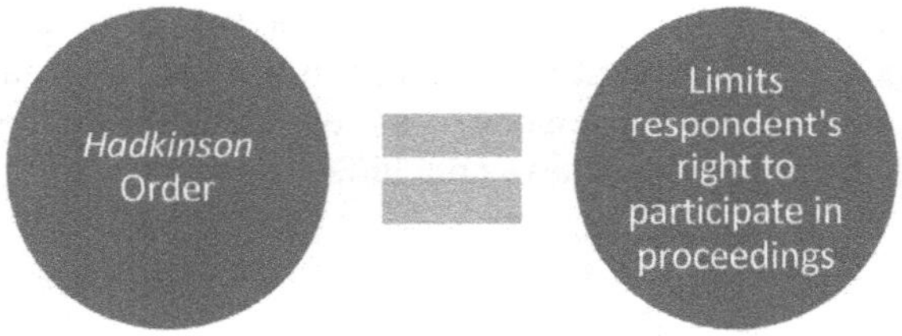

5.05 The modern formulation of this historical power derived from canon law was framed by Denning LJ in *Hadkinson v Hadkinson*[3]:

Key citation: *Hadkinson v Hadkinson*[4]

Denning LJ[5] [emphasis added]:

> 'It is a strong thing for a court to refuse to hear a party to a cause and it is only to be justified by grave considerations of public policy. It is a

3 [1952] P 285 at 298.

4 [1952] P 285 at 298.

5 Although Denning LJ was giving in effect a minority judgment, all the judges came to the same conclusion. Denning LJ's reasons were slightly different (with more emphasis on the discretion than the duty) to those of Somerville and Romer LJJ. Nevertheless, it is Denning LJ's judgment which now represents the modern practice as appears from the speeches of Lord Bridge of Harwich and Lord Oliver of Aylmerton in *X Ltd v Morgan-Grampian (Publishers) Ltd* and Others [1991] 1 AC 1, [1990] 2 WLR 1000 (paras 46 and 47; 50 and 51 respectively).

> step which a court will only take when the contempt itself impedes the course of justice and there is no other effective means of securing his compliance…
>
> … the fact that a party to a cause has disobeyed an order of the court is not of itself a bar to his being heard, but **if his disobedience is such that, so long as it continues, it impedes the course of justice in the cause**, by making it more difficult for the court to ascertain the truth or to enforce the orders which it may make, then **the court may in its discretion refuse to hear him until the impediment is removed or good reason is shown why it should not be removed**.'

5.06 In order for the court to make a *Hadkinson* order it is necessary for the applicant to prove that the respondent is in contempt of court. Once contempt has been established, the court must consider other matters that are relevant to whether it should exercise its discretion to make an order.

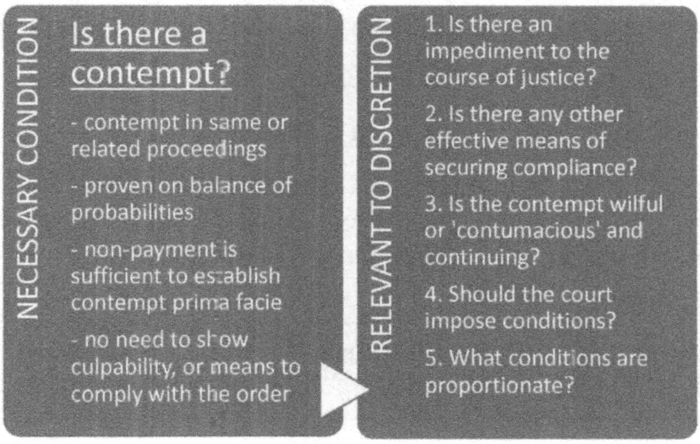

Proving the contempt

5.07 The applicant must first show the respondent is in contempt of court in order to engage the power to make a *Hadkinson* order. The remedy is not limited to circumstances where the respondent is in breach of a court *order*. 'Contempt' may be established by breach of an order, breach of an undertaking[6] or contempt in the face of the court.

5.08 For the purposes of engaging the *Hadkinson* jurisdiction, contempt does not need to be proved to the criminal standard[7]. It is a civil remedy, effectively a case management power with the underlying aim of achieving 'procedural

6 See for example *Gordon v Gordon and Gordon (Co-respondent)* [1904] P 163, though the point was obiter dicta as the Court of Appeal decided to hear the wife despite her contempt for breach of an undertaking.

7 Here a distinction is made between proving contempt for the purposes of obtaining a *Hadkinson* order, and contempt for the purposes of other remedies such as committal (see **Chapter 3**) and judgment summons (see **Chapter 4**).

justice' rather than sanction[8]. As the liberty of the subject is not at stake, contempt only needs to be established to the civil standard, the balance of probabilities.

5.09 Where the breach relied upon is non-payment of a sum required by court order, the mere fact of non-payment is sufficient to establish contempt for *Hadkinson* purposes.

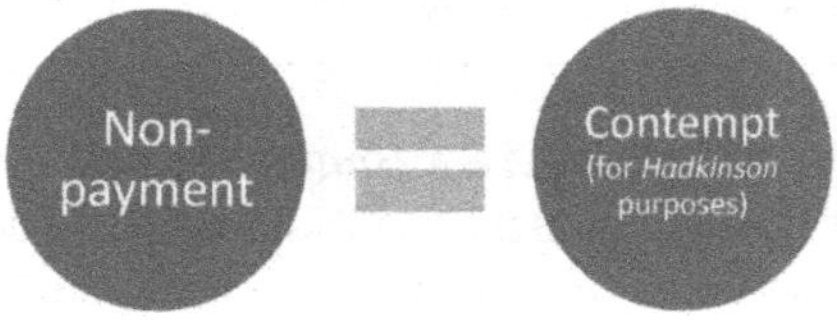

The contempt is established by mere non-compliance, regardless of whether the reasons were justified or not. Thus, there is no need to prove that the respondent:

- Was culpable or wilful in their contempt;
- Had the means to pay the sum when they defaulted[9].

Such features, if proved, will be relevant to the exercise of the court's discretion as to whether to debar a contemnor from being heard, or whether to impose conditions before permitting the contemnor to participate.

Key citation: *Mubarak v Mubarik*[10]

Ryder J:

> '... simple disobedience with an order is sufficient to find the contempt and that, although the existence of wilful contempt is a component that the court must consider, it is relevant to the exercise of discretion not whether the discretion exists on the facts of the instant case.'

8 Per Bodey J in *Mubarak v Mubarik (No 2)* [2006] EWHC 1260 (Fam), [2007] 1 WLR 271, [2007] 1 FLR 722 at para 71.

9 Per Court of Appeal in *Baker v Baker (No 2)* [1997] 2 FCR 249, [1997] 1 FLR 148 at 152-153. In that case the husband's contempt had been (rightly, per the Judgment of the CA) admitted at first instance, but since he sought to re-open his concession on appeal, the CA gave active consideration to the requirement of proving contempt. Ultimately these observations were *obiter dicta* since he was not permitted to revise his case on appeal, but when the point was argued at first instance in *Mubarak v Mubarik* [2004] EWHC 1158 (Fam), [2004] 2 FLR 932 before Ryder J, and *Mubarak v Mubarik (No 2)* [2006] EWHC 1260 (Fam), [2007] 1 WLR 271, [2007] 1 FLR 722 before Bodey J, it was held that mere non-payment would suffice, with the degree of disobedience or culpability being relevant only to the exercise of the discretion. The Court of Appeal has since approved this statement of the law in *Orenga de Gafforj v Orenga de Gafforj* [2018] EWCA Civ 2070; [2019] 1 FCR 73 per Peter Jackson LJ at para 12.

10 Per Ryder J in *MA v MI* [2004] EWHC 1158 (Fam), [2004] 2 FLR 932 at para 53.

5.10 The relevant breach does not need to relate to a particular type of order. The jurisdiction may be triggered by any of the following (not an exhaustive list):

- Removal of a child from jurisdiction in breach of an order[11]
- Non-payment of a lump sum[12]
- Non-payment of periodical payments[13]
- Non-payment of maintenance pending suit[14]
- Non-payment of child maintenance or school fees[15]
- Failure to comply with a property adjustment order
- Failure to comply with other provisions of a financial remedy order[16]
- Breach of a disclosure order[17]

5.11 Ongoing default will be treated as a continuing contempt and is more likely to result in the discretion being exercised so as to make a debarring order: see *Laing v Laing*[18].

5.12 The order that has been breached does not need to have been made in the same proceedings as that in which the relief is sought, but the power has only ever been used in a family law context where the proceedings were either the same or closely related (for example a variation application where the original order has been breached, or an appeal when the appellant is in default of maintenance or costs allowances owed to the respondent on appeal)[19].

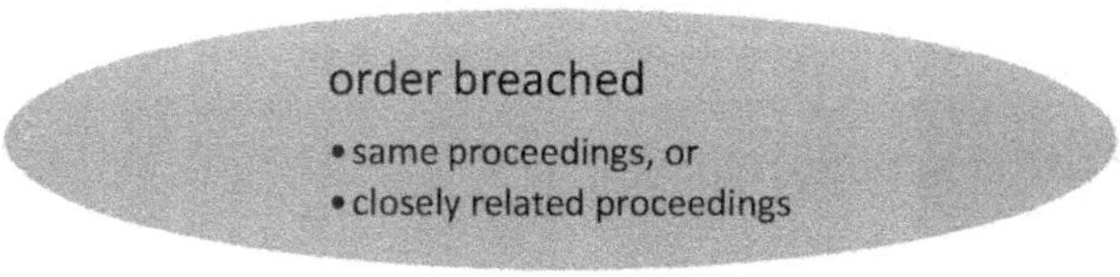

5.13 In *DS v HR*[20], Cohen J made a *Hadkinson* order in separate but factually related proceedings involving some of the same parties. He refused to hear a father's appeal of a costs order made in proceedings under the Family Law Act 1996, Part IV until the appellant had purged his contempt of a child maintenance clause in a financial remedies order.

11 *Hadkinson v Hadkinson* [1952] P 285.
12 *Mubarak v Mubarik* [2004] EWHC 1158 (Fam), [2004] 2 FLR 932.
13 *Laing v Laing* [2005] EWHC 3152 (Fam), [2007] 2 FLR 199.
14 *Laing v Laing* [2005] EWHC 3152 (Fam), [2007] 2 FLR 199.
15 *DS v HR (Hadkinson Order)* [2019] EWHC 2425 (Fam), [2020] 1 FLR 945.
16 *C v C (Appeal: Hadkinson Order)* [2010] EWHC 1656 (Fam), [2011] 1 FLR 434.
17 *M v M (Financial Provision)* [2010] EWHC 2817 (Fam), [2011] 1 FLR 1773.
18 *Laing v Laing* [2005] EWHC 3152 (Fam), [2007] 2 FLR 199.
19 *DS v HR (Hadkinson Order)* [2019] EWHC 2425 (Fam), [2020] 1 FLR 945; *Orenga de Gafforj v Orenga de Gafforj* [2018] EWCA Civ 2070; [2019] 1 FCR 73.
20 *DS v HR (Hadkinson Order)* [2019] EWHC 2425 (Fam), [2020] 1 FLR 945.

Case summary: *DS v HR*[21]

Facts:

This was the first reported case in which a *Hadkinson* order was made in different but related proceedings. In this case, FLA 1996 and MCA 1973 proceedings were both before the court but being heard separately. Further, the FLA 1996 claim involved additional parties who were not joined to the MCA 1973 proceedings.

Held by Cohen J:

Despite being heard separately, in H's mind the FLA and MCA proceedings were intrinsically linked: H's motive for refusing to pay child maintenance arose from his objection to the costs order made in the FLA 1996 proceedings.

Each stage of the *Mubarak* test formulated by Ryder J)[22] was made out. H had no defence to the non-payment of child maintenance and the sum of money was, to him, a small amount, not to mention it being a sum he had agreed to pay. It was proportionate and appropriate to make a *Hadkinson* order that unless H paid the arrears of child maintenance within two months, his appeal of the FLA 1996 costs order would be struck out.

Exercise of the discretion

5.14 A *Hadkinson* order is a draconian power. At first blush, to debar a party from participating in part or all of proceedings offends against his or her access to justice and ECHR Article 6 rights to a fair trial. These points were considered by in *Mubarak v Mubarik*[23] by Ryder J who gave detailed guidance on the exercise of the discretion in a post-ECHR legal context.

21 *DS v HR (Hadkinson Order)* [2019] EWHC 2425 (Fam), [2020] 1 FLR 945.
22 *Mubarak v Mubarik* [2004] EWHC 1158 (Fam), [2004] 2 FLR 932 at para 59.
23 *Mubarak v Mubarik* [2004] EWHC 1158 (Fam), [2004] 2 FLR 932.

Case summary: *Mubarak v Mubarik*[24]

Facts:

In 1999 a final order was made which required H to pay a lump sum of £4.875 million in addition to periodical payments. W pursued a judgment summons against H after he failed to pay the lump sum; her application was ultimately unsuccessful.

H applied to vary the periodical payments while he remained in default of the lump sum order. He had also been criticised for his failure to make proper disclosure, in particular of the value of a group of companies controlled by an offshore trust.

W argued that as a result of H's ongoing contempt the court should refuse to hear his application, or make his participation subject to conditions.

Held by Ryder J:

It was reasonable to impose conditions on hearing H's application. These must be *proportionate* to the wilful and continuing nature of the contempt. The conditions were:

- H was required to notify the trustees that he irrevocably accepted he was bound by the original decision in certain respects and requested the trust to act accordingly.
- H must not oppose certain steps taken by W to aid enforcement.

Hadkinson conveyed a discretionary power, not a duty. Mere disobedience of an order was not of itself a bar to that party being heard, but if a party's disobedience is such that, so long as it continues, it would impede the course of justice by making it more difficult for the court to ascertain the truth of, or to enforce the orders which it makes, the court may in its discretion refuse to hear the contemnor until the impediment is removed, unless good reason is shown why the impediment should not be removed.

The court must consider the following questions, with 1 being a necessary condition and 2–4 being relevant to the exercise of discretion (at para [59]):

1. Is the respondent in contempt?
2. Is there an impediment to the course of justice?
3. Is there any other effective means of securing compliance with the court's orders?
4. Should the court exercise its discretion to impose conditions having regard to the question: is the contempt wilful (ie is it contumacious and continuing)?
5. If so, what conditions would be proportionate?

24 *Mubarak v Mubarik* [2004] EWHC 1158 (Fam), [2004] 2 FLR 932.

5.15 It is clear from *Mubarak* and other judicial statements that in order to comply with Article 6 of the ECHR[25] the court must use the *Hadkinson* power sparingly. It is a *remedy of last resort*, to be exercised only in circumstances where the court is satisfied that:

- There is no other method of securing compliance with the court's orders;

  and

- The disobedience, so long as it continues, is an impediment to justice (either by making it more difficult for the court to ascertain the truth or to enforce its own orders);

  and

- Any debarring order or participation conditions must be proportionate to the breach.

5.16 In *Mubarak v Mubarik*[26] at para [59] Ryder J set out a list of questions which the court should consider when deciding whether to make a *Hadkinson* order. These were approved by the Court of Appeal in *Assoun v Assoun*[27] and *Orenga de Gafforj v Orenga de Gafforj*[28]:

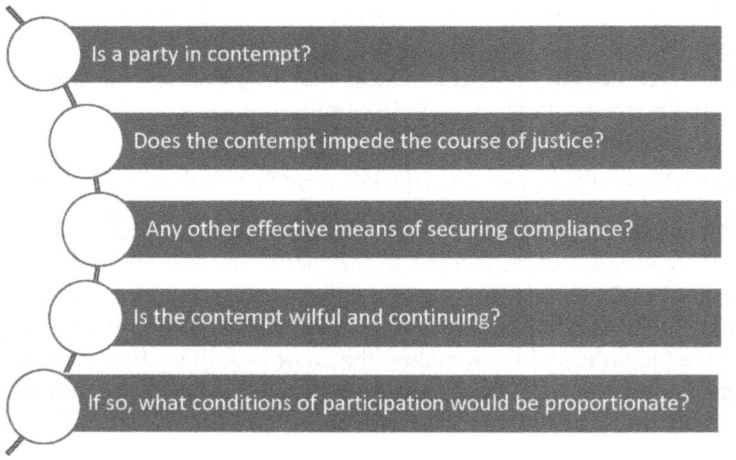

5.17 In *Laing v Laing*[29] at para [18] Sir Mark Potter P described impeding the course of justice as:

> 'making it more difficult for the court to ascertain the truth or to enforce the orders it makes'

25 Convention for the Protection of Human Rights and Fundamental Freedoms.

26 *Mubarak v Mubarik* [2004] EWHC 1158 (Fam), [2004] 2 FLR 932.

27 *Assoun v Assoun* [2017] EWCA Civ 21; [2017] 2 FCR 519, [2017] 2 FLR 1137, [2017] 2 FCR 519 at para 12.

28 *Orenga de Gafforj v Orenga de Gafforj* [2018] EWCA Civ 2070, [2019] 1 FCR 73 per Peter Jackson LJ at para 11 (albeit the same principles were stated but the sequence was changed).

29 [2005] EWHC 3152 (Fam), [2007] 2 FLR 199.

He noted that this was the approach taken in *Baker v Baker (No 2)*[30] and *Mubarak v Mubarik*[31].

Case summary: *Laing v Laing*[32]

Facts:

H had been ordered to pay periodical payments of £22,500 pa. He stopped paying at a time when he had the means to pay and he applied for a downward variation following his retirement. By the date of the interim hearing H was in breach of the order and had accrued arrears. DJ Segal ordered him to pay £13,000 in respect of the arrears and a reduced sum of £1,000 pm. The court made the continuation of the variation application conditional upon payment of these sums.

H appealed, arguing that:

(i) *Hadkinson* orders were only available when there is a breach of a capital order;

(ii) *Hadkinson* relief is a 'last resort in the grossest of cases';

(iii) The debarring order pre-judged the husband's variation application;

(iv) H's default did not impede the course of justice;

(v) There was another effective means of securing compliance;

(vi) It is common after applying for a downward variation to cease paying.

Held by Sir Mark Potter (dismissing the appeal):

The mere fact that a husband may have a legitimate argument for downward variation does not legitimate a wilful failure to pay if he has ample means to do so.

The concept of 'last resort' falls to be viewed in the context of the case including the immediacy of the need for enforcement. W's needs were immediate given her financial circumstances.

The alternative remedy of judgment summons was likely to be ineffective.

This decision was not a 'green light' for similar applications where it was not clear that the defaulter had the means to pay and where there may well be substantial remission of arrears.

30 *Baker v Baker (No 2)* [1997] 2 FCR 249, [1997] 1 FLR 148.
31 *Mubarak v Mubarik* [2004] EWHC 1158 (Fam), [2004] 2 FLR 932.
32 *Laing v Laing* [2005] EWHC 3152 (Fam), [2007] 2 FLR 199.

5.18 The *Hadkinson* remedy is said to be 'flexible'[33], requiring a careful consideration of the competing rights of the contemnor and the *Hadkinson* applicant. The power may only be used insofar as is necessary to achieve the desired effect of securing compliance with the court's orders without undue or disproportionate infringement of the contemnor's right to be heard.

5.19 If the court concludes that there is another effective means of securing compliance with its orders, it would be improper to make a *Hadkinson* order, even in circumstances where the breach is obvious and indefensible. It is not to be used as a method of sanction, but a means of procuring compliance[34].

5.20 In *M v M*[35], Bodey J refused to make a Hadkinson order against a husband who was in arrears of maintenance owed to the wife in the sum of c £200,000.

Case summary: *M v M (Maintenance Pending Suit: Enforcement on Dismissal of Suit)*[36]

Facts:

H applied to discharge an MPS order and to remit arrears of £200k. He had paid nothing owing under the terms of the order and while in breach of its terms he had obtained a divorce in Nigeria such that W's English petition had been dismissed. H argued that the English court no longer had jurisdiction for the divorce suit. W sought to enforce the arrears. She contended H should be debarred from making his applications as he was in breach of the order.

Held by Bodey J (refusing the application for a *Hadkinson* order):

> '[52]… [A *Hadkinson* order] is a remedy of last resort, for use where the circumstances are such that adequate justice cannot be done to the aggrieved party whilst the defaulter remains in breach. Hence one particular factor to be taken into consideration is whether or not there is any other way to secure effective compliance with the order concerned. Even where there is not, there will be some circumstances in which the defaulter has to be permitted to challenge the very order in respect of which he or she is in breach.

33 See Cohen J in *DS v HR (Hadkinson Order)* [2019] EWHC 2425 (Fam), [2020] 1 FLR 945, adopting the language of Peter Jackson LJ in *Orenga de Gafforj v Orenga de Gafforj* [2018] EWCA Civ 2070, [2019] 1 FCR 73 at para 15.

34 *M v M (Maintenance Pending Suit: Enforcement on Dismissal of Suit)* [2008] EWHC 2153 (Fam), [2009] 1 FLR 790.

35 *M v M (Maintenance Pending Suit: Enforcement on Dismissal of Suit)* [2008] EWHC 2153 (Fam), [2009] 1 FLR 790.

36 [2008] EWHC 2153 (Fam), [2009] 1 FLR 790.

> [53] Here, there is an alternative means by which effective compliance with the maintenance pending suit order can be achieved, namely by the process of the charging order and the order for sale already in place, absent any contrary order emerging from this judgment. I do not therefore propose to debar the husband from participating at this hearing, nor from advancing such arguments and seeking such reliefs as he may be advised.'

NB this decision was upheld in *M v M (Maintenance Pending Suit: Enforcement on Dismissal of Suit)*[37].

5.21 It is easier to obtain a *Hadkinson* order preventing a contemnor from being heard at an *interim* hearing or on a *discrete issue* within proceedings than it is to debar a party from participating in a final hearing or a substantive application.

5.22 In *M v M*, King J made a full *Hadkinson* order preventing the husband from being heard in response to a MPS application, but took no steps to limit his participation in the substantive proceedings, indeed emphasised the desirability of his engagement in future. The judge considered that the relative prejudice to the husband in constraining his participation in a discrete, interim application (which could be varied in future) was considerably lower than debarring him from the proceedings as a whole.

Case summary: *M v M (Financial Provision)*[38]

Facts:

Following separation, H ceased all financial provision for W and the children (apart from school fees). H failed to serve an affidavit of means (in breach of an order) and failed to attend the hearing, though he instructed leading and junior counsel to represent him. There was no explanation for his failure to provide evidence as ordered.

Held by King J (granting a *Hadkinson* order preventing H's participation in the MPS application):

H's contempt had been directed specifically at undermining the very application before the court. He had set out to deprive the court of the information it needed and to which it was entitled. A *Hadkinson* order in

37 2009] EWCA Civ 1427, [2010] 1 FLR 1413.

38 *M v M (Financial Provision)* [2010] EWHC 2817 (Fam), [2011] 1 FLR 1773, King J.

these circumstances did not fall foul of the ECHR Art 6. The contempt was wilful and impeded the course of justice.

The MPS jurisdiction was 'commonplace' and the court was unlikely to fall into error if H were not permitted to make legal submissions. Further, H could apply to vary the order if at any stage he should he re-engage with proceedings. There was therefore considerably less prejudice to H in debarring him from participating in a MPS application than a final hearing.

5.23 There is no reported case where a party has been debarred from participating, whether as applicant or respondent, in *a final hearing of substantive financial remedies proceedings* (as opposed to a variation application or an application to appeal or set aside an order). There is some doubt as to whether such an order would ever be appropriate, as it would undermine the court's ability to discharge its duties under the MCA 1973, s 25 and fulfil its investigative inquisitorial functions. In *Young v Young*[39], Moor J declined to make an order prohibiting a husband contemnor from being heard at a final hearing. Although he was satisfied the court had the power to make such an order, Moor J considered the exercise of such power had the potential to lead to injustice by impeding the court's inquisitorial function under the MCA 1973, s 25.

Key citation: *Young v Young*[40]

Moor J:

> '...I was concerned about extending the Hadkinson jurisdiction to contested final hearings for financial remedies. The court has to apply s 25 of the Matrimonial Causes Act 1973. It has to get to the bottom of the financial affairs of the parties. It is important that the court makes a proper investigation and produces a judgment that is not only fair but also right and correct. I consider that restricting the right of one party to participate in that exercise is difficult and, at times, has the potential to lead to injustice. It is, of course, right that the husband has been found to be in contempt of court to the criminal standard of proof. The wife is entitled to be very aggrieved about that. I do accept that it is has put her to considerable additional expense in costs. I will have to consider this contempt when I decide where the truth now lies. Nevertheless, having considered all that, and whilst making it abundantly clear that this court expects and requires its order to be obeyed, I took the view that it was not right to restrict the husband's participation in this final hearing.'

39 [2013] EWHC 3637 (Fam), [2014] 2 FCR 495 [2014] 2 FLR 786 at paras 89-90.
40 [2013] EWHC 3637 (Fam), [2014] 2 FCR 495 [2014] 2 FLR 786 at para 90.

5.24 Likewise, Holman J refused to make a debarring order against a husband in contempt in *LKH v TQA AL Z*[41]. The husband had failed to file a Form E and was in breach of orders to pay MPS, legal funding and costs. Notwithstanding these breaches, Holman J concluded that a full *Hadkinson* order would not serve the interests of justice, since such an order risked relevant evidence not being before the court on the substantive application. Instead, he concluded that a '*Mubarak*' pound for pound order was more appropriate and proportionate to the facts of the case. Such orders are considered in greater detail below in **5.32** et seq.

5.25

Case summary: *LKH v TQA AL Z*[42]

Facts:

The case involved a 'grave picture of non-compliance by H' who had failed to file a Form E and had breached orders for MPS, legal funding and costs. His overall arrears exceeded £200,000.

H filed a statement stating that his net wealth was $45 million, but his assets were illiquid and unrealisable. He claimed he was unable to make the payments owing to W, yet he had paid his own solicitors £95,000 and had incurred further costs with them. W owed her solicitors in excess of £200,000.

W sought an order that for every £1 paid to H's solicitors, H must pay £100 to her solicitors and a further order debarring H from entering an appearance while he remained in contempt.

Held by Holman J (refusing a full *Hadkinson* order but making *Mubarak* order):

A full *Hadkinson* order was a 'very extreme course'. It would be rare indeed to prevent a party from engaging in the *substantive financial remedy proceedings*, which required both parties to be fully engaged for the court to discharge its inquisitorial function.

It was appropriate to make a *Mubarak* £1 for £1 order (not the £100 for £1 order sought by W) in addition to the interim maintenance order already in existence, as it was 'frankly, intolerable and an affront to justice that in the last month this man paid £95,000 to his new solicitors

41 *LKH v TQA AL Z (Interim maintenance and pound for pound costs funding)* [2018] EWHC 2436 (Fam), [2018] 4 WLR 135, [2018] 3 FCR 553.

42 *LKH v TQA AL Z (Interim maintenance and pound for pound costs funding)* [2018] EWHC 2436 (Fam), [2018] 4 WLR 135, [2018] 3 FCR 553.

> at the very time when he was already in arrears and getting further into arrears with his wife' para [23].
>
> The 'rationale of such an order must be that of an equal or level playing field,' and thus the Mubarak jurisdiction cannot 'properly be applied to require a payer (usually the husband) to pay substantially more to the other party than to his own solicitors' para [17].

5.26 While *Hadkinson* orders may be made against both applicants and respondents[43], in balancing the competing prejudices to a party being kept out of funds against the rights of a contemnor to take part in proceedings, a court will more readily debar a contemnor applicant from being heard than it will a respondent. This is not a statement of principle but an application of the court's discretion: *Mubarak v Mubarik (No 2)*[44].

Conditions

5.27 Any conditions on a party's right to be heard must be proportionate to the breach[45]. There must further be some causal link between compliance with those conditions and the removal of an impediment to justice[46]. Since the power is 'flexible'[47] courts can be creative as to what conditions may be appropriate in different cases.

5.28 The following table contains illustrations of *Hadkinson* conditions in practice:

Examples of *Hadkinson* conditions	
Hadkinson[48]	Contemnor must return child to the jurisdiction of England and Wales before her appeal of the return order would be heard.
Baker (No 2)[49]	Contemnor must pay lump sum ordered before his application to vary parts of the order would be heard.

43 In contrast to the pre-1952 statements of the principle, which frequently emphasised the 'general rule' that a person in contempt may not initiate proceedings of his own while recognising that such parties may legitimately need to respond to applications made by others or to challenge the lawfulness of orders made against them: see Gordon *v Gordon and Gordon (Co-respondent)* [1904] P 163; and the Judgment of Romer LJ in *Hadkinson v Hadkinson* [1952] P 285.

44 *Mubarak v Mubarik (No 2)* [2006] EWHC 1260 (Fam), [2007] 1 WLR 271, [2007] 1 FLR 722.

45 *Mubarak v Mubarik* [2004] EWHC 1158 (Fam), [2004] 2 FLR 932 at paras 51 and 59, expressly approved by the Court of Appeal in *Assoun v Assoun* [2017] EWCA Civ 21, [2017] 2 FCR 519, [2017] 2 FLR 1137, [2017] 2 FCR 519 at para 12.

46 *Mubarak v Mubarik* [2004] EWHC 1158 (Fam), [2004] 2 FLR 932 at paras 48 and 51, expressly approved by the Court of Appeal in *Orenga de Gafforj v Orenga de Gafforj* [2018] EWCA Civ 2070; [2019] 1 FCR 73 at para 15.

47 *Orenga de Gafforj v Orenga de Gafforj* [2018] EWCA Civ 2070; [2019] 1 FCR 73 at para 15.

48 *Hadkinson v Hadkinson* [1952] P 285.

49 *Baker v Baker (No 2)* [1997] 2 FCR 249, [1997] 1 FLR 148.

Mubarak[50]	Contemnor must notify trustees that he will accept and be irrevocably bound by the court's decision and to request the trustees to act accordingly before his variation application would be heard.
	In addition, contemnor must not oppose certain steps being taken to aid enforcement.
Laing[51]	Contemnor must pay arrears of maintenance plus ongoing maintenance (at a reduced rate) before substantive application to vary /discharge order would be heard.
Mubarak (No 2)[52]	For every £1 the contemnor paid in future to his own lawyers, he must pay £1 into an account held to the order of the court, to be released to the wife's solicitors at the conclusion of the case.
C v C[53]	Contemnor must bring £1m onshore and pay it into a solicitors' account, held to the order of the court, before his appeal would be heard. In default of payment by a designated date, his appeal would be dismissed.
M v M[54]	Outright debarring order preventing H from defending MPS application.
Assoun[55]	Contemnor must pay outstanding sums before his application to vary/ terminate order for periodical payments would be heard.
	The Court of Appeal also attached conditions to the grant of leave to appeal: the contemnor must pay a Texan court bond of $62,500 and pay into court of £30k costs security before the appeal would be heard.
De Gafforj[56]	Contemnor must pay outstanding LSPO and the costs of *Hadkinson* application; in default of which his appeal would be dismissed. NB: the husband was not required to pay smaller sums being MPS arrears and unpaid historic costs as a condition of his appeal; these remained owing.
DS v HR[57]	Contemnor must discharge child maintenance arrears before his appeal of a costs order made in related proceedings would be heard.
Taiga v Ogbedo[58]	Contemnor must pay outstanding costs orders (£14,771) before he would be heard on various applications primarily relating to implementation of historic orders.
BSA v NVT[59]	Contemnor must pay an unpaid costs allowance for historic costs and an unpaid costs order, failing which his appeal would be dismissed. NB: the contemnor was in breach of lump sum payments exceeding this figure (including two lump sums and a further costs order) but these breaches were not held to be an immediate impediment to justice, so payment of those additional sums was not made a condition of his appeal proceeding. As above, they remained outstanding.

50 *Mubarak v Mubarik* [2004] EWHC 1158 (Fam), [2004] 2 FLR 932. NB Ryder J further directed that he *would* hear the husband on the limited factual issue of his means and motivation to pay, as this would be relevant to the exercise of the *Hadkinson* discretion.

51 *Laing v Laing* [2005] EWHC 3152 (Fam), [2007] 2 FLR 199.

52 *Mubarak v Mubarik (No 2)* [2006] EWHC 1260 (Fam), [2007] 1 WLR 271, [2007] 1 FLR 722.

53 *C v C (Appeal: Hadkinson Order)* [2010] EWHC 1656 (Fam), [2011] 1 FLR 434. NB when making this order, King J observed the Court of Appeal had made a similar condition to the grant of leave when Ms Radmacher was given leave to appeal in *Radmacher v Granatino* [2008] EWCA Civ 1304, [2009] 1 FLR 1566, in light of what they found to be her 'gross and subsisting breaches' of past orders.

54 *M v M (Financial Provision)* [2010] EWHC 2817 (Fam), [2010] 10 WLUK 417, [2011] 1 FLR 1773.

55 *Assoun v Assoun* [2017] EWCA Civ 21, [2017] 2 FCR 519, [2017] 2 FLR 1137.

56 *Orenga de Gafforj v Orenga de Gafforj* [2018] EWCA Civ 2070; [2019] 1 FCR 73.

57 *DS v HR (Hadkinson Order)* [2019] EWHC 2425 (Fam), [2020] 1 FLR 945.

58 *Taiga v Ogbedo* [2020] EWHC 3578 (Fam).

59 *BSA v NVT* [2021] EWHC 2202 (Fam).

Exceptions to Hadkinson orders

5.29 Even before the Human Rights Act 1998, there were certain recognised exceptions to the *Hadkinson* principle[60]. In cases falling within these exceptions, contemnors should always be heard. They are summarised in the following diagram:

5.30 These exceptions remain good law. Since the *Hadkinson* power is discretionary and to be used 'sparingly', there will be other circumstances, not falling within the exceptions identified above, where courts are likely to determine contemnors should be heard. Following Moor J in *Young v Young*[61], and Holman J in *LKH v TQA AL Z*[62], this is likely to include final hearings in proceedings where the court has a quasi-inquisitorial function, including financial remedy and child welfare applications.

Procedure

5.31 A *Hadkinson* application is an interim application governed by Family Procedure Rules 2010 ('FPR 2010'). Notice should almost always be given. Evidence must be filed with the application form. In an exceptional case, a *Hadkinson* application may be made on short or no notice to the respondent, but only if justified by urgency or other grounds: *Assoun v Assoun*[63].

60 *Hadkinson v Hadkinson* [1952] P 285 per Romer LJ at 289.

61 [2013] EWHC 3637 (Fam), [2014] 2 FCR 495, [2014] 2 FLR 786, [2014] 2 FCR 495 at para 89.

62 *LKH v TQA AL Z (Interim maintenance and pound for pound costs funding)* [2018] EWHC 2436 (Fam), [2018] 4 WLR 135, [2018] 3 FCR 553 at paras 19 and 20.

63 *Assoun v Assoun* [2017] EWCA Civ 21, [2017] 2 FCR 519 [2017] 2 FLR 1137.

Case summary: *Assoun v Assoun*[64]

Facts:

H applied to vary a periodical payments order of which he was in arrears. W sought a *Hadkinson* order but only gave notice of this when position statements were exchanged the day before the first appointment. The court made the debarring order.

H appealed, arguing there had been procedural unfairness, specifically that the lack of notice had prevented him from adducing evidence demonstrating his lack of means.

Held by the Court of Appeal (dismissing the appeal):

> '[16]...the responsibilities described in the rules, practice directions and pre-action protocols apply to both parties. For example, an application for a Hadkinson order should have been made under part 18 FPR on an application notice stating the order being applied for and the reasons for the same. The application notice has a statement of truth which has to be signed by the applicant in accordance with part 17 FPR if the applicant wishes to rely on matters set out in the application as evidence. Rule 18.8 sets out the provisions for service. In any future case I would expect there to be meticulous attention to the appropriate inter partes procedure unless the applicant has grounds to establish the need for an expedited and/or without notice application. Applicants should expect the court to scrutinise adherence to the rules and practice directions of the court and to refuse or adjourn an application that does not comply with them.'

When granting leave the CA had directed the husband to file evidence of his means to be considered at the appeal. The appellate court's conclusion was that his disclosure was not full and frank.

C *MUBARAK* ORDERS

Definition

5.32 A '*Mubarak*' or 'pound for pound' order is one requiring a respondent, as a condition of participation in the proceedings, to pay to the applicant or the applicant's solicitors a sum equal to that which the respondent pays or incurs with

64 [2017] EWCA Civ 21, [2017] 2 FCR 519, [2017] 2 FLR 1137.

the respondent's own lawyers. Such an order was made by Bodey J in *Mubarak v Mubarik*[65].

5.33 A *Mubarak* order is a species of *Hadkinson* order since it places a condition upon the contemnor's participation in the proceedings. However the order first devised by Bodey J in 2006 within the protracted *Mubarak* proceedings, has led to a separate sub-class of the *Hadkinson* jurisprudence.

5.34

Case summary: *Mubarak v Mubarik (No 2)*[66]

Facts:

H was in breach of an order to pay a lump sum of £4.875 million made seven years previously. Various attempts at enforcement had been unsuccessful.

H had not complied with the conditions imposed by Ryder J on a previous *Hadkinson* application, so his application to reduce the periodical payments had been adjourned, as had W's application to enforce them.

In 2005 H had stopped paying all sums to W and since then she had been solely dependent on loans from friends and commercial entities. The case returned before Bodey J on various applications by W inter alia to set aside transactions with a view to aiding enforcement.

W sought a further *Hadkinson* order. H argued, inter alia, that such an order should not be made against him when he was a respondent to W's applications.

Held by Bodey J (making a pound for pound order):

The *Hadkinson* procedure could be used against a respondent, although the fact that H was a respondent was relevant to the exercise of discretion. The balance of justice would require additional safeguards.

It would be wrong simply to debar H from defending W's applications in which jurisdictional questions fell to be decided. However, terms would be imposed on his participation:

1) H to inform trustees irrevocably that he would be bound by the court's decision and he wished them to assist him in meeting his obligations under the orders, and

65 *Mubarak v Mubarik (No 2)* [2006] EWHC 1260 (Fam), [2007] 1 WLR 271, [2007] 1 FLR 722.
66 *Mubarak v Mubarik (No 2)* [2006] EWHC 1260 (Fam), [2007] 1 WLR 271, [2007] 1 FLR 722.

2) For every £1 H paid henceforth to his lawyers, he must pay £1 into a joint account in the names of the parties' solicitors to be held to the order of the court, to be paid to W's solicitors at the end of the final hearing unless the court actively ruled otherwise.

These conditions were proportionate. The first condition did no more than to require H to comply with the orders of the court. The second condition sought to moderate his ability to employ a first rate legal team while failing to pay W any monies owed to her.

The standard of proof for establishing contempt in a *Hadkinson* context was the balance of probabilities. Mere default of an order was sufficient to trigger the jurisdiction. Culpability was relevant to discretion.

5.35 *Mubarak (No 2)*[67] has been followed in other cases where a court has made a contemnor's participation in the proceedings conditional upon compliance with a pound for pound order. For example, in *Mann v Mann*[68] and *LKH v TQA AL Z*[69], the court mandated a respondent's solicitors to pay to the applicant's representatives a prescribed sum each time the respondent made a payment to them.

5.36 The rationale behind a *Mubarak* order is that where a party is in breach of a court order to pay a sum, it is 'an affront to the court's sense of justice[70]' for that party to find the means to pay their own legal representatives in the pursuit of evading that liability (either by resisting enforcement or by seeking to vary or set aside the order) while maintaining there is insufficient liquidity to purge the contempt. Such orders are less punitive than other forms of *Hadkinson* order because they do not require a respondent to do any more than reallocate funds they are already spending for the purposes of proceedings.

5.37 Under an injunctive *Mubarak* order the payments made to the applicant are linked to the amount the respondent pays on legal fees. However, unlike a Legal Service Payment Order, the purpose of the order is not necessarily to provide litigation funding for the applicant; it may instead be to afford security for a claim yet to be determined or to aid enforcement of past or prospective orders. For this reason, it is not necessary for payments to be made to the applicant or the applicant's solicitors (and therefore to be used to discharge the applicant's legal costs); the payments may alternatively be paid into court or to some other secure fund.

67 *Mubarak v Mubarik (No 2)* [2006] EWHC 1260 (Fam), [2007] 1 WLR 271 [2007] 1 FLR 722.
68 *Mann v Mann* [2014] EWHC 2032 (Fam).
69 *LKH v TQA AL Z (Interim maintenance and pound for pound costs funding)* [2018] EWHC 2436 (Fam), [2018] 3 FCR 553, [2018] 4 WLR 135, at paras 21-23.
70 *Mann v Mann* [2014] EWHC 2032 (Fam), at para 28.

Limitations

5.38 There is no reported case where a respondent has been ordered to pay *more* to the applicant than they pay to the respondent's own lawyers. Indeed, some judicial guidance indicates such an order would not be an appropriate use of the power: see *LKH v TQA AL Z*[71].

Key citation: *LKH v TQA AL Z*[72]

Holman J (para 17):

> 'The rationale of [a *Mubarak* order] must be that of an equal or level playing field, and it does not seem to me that the Mubarak jurisdiction can properly be applied to require a payer (usually the husband) to pay substantially more to the other party than to his own solicitors. So in my view, the jurisdiction should correctly be regarded as a pound for pound one, so that from now on, with every pound he chooses to pay his own lawyers, he must pay an equal pound to the wife's lawyers up to, of course, the overall ceiling ordered by the order of 19 April 2018.'

5.39 It is respectfully suggested that Holman J's comments about an 'equal or level playing field' may be more relevant to cases where the purpose of the *Mubarak* order is to discharge a legal services payment order to provide funding for future legal fees, than when it is to discharge another type of order of which the respondent is in contempt. It could also be argued that where a court has concluded that an order for MPS or LSPO was urgently required in a particular sum, it might be necessary for there to be an enhanced rate of payment to the applicant up to that total in order to achieve a 'level playing field'.

5.40 In drafting *Mubarak* orders, an applicant must always be mindful of the potential for the respondent to avoid making payment by complying with the letter but not the spirit of the order. For example, if the respondent's solicitor holds a sizeable fund on account when the order is made, an order that for 'every £1 *paid* by the respondent to his solicitor, he shall pay £1 to the applicant's solicitor,' will not trigger any payments being made to the applicant during the period in which the respondent's solicitors are able to meet ongoing costs incurred from the funds they are already holding on account. The same difficulty would apply

71 *LKH v TQA AL Z (Interim maintenance and pound for pound costs funding)* [2018] EWHC 2436 (Fam), [2018] 4 WLR 135, [2018] 3 FCR 553.

72 *LKH v TQA AL Z (Interim maintenance and pound for pound costs funding)* [2018] EWHC 2436 (Fam), [2018] 4 WLR 135, [2018] 3 FCR 553.

if the respondent's fees had already reached a sufficiently high level that his representatives were willing to continue to act 'on credit', even if temporarily so. Such potential pitfalls can be avoided if the order is drafted to use the word 'incurred' instead of 'paid', as this will create an obligation on the respondent (or the respondent's solicitors) to make payments to the applicant if further work is conducted by the respondent's solicitors, whether or not the solicitors receive any further payments from the respondent.

5.41 Similarly, a *Mubarak* order should anticipate changes in the respondent's legal representation, either to a new firm of solicitors, or to direct access counsel, and be drafted accordingly.

5.42 There is nothing to prevent a respondent from acting in person. Linking payments being made to the applicant to sums the respondent spends on legal fees will not assist an applicant if the respondent chooses to proceed as a litigant in person. In those circumstances a *Mubarak* order may have the effect of separating the respondent from his or her lawyers, but not in securing payment for the applicant or compliance with the court order.

Illustrations

5.43 *Mubarak* injunctions can be drafted in different ways, depending on the purpose they are intended to serve.

Illustrations of *Mubarak* injunctions	
ORDER	COMMENTS
For every £1 **paid** by a contemnor to their (ie the contemnor's) own solicitors, they (the contemnor) shall pay to the applicant's solicitor the sum of £1.	• This order can alternatively be expressed: – as a straightforward injunction, or – as a *Hadkinson* order, depending on whether participation in proceedings is made conditional on compliance with the order to make payments. • If purpose of the order is to enable the applicant to obtain legal services it will be a type of LSPO and the relevant statutory test should be applied. • If the purpose of the order is to discharge arrears, payments should be capped at the level of the arrears. • Note the word 'paid' rather than 'incurred'. If the contemnor engages legal services on credit, the applicant will not receive any more funds.
For every £1 **incurred** by a contemnor with their (ie the contemnor's) own solicitors, they (the contemnor) shall pay to the applicant's solicitor the sum of £1.	• As above, but the order requires the respondent to pay the applicant even if the respondent ceases to pay their own solicitors, provided they continue to engage them

For every £2 **received** by the contemnor's solicitors, they (ie the contemnor's solicitors) shall pay to the applicant's solicitors the sum of £1.	• The principle is as above, but the onus is placed on solicitors to implement the payment. • As with the first illustration if the contemnor receives legal services on credit the applicant will not receive anything.
For every £1 paid by the contemnor to their own (ie the contemnor's) solicitors, they (the contemnor) shall pay to the applicant's solicitors the sum of **£50**.	• There are no reported cases of such an order, where the rate of payment towards the applicant's legal fees is faster than those paid by the respondent to their own solicitors, but there is arguably but no principled reason why the rate at which the contemnor pays the applicant cannot be proportionate (rather than equivalent) to the rate paid to their own solicitors[73]. • If the purpose is to enable legal fees to be paid, there may be more reason to make the payments at an equivalent rate; if the purpose, however, is to discharge an unpaid debt, it might be appropriate for the court to direct payment at a higher or lower rate to the applicant than to the contemnor's own lawyers.
For every £1 paid by the contemnor to their own (ie the contemnor's) solicitors, they (the contemnor) shall pay into court (or to a joint solicitors' account) the sum of £1, to be held to the order of the court pending final determination of the claim.	• This provides security to an applicant during proceedings, but the payments will not be made available to discharge the applicant's on-going legal fees unless a further order is made by the court to that effect.

73 Note however Holman J's refusal to make such an order in *LKH v TQA AL Z (Interim maintenance and pound for pound costs funding)* [2018] EWHC 2436 (Fam), [2018] 4 WLR 135, [2018] 3 FCR 553 at para 17 in particular.

CHAPTER 6

Execution and the direction and authorisation of third parties

Content at a glance:

A INTRODUCTION

6.01 This chapter provides an overview of miscellaneous tools available to the court such as the execution of documents and the delegation of authority that can be used as aids to enforcement.

B EXECUTION OF DOCUMENTS

6.02 Orders will often require a party to undertake certain transactions or execute documents that are necessary to give effect to orders and undertakings. It is not uncommon for a party to such an order to be dilatory or simply to refuse to take these steps themselves.

6.03 In such circumstances, the court has the power to execute the documents as if they stood in the shoes of the relevant party, or alternatively to confer that power upon a nominated third party, thereby cutting the recalcitrant party out of the enforcement process entirely.

6.04 The statutory source of this power is Senior Courts Act 1981 ('SCA 1981'), s 39:

> **'39 Execution of instrument by person nominated by High Court**
>
> (1) Where the High Court or family court has given or made a judgment or order directing a person to execute any conveyance, contract or

other document, or to indorse any negotiable instrument, then, if that person –

(a) neglects or refuses to comply with the judgment or order; or

(b) cannot after reasonable inquiry be found,

that court may, on such terms and conditions, if any, as may be just, order that the conveyance, contract or other document shall be executed, or that the negotiable instrument shall be indorsed, by such person as the court may nominate for that purpose.

(2) A conveyance, contract, document or instrument executed or indorsed in pursuance of an order under this section shall operate, and be for all purposes available, as if it had been executed or indorsed by the person originally directed to execute or indorse it.'

6.05 It is to be noted that this power is not limited to conveyances of land (although that is the most common usage) but applies to any conveyance, contract or other document. This can include, for example, documents to transfer particular investments or bank accounts.

6.06 The following are examples of occasions on which the power has been used:

- In *Yuzu Hair & Beauty Limited v Selvathiraviam*[1] Zacaroli J determined that the SCA 1981, s 39 could be used to permit a nominated person (in that case a High Court Master of the Chancery Division) to sign a document giving instructions to a bank to provide details of information pertaining bank accounts held by the defendant. The defendant had been required by a freezing order to obtain that information from the bank pursuant to ancillary disclosure requirements in relation to their assets.
- In *Gee v Gee & Gee*[2] HHJ Matthews (as a judge of the High Court) used the SCA 1981, s 39 to obtain the execution of a stock transfer form, following a judgment on a proprietary estoppel claim requiring the defendants to transfer a specified number of shares in a company to the claimant in satisfaction of their interests. In that case the nominated person was not a judge but a family member of the claimant and co-owner and director of the company.

6.07 Execution of a document includes not just signing, but delivering it up: see Nugee J (*obiter dicta*) in *Arrowgame Ltd & Goodman v Wildsmith & others*[3].

6.08 There are a number of requirements which must be fulfilled before the power can be exercised. It is incumbent on the applicant for a s 39 order to show, on evidence, that the defendant has 'neglected or refuses to comply with

1 [2020] EWHC 3695 (Ch).
2 [2020] EWHC 1842 (Ch).
3 [2016] EWHC 3608 (Ch).

the judgment or order' or that they cannot be found (per s 39(1)(a)): *Gee v Gee & Gee*[4], at para [26], where HHJ Matthews referred to this is a 'jurisdictional requirement'.

6.09 HHJ Hess set out the procedure in *Welch v Welch*[5] where (not atypically) a final financial remedy order had provided for an order for sale of a particular property 'forthwith' [i.e. by no specified date]. It is:

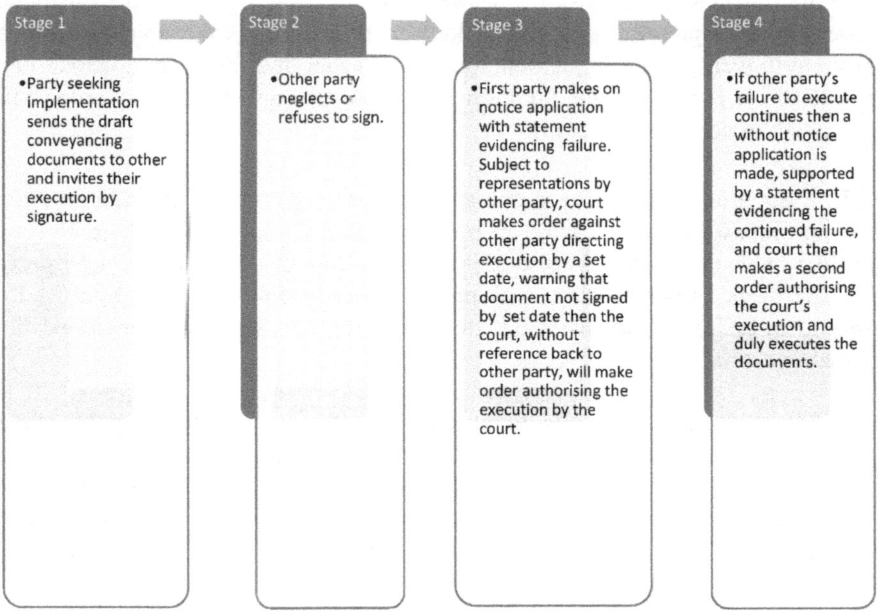

6.10 It is important to note that one cannot leap straight from a 'shall transfer forthwith [or by other even unspecified by date]' to a s 39 order. What is required is a clear order directed at the respondent requiring expressly that they 'shall execute [a specific document(s)] by [a specific time/date]'. Unless such an order has been made (hence stage 3) then a s 39 order cannot be made.

6.11 There is some debate as to whether an *anticipatory* order can be made (ie truncating Stages 3 and 4 above, such that a s 39 order is made in advance that provides for an automatic substituted execution *if* the date ordered in Stage 3 (or the original order being enforced) is not abided by (thereby obviating the need for Stage 4 at all)). In *Welch v Welch*[6] HHJ Hess had made such an order (at an early stage of the case) but McCombe LJ had granted permission to appeal (clearly with some scepticism) against it on the point that it was only if the person in question had *already* been presented with an order to sign and refused that a s 39 application could then be made. However, this was not determined conclusively,

4 [2020] EWHC 1842 (Ch).
5 [2017] EWFC B32, [2017] 3 FCR 405.
6 [2017] EWFC B32, [2017] 3 FCR 405.

as the appeal was not in the end heard. HHJ Hess (in the later stage of proceedings in the above cited decision) noted that the editors of the White and Red books, and the *obiter dicta* remarks in *Savage v Norton*[7] supported the proposition that in certain circumstances the court had the power to make anticipatory orders, but he did not determine the issue either way (for it was not by then before him).

6.12 It is suggested the safest route is to avoid a truncated anticipatory order, if possible, to obviate the risk of the *Welch* point being argued by the obstinate non-complier. That said, a court is likely to do all things possible to avoid a party circumventing the implementation of an order and the more obstinate the defaulter is or is likely to be, the more likely it is that an anticipatory order will be viewed favourably by a court.

6.13 Such an anticipatory order can be made by consent, including in the original order itself, as it was for example in *Khan v Mahmood*[8], where Marcus Smith J (on a successful appeal against a declaration of ownership of a property resulting in the appellate court making a fresh order for a transfer) approved a consent order for a 'forthwith' transfer provision but which also included the following term:

> 'If the Respondent fails to execute any document necessary to effect the Transfer within 7 days of being requested to do so in writing by the Appellant, or an authorised representative of the Appellant, a District Judge shall execute such documentation in place of the Respondent pursuant to section 39 of the Senior Courts Act 1981.'

C MATRIMONIAL CAUSES ACT 1973, s 24A

6.14 In respect of orders for transfers of real property and orders for sale of properties, Matrimonial Causes Act 1973 ('MCA 1973'), s 24A includes provisions that can be used as aids to enforcement.

6.15 The relevant parts of the statute provide as follows [emphasis added]:

> **'24A Orders for sale of property**
>
> (1) Where the court makes an order under section 22ZA or makes under section 23 or 24 of this Act a secured periodical payments order, an order for the payment of a lump sum or a property adjustment order, then, on making that **order or at any time thereafter**, the court may make **a further order** for the sale of such property as may be specified in the order, being property in which or in the proceeds of

7 [1908] 1 Ch 290.
8 [2021] EWHC 597 (Ch), [2021] WTLR 639.

sale of which either or both of the parties to the marriage has or have a beneficial interest, either in possession or reversion.

(2) Any order made under subsection (1) above **may contain such consequential or supplementary provisions as the court thinks fit** and, without prejudice to the generality of the foregoing provision, may include –

(a) provision requiring the making of a payment out of the proceeds of sale of the property to which the order relates, and

(b) provision requiring any such property to be offered for sale to a person, or class of persons, specified in the order.

(3) Where an order is made under subsection (1) above on or after the grant of a decree of divorce or nullity of marriage, the order shall not take effect unless the decree has been made absolute.

(4) Where an order is made under subsection (1) above, the court may direct that the order, or such provision thereof as the court may specify, shall not take effect until the occurrence of an event specified by the court or the expiration of a period so specified.

(5) ….

(6) ….'

6.16 The first point to note is that the powers are available 'at any time [at or after the original order was made]'. Secondly, they are very wide, ie 'such consequential or supplementary provisions as the court thinks fit'.

6.17 MCA 1973, s 24A can be used to give the putative enforcing party sole conduct of a sale. The provision in s 24A(2)(a) permits payments to made from proceeds of sale to third parties (or in the case of the enforcing party who is also a recipient of the benefit of a lump sum order, to that party). This latter provision could be of obvious utility, but it should be noted there will already need to be some other order providing for the transfer of a property or its sale to which this condition can be attached; the section does not enable a party to seek a new property adjustment order for the sole purpose of obtaining an order for sale to which a payment condition can be attached.

D *BLIGHT V BREWSTER* ORDERS

6.18 A *Blight v Brewster*[9] order is an order that can be directed towards a non-payer's pension, to require that person's right to elect to take such draw down as the pension permits to be triggered. By this mechanism a sum of cash may be

9 *Blight & others v Brewster* [2012] EWHC 165 (Ch), [2012] 1 WLR 2841, [2012] BPIR 476.

able to be produced as owed to the debtor by his pension provider, over which a third peart debt order or receivership could bite and hence in effect ultimately be paid to the enforcing party in compliance with a defaulted upon lump sum (or other payment) order.

6.19 This is a relatively new species of order. Its availability depends initially on the debtor having a pension that is capable of being drawn down, for example a UK private pension fund with the familiar right to elect to take a 25% lump sum tax free. Whether this is available (and it may be available in part, if a partial but not complete draw down has already taken place) is a matter of fact, and dependent on the terms and history of the relevant pension. In the UK this is likely to be in respect of a debtor who is over 55 years old (given the age at which tax free lump sums can first be taken, although differing pensions may have other provisions).

6.20 This was a route attempted in *Field v Field*[10], where the husband had not paid a required lump sum order. Wilson J however rejected it and held that forcing a debtor to make the election would be a 'free standing' injunction and as such was impermissible.

6.21 However, the Privy Council doubted that *Field* was correctly decided, albeit *obiter dicta*, in *Tasarruf Mevduati Sigorta Fonu v Merrill Lynch Bank and Trust Company (Cayman) Ltd*[11] at para [63]:

> 'The second objection was based on the decision of *Field v Field* [2003] 1 FLR 376. In that case a husband had defaulted on an order to pay a lump sum to his former wife. The husband had a non-assignable right to elect for a lump sum payment under his employer's pension scheme. It was held that the pension could not be reached by the wife through an order requiring the husband to elect a lump sum payment and appoint a Receiver to receive the proceeds. Wilson J thought that to make such an order would amount to 'a free-standing enforcement procedure in its own right,' which was not permitted by section 37; at [17]. The basis for such characterisation of the order in that case is not clear. In the present case the order would be ancillary to TSMF's rights as judgment creditors. The Board considers there is force in the criticism of the reasoning of this decision in Gee, Commercial Injunctions, 5th ed 2004, paras 16.017-018, but as indicated above, this is not a question which falls to be decided on this appeal.'

6.22 In *Blight & others v Brewster*[12], Mr Gabriel Moss QC sitting as a deputy High Court Judge made an order requiring the debtor to make the pension election.

10 [2003] 1 FLR 376.
11 [2011] UKPC 17, [2012] 1 WLR 1721, [2011] BPIR 1743, [2011] WLTR 1249.
12 [2012] EWHC 165 (Ch), [2012] 1 WLR 2841, [2012] BPIR 476.

He held expressly that the Privy Council *obiter dicta* remarks in *Tasarruf* were to be preferred to the ratio of *Field* (see paras [58]–[78]).

6.23 The *Blight* order made was:

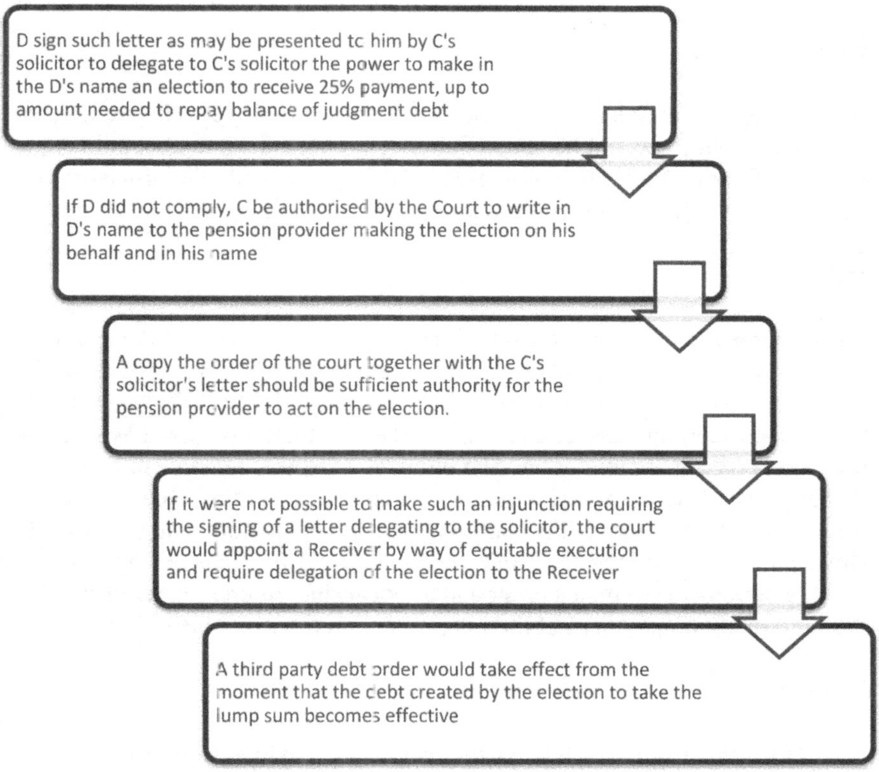

6.24 The *Blight* procedure has been considered since in the following cases decided by Mostyn J:

- *Goyal v Goyal No 3*[13]
- *Maughan v Wilmot*[14]

6.25 In *Goyal*[15], Mostyn J expressly relied on *Blight* to make a 'bolstering injunction' requiring the husband to procure payments from an annuity policy to be made to him and preferably directly to the wife, in satisfaction of a periodical payments order that she should receive two thirds of the quarterly income he received from that policy.

13 [2017] EWFC 1, [2017] 2 FCR 159.
14 [2020] EWHC 885 (Fam), [2020] 2 FCR 429.
15 [2017] EWFC 1, [2017] 2 FCR 159.

Case Summary: Goyal v Goyal No 3[16]

Facts:

H had or appeared to have an Indian pension/annuity policy. He had argued that (i) the policy was not his; and (ii) in any event it was not susceptible to a Pensions Sharing Order being overseas and falling outside the provisions of MCA 1973, s 24B (see *Goyal v Goyal No 2*[17]).

Held:

The pension/annuity was not susceptible to a Pension Sharing Order as it was overseas and s 24B could not bite on overseas pension. Nor was it necessarily susceptible to a variation of settlement order under MCA 1973, s 24(1)(c), because at the initial substantive hearing the court had dismissed W's claim for a property adjustment order. The judge also expressed concern that even if that power had been available, its exercise was questionable due to its ostensible extra territorial effect, although this point did not fall to be decided. However, he determined the same outcome could be achieved by another route: a periodical payments order and a 'bolstering' injunction requiring the husband to obtain payment of the maximum annuity available to him.

Key citation:

> '14. I therefore vary the existing periodical payments order to provide that it has two limbs. The first limb will be the monthly amount payable by the husband under Judge Brasse's order as varied by me (as to which, see below). The second limb will provide that the husband will pay to the wife two-thirds of the quarterly income deriving from the annuity policy as it arises. … There will be a bolstering injunction made against the husband requiring him to procure that these payments go to the wife. This injunction is made pursuant to the principle expounded in *Blight v Brewster* following the Privy Council in *Tasarruf Mevduati Sigorta Fonu v Merrill Lynch Bank and Trust Company (Cayman) Limited* [2011] UKPC 17. On service of that injunction on HDFC Life the existing freezing order, initially made by the Court of Appeal and repeated by me, will be discharged. I would like to think that HDFC Life will, on service on them of this judgment, my order, and the bolstering injunction, pay the sums directly to the wife's account, but that is a matter beyond my power to direct.'

16 [2017] EWFC 1, [2017] 2 FCR 159.
17 [2016] EWFC 50, [2017] 1 FCR 188, [2017] 2 FLR 236, [2016] 4 WLR 170.

6.26 In *Maughan v Wilmot*[18] Mostyn J again identified that a *Blight* order could require the drawdown of the husband's pension funds. On the facts of that case he did not make such an order; he was asked instead to appoint a receiver (which he did).

6.27 Although gaining (so far) only limited traction in family cases, the *Blight* order has been used in two civil cases, as an aid to enforcement of prior judgments for the payment of money:

- *Bacci & Others v Green & Others*[19]
- *Brake & Another v Guy & Others*[20]

6.28 In *Bacci*, the applicants sought orders to the following effect:

- The debtor delegate to the creditors (or rather their solicitors) the right to call for a lump sum under a pre-existing occupational pension scheme, and the right to call for a pension under the scheme, upon the debtor turning 55 years old (which was imminent*)*
- The claimants in exercising their delegated authority would require the payments to be made from the pension company to an account in the debtor's name which they nominated
- At the same time a third party debt order should be made to bite against the receiving account, to make payment of the sum owed to the creditor from it.

6.29 In *Bacci* the defendant debtor argued an absence of jurisdiction to make such an order (an effective attack on *Blight* itself), but this argument failed. The Deputy High Court Judge was robust in his rejection of the defences raised by the creditor at para [56]) [emphasis added]:

> '(2) In my view, there is no public policy which prevents the s. 37(1) jurisdiction from being exercised. On the contrary, the overriding public policy consideration is that contained in s.281(3) of the 1986 Act, which was expressly referred to in the January 2019 Order when granting the Claimants summary judgment. **Fraudsters should not prosper.** I refer in particular to [60] and [70] of the judgment of Mr Gabriel Moss QC, [in ***Blight***]
>
> (3) In the exercise of my discretion, I find that it is just, equitable and convenient to make the orders sought by the Claimants, subject to the necessary amendments to take account of the points made by the Trustees and Mrs Green set out above. **There are compelling reasons for the Claimants, who are amongst those who have been**

18 [2020] EWHC 885 (Fam), [2020] 2 FCR 429.
19 [2022] EWHC 486 (Ch).
20 [2022] EWHC 1746 (Ch).

defrauded by Mr Green to be able to have access to his money to satisfy the judgment debt.'

6.30 In *Brake*, similar (but not identical) relief was sought, delegating to the creditor's representative the rights of the debtor to require the liquidation of his SIPP (it being held in investments, not cash) and its drawdown (he having already previously taken his tax free lump sum). The effect of such orders would be to create a debt owed by the pension trustees to the debtor against which a Third Party Debt Order would bite.

6.31 Unsurprisingly in the light of *Bacci* no submission was made that the court did not have the power to make the order sought. Rather, the debtor submitted that injunction sought should not be made as it was not just of convenient to do so because:

- It was not a case where the tax free lump sum was available (it having already been taken) so any further draw down would involve creating a tax liability on that event, and one which may be less tax efficient than how he might otherwise have chosen to take pension payment.
- The *Blight* and *Bacci* cases had been decided in respect of debtors whose liabilities had arisen through fraudulent conduct, whereas Mr Brake's debt arose from costs orders following an unsuccessful claim for breach of confidence/misuse of private information and his unsuccessful appeal of that decision.

6.32 The court was not impressed with either argument, and expressly held that the reasons why the liability being enforced had arisen were not relevant to the enforcement remedy sought. As for the tax argument that was raised, the court held at para [72]:

> 'Moreover, the fact that any drawdown by Mr Brake would be subject to tax is in itself of minor importance. For example, if a judgment creditor obtains a charging order on assets owned by the judgment debtor, and thereafter obtains an order for their sale, that sale may involve a liability to capital gains tax on the part of the judgment debtor. But no one suggests that, merely because there is a tax liability arising as a result of the sale, therefore the sale should not have been ordered, or should not take place. Selling assets to raise money to pay debts often involves costs which reduce the value available to pay creditors. (I accept of course that, if the amount of tax would be so great that as a result there was no real benefit to the judgment creditor, the court might well decide not to order the sale.)'

6.33 The judge ultimately decided to grant the orders sought, and in doing so said at para [90] [emphasis added]:

> 'In my judgment, it is indeed just and convenient for the court to make an injunction ordering Mr Brake to exercise his right to draw down his

remaining pension entitlement from the third party. Mr Brake has been ordered to pay to the successful respondents their costs of his unsuccessful appeal. **He has an asset which can be realised for their benefit. The authorities make clear that it does not matter that the asset concerned is a pension entitlement. The old paternal policy of preventing pension scheme members realising more than a proportion in cash and requiring the remainder to be used in the purchase of an annuity has gone.**'

6.34 The Court of Appeal decision in *re Henry, Horton v Henry*[21] is also authority for the existence of the *Blight* remedy. At para [39], Gloster LJ (delivering the judgment of the court with the agreement of McFarlane LJ and Sir Stanley Burnton) observed that:

> '…, prior to bankruptcy, a judgment creditor may, by injunction, compel a judgment debtor to make an election to draw down his pension … in order to satisfy [a judgment debt].'

6.35 It is worth practitioners noting the following points arising from the above cases:

- The pension trustees were joined as parties in *Bacci* and *Brake* (albeit they took neutral views as to the merits of the order, and raised technical and/or procedural points to ensure their position as fiduciaries was not prejudiced). The joinder of a pension scheme (especially if UK-based) is likely to be an appropriate step to ensure the orders obtained are in the correct form and all relevant parties are bound.
- The cases have between them approved *Blight* orders over a variety of pension schemes: a SIPP, an occupational pension scheme and a personal pensions scheme.
- All cases involved a careful consideration of the precise terms of the pension scheme rules and governing documents, to ensure that what was being sought was available, appropriate and permissible.
- The application does not have to be in respect of the commutable tax free lump sum, but can encompass all the potential benefits that would otherwise be available to the beneficiary of the scheme.
- The cases seeking payments of lump sums or single payments were bought in conjunction with applications for third party debt orders as a necessary link in the chain to get the funds from the pension company in cash, to the recipient member, then to creditor. Whether and to what extent these are required or appropriate depends to a large extent on the structure of the benefits.

21 [2016] EWCA Civ 989, [2017] 1 WLR 391, [2016] BPIR 1426.

- There is no substitute for considering the relevant pension information in detail, and if necessary seeking orders for the disclosure of documents and information (if not already disclosed in the substantive proceedings) before formulating the precise relief and orders sought.

E *BLIGHT v BREWSTER* ORDERS IN NON-PENSION CASES

6.36 There appears to be no obvious reason why a *Blight* order should be confined to pensions.

6.37 Although no family case has yet been determined that demonstrates its use in relation to non-pension assets, there is no obvious reason why it could not be. It was posited as a potential remedy (in conjunction with a third party debt order) against cash funds held on behalf of a party in a bank account in *Flexidig Limited v M & M Contractors (Europe) Limited*[22] (although the application for the order was not pursued).

6.38 In *Tasarruf*[23] the debtor had a right to revoke a discretionary trust on the basis that such a revocation would render him the owner in equity of the assets. The Court ordered him to delegate the power of revocation to receivers who then satisfied debts with the assets. The receivers had already been appointed; had they not been, the power of revocation could instead have been delegated to the creditor.

6.39 In *JSC VTB Bank v Skurikhin & Others*[24] it was observed at para [108] that:

> 'If, however, the judgment debtor has a right to call for assets, the Court can compel him to exercise that right or can appoint a receiver over it'

6.40 The court clearly considered that the power was not confined to cases involving pension assets. It went on to say that:

> 'That same rationale must apply where it is demonstrated that an individual has a right to instruct trustees to apply assets held within a trust (or a Liechtenstein foundation) in accordance with that individual's direction.'

6.41 In a family law context, it appears to have been an idea at least floated but not determined (nor argued) in relation to a husband's interest under a trust in *AF v SF*[25]at para [57].

22 [2021] EWHC 784 (TCC).
23 [2011] UKPC 17, [2012] 1 WLR 1721, [2011] BPIR 1743, [2011] WLTR 1249.
24 [2019] EWHC 1407 Comm.
25 [2019] EWHC 1224 (Fam), [2020] 1 FLR 121.

6.42 Much will turn on the precise nature of the debtor's rights in relation to the asset against which enforcement is sought. Practitioners should give careful consideration to the particular rights in question and whether the debtor can compel the entity which holds the asset to act at his direction (as opposed to the entity having a discretion to do so). A *Blight* remedy may be available in relation to assets in respect of which a debtor holds rights which he is entitled to exercise (for example stock options or restricted equity units).

CHAPTER 7

Freezing orders and avoidance of dispositions

Content at a glance:

A INTRODUCTION

7.01 The court has various powers at its disposal to aid enforcement and prevent attempts to defeat or reduce claims after financial relief has been granted.

7.02 This chapter focuses on the following potential remedies for preventing or setting aside dispositions in financial remedy proceedings[1]:

- Matrimonial Causes Act 1973 ('MCA 1973'), s 37.
- Senior Courts Act 1981 ('SCA 1981'), s 37 and the inherent jurisdiction.
- Insolvency Act 1986 ('IA 1986'), s 423.

B MATRIMONIAL CAUSES ACT 1973, s 37

A specific matrimonial tool

Operates to set aside or prevent dispositions

Reliant on intention which, in certain circumstances, may be presumed

1 It should be noted that there are other potential remedies which enable a court to grant injunctive relief. For instance, Civil Jurisdiction and Judgments Act 1982, s 25 empowers the High Court to grant interim relief in support of proceedings either commenced or to be commenced in a foreign jurisdiction.

Overview

7.03 The court has the power to prevent and avoid dispositions designed to defeat an applicant's claims for financial relief by virtue of the MCA 1973, s 37. This is a bespoke statutory tool for financial remedy cases[2] and will usually be the first of the court's powers to consider.

7.04 MCA 1973, s 37 provides two kinds of remedy relevant to enforcement:

- A pre-emptive injunction preventing any future disposal, dealing or transfer, including out of the jurisdiction, of any property, ie a freezing injunction.

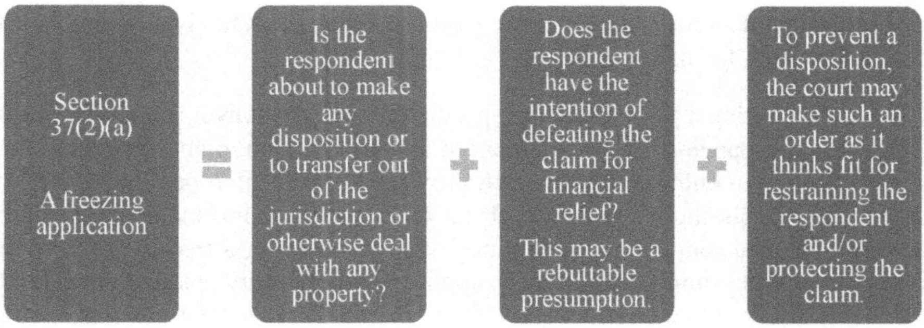

- The set aside of a reviewable disposition.

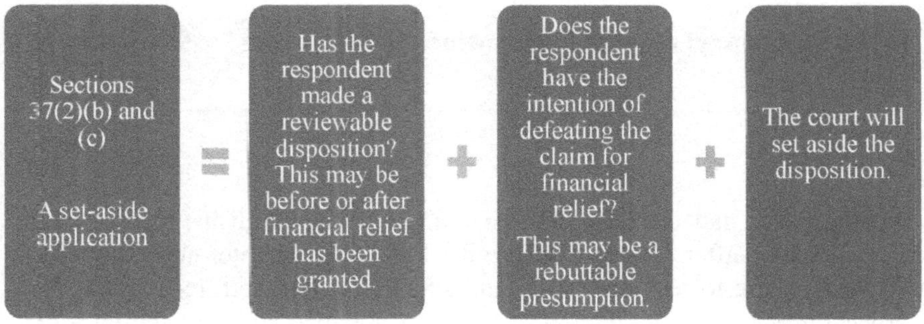

Financial relief

7.05 Financial relief is defined for these purposes as an application under any of the following provisions of MCA 1973:

- Section 22 (Maintenance Pending Suit)
- Section 23 (Periodical Payment and Lump Sum Orders)

2 *AC v DC (Financial Remedy: Effect of Section 37 Avoidance Order)* [2012] EWHC 2032 (Fam), [2013] 2 FLR 1483. There are *broadly* equivalent powers under the MFPA 1984, ss 23-24, the Civil Partnership Act 2004, Sch 5, Part 14 and the Inheritance (Provision for Family and Dependants) Act 1975, ss 10-13 albeit in respect of the latter, in *Dellal v Dellal* [2015] EWHC 907 (Fam), [2015] WTLR 1137, Mostyn J observed that there are '*real conceptual and structural differences*' between an order under I(PFD)A 1975, s 10 and one under MCA 1973, s 37(2)(b).

- Section 24 (Property Adjustment Orders)
- Section 24B (Pension Sharing Orders)
- Section 27 (Financial Provision Orders in cases of failure to maintain)
- Section 31 (Applications for variation) save for s 31(6)
- Section 35 (Alteration of a Maintenance Agreement)

The requisite intention

7.06 In each situation, the court must be satisfied on the balance of probabilities that the respondent has acted with the requisite intention, namely an intention to defeat the claim for financial relief.

7.07 'Defeating a person's claim' specifically includes (albeit is not limited to) frustrating or impeding the enforcement of any order which might be or has been made[3]. Within an enforcement context, proving this will often be relatively easy as the asset in question will be the object of a property adjustment order or the obvious/intended source of a lump sum payment. However, a freezing injunction is not permissible simply to provide an applicant with security post-judgment[4] and care must be taken to demonstrate that the case does not involve a situation where the respondent is simply doing what they wish with an asset that is theirs.

Case summary: *Ahmed v Mustafa*[5]

Facts:

A final order had provided for the transfer of an English property from H to W. Soon after the transfer, W gifted it to her daughter at a time when H was seeking to restrain her by anti-suit injunction from re-litigating the proceedings in Cyprus. At first instance, H obtained an order setting aside the property transfer to W's daughter.

Held by the Court of Appeal, McFarlane LJ:

The property transfer to W's daughter was a consequence of the order, not an attempt to defeat it. It could not be said that the disposition frustrated or impeded the enforcement of the order. Thus, the order setting aside the property transfer was reversed on appeal.

3 MCA 1973, s 37(1). In *Akhmedova v Akhmedov* [2021] EWHC 545 (Fam), [2021] 4 WLR 88, it was held that the use of the words '*frustrate*' and '*impede*' was intended to capture '*not only dispositions which make enforcement impossible, but also dispositions which make it slower or more difficult to enforce.*'

4 *Crowther v Crowther & Others* [2020] EWCA Civ 762, [2020] 3 FCR 602.

5 [2014] EWCA Civ 277, [2016] 1 FCR 50, [2015] 1 FLR 139.

7.08 There is a rebuttable presumption that the respondent has or had the requisite intention where the court is satisfied that the disposition has the consequence of defeating the applicant's claim and either:[6]

- The disposition took place less than three years before the date of the application; or
- The disposition is about to take place.

Case summary: *AAZ v BBZ* sub nom. *Akhmedov v Ahkmedova*[7]

Facts:

W sought an order under MCA 1973, s 37 and IA 1986, s 423 setting aside a deed of trust under which H purported to assign to a Bermudan 'Cipher' trust virtually his entire wealth. The disposition was made four days prior to H signing a statement in the ongoing financial remedy proceedings.

Held by Haddon-Cave J:

The disposition was clearly made within the past three years such that the presumption applied. H produced no evidence to rebut the presumption and the disposition was accordingly set aside.

7.09 Where the relevant disposition took place outside the three-year period (a relatively unusual scenario in enforcement cases), the applicant must prove that the respondent had the relevant intention. It should be noted that:

- The court is concerned with the respondent's intention in a subjective sense. This requires an investigation of the respondent's state of mind[8].
- The court is entitled to rely on inferences to ascertain a respondent's true intentions and the court may infer intention from the natural consequences of the respondent's actions[9].
- The intention to defeat the claim need not be the sole or dominant intention[10].

6 MCA 1973, s 37(5).
7 [2016] EWHC 3234 (Fam), [2018] 1 FLR 153.
8 *Kemmis v Kemmis (Welland Intervening)* [1988] 1 WLR 1307, [1988] 2 FLR 223 per Lloyd LJ at 1326.
9 *Kemmis v Kemmis (Welland Intervening)* [1988] 1 WLR 1307, [1988] 2 FLR 223 per Lloyd LJ at 1326.
10 *Kemmis v Kemmis (Welland Intervening)* [1988] 1 WLR 1308, [1988] 2 FLR 223 per Nourse LJ at 1331; *Kremen v Agrest & Fishman* [2010] EWHC 2571 (Fam); [2011] 2 FLR 478.

- Timing can be highly relevant. If the disposition predates the divorce and/or marital difficulties by some years, this would weigh against the existence of the requisite intention[11].
- Purpose is also highly relevant. If it can be shown that the disposition was made for an apparently legitimate, innocent or benevolent purpose, the court may decline to set it aside[12].

Case summary: *Mubarak v Mubarik*[13]

Facts:

The parties settled a trust in Jersey into which had been transferred their respective shares in the family company in 1997. In 2005, in attempting to enforce a financial remedy order, W applied to set aside the transfer under MCA 1973, s 37.

Held by Holman J (refusing the application):

> 'The fact is that the husband plainly did have legitimate and appropriate intentions, namely orderly succession and, very critically, avoidance of tax, which are capable of fully and wholly explaining and justifying the setting up of the trust and the transfer of the shares. All the available documentary evidence supports those intentions and gives no hint of any other.'

Meaning of disposition of property and reviewable disposition

7.10 Whilst property is not defined under MCA 1973, s 37, in *Mubarak*[14] Holman J adopted the well-known dicta of Lord Wilberforce in *National Provincial Bank Ltd v Ainsworth*[15] which requires that property '… must be definable, identifiable by third parties, capable in its nature of assumption by third parties, and have some degree of permanence or stability.'

7.11 'Disposition' includes any conveyance, assurance or gift of property of any description, whether made by an instrument or otherwise, in which either or both of the parties has or had a beneficial interest (either in possession or

11 *Mubarak v Mubarik* [2007] EWHC 220 (Fam), [2007] 2 FLR 364.
12 *Mubarak v Mubarik* [2007] EWHC 220 (Fam), [2007] 2 FLR 364.
13 *Mubarak v Mubarik* [2007] EWHC 220 (Fam), [2007] 2 FLR 364.
14 *Mubarak v Mubarik* [2007] EWHC 220 (Fam), [2007] 2 FLR 364.
15 [1965] AC 1175 at 1247G–1248A.

reversion)[16]. It will therefore include transfers to entities such as offshore trusts[17]. A disposition of property does not include:

- a provision contained in a will or codicil[18].
- an instrument of exclusion from a discretionary trust[19].
- the expiration of a tenancy[20].
- dealings with underlying company assets (absent a finding that the company is a party's alter ego and/or the assets are held on trust)[21].
- directly or indirectly engaging in any business which was, or might be, in competition with a business in which either party to the marriage held shares[22].

7.12 Setting aside a disposition requires the disposition to be reviewable. A disposition is not reviewable if it was made for valuable consideration to a person acting in good faith and without notice of any intention on the part of the respondent to defeat the applicant's claim[23]. The following points are worth noting:

- A sale at an undervalue, although possibly satisfying the 'valuable consideration' test, may communicate an improper motive on the respondent's party to the transferee so that the latter will not take in good faith (a fact-specific concept)[24].
- Though a sale may be at full value, the transaction may be set aside if the transferee had actual or constructive notice of the respondent's intention to defeat the applicant's claims[25].
- Though the legal burden of proof remains on the applicant to prove that the transferee had notice of the respondent's intentions the evidential burden

16 MCA 1973, s 37(6).

17 See for instance *AAZ v BBZ* and *AC v DC (Financial Remedy: Effect of s 37 Avoidance Order) (No 1)* [2012] EWHC 2032 (Fam), [2013] 2 FLR 1483: the latter being a case which involved the transfer of assets to a Manx employee benefit trust.

18 MCA 1973, s 37(6).

19 *Mubarak v Mubarik* [2007] EWHC 220 (Fam), [2007] 2 FLR 364 where Holman J considered that an instrument of exclusion did not dispose of property; it simply removed a beneficiary's right to be considered as a potential recipient of property.

20 *Newlon Housing Trust v Alsulaimen & Anor* [1998] UKHL 35, [1999] 1 AC 313.

21 *C v C sub nom Christoforou v Christoforou* [2015] EWHC 2795 (Fam) applying *Crittenden v Crittenden* [1990] 2 FLR 361, *McGladdery v McGladdery* [2000] 1 FCR 315, [1999] 2 FLR 1102 and *Prest v Petrodel Resources Ltd and Ors* [2013] UKSC 34, [2013] 2 AC 415, [2013] 3 WLR 1, [2013] 3 FCR 210, [2013] 2 FLR 732 – this issue fell to be properly considered under SCA 1981, s 37.

22 *R v R* [2013] EWHC 4244 (Fam), [2014] 2 FLR 699 – again, this issue fell to be properly considered under SCA 1981, s 37.

23 MCA 1973, s 37(4).

24 As to the meaning of 'good faith' see *Kemmis* and *Midland Bank Trust Co Ltd v Green* [1981] AC 513.

25 See for instance *Everclear v Agrest* [2011] EWCA Civ 232; [2011] 2 FLR 506 where the husband transferred a bearer share to a friend who then sold it for valuable consideration to another friend. Notice was established on the facts. The first instance decision of *Kremen v Agrest (No.2)* [2010] EWHC 3091 (Fam), [2011] 2 FLR 490 was accordingly upheld.

shifts to the transferee due to the obvious difficulties of an applicant having to prove a a matter about which they have no direct knowledge[26].

7.13 A reviewable disposition must have been made by the 'other party to the proceedings'[27]. However, dispositions made by the respondent's servants, agents, nominees or trustees may be considered to have been made by him personally where they are indistinguishable from him i.e. his alter ego[28]. Practitioners may also encounter cases where a property which been transferred by the other party to the proceedings to a third party is then further transferred by that third party to a different third party (a situation considered in *Ansari v Ansari & Ors*[29])

Case summary: *Ansari v Ansari & Ors*[30]

Facts:

The Court of Appeal considered the situation where the original transferee subsequently made an onward transfer of property.

Held by the Court of Appeal, Longmore LJ:

> '19. The words of sub-section (3) are undoubtedly very wide. Eastham J decided in *Green v Green* that they were not wide enough to set aside a disposition other than that made by a party to the proceedings for financial relief and HHJ Raynor correctly held that he was bound by that decision. We are not bound and can consider the matter afresh.
>
> 20. The broad question is whether the court can set aside a disposition which is made subsequently to the reviewable disposition. One can envisage a case in which a husband sells to X who knows the husband intends to defeat the wife's claim and X then sells to Y who likewise knows that such is the husband's intention. If all parties conspire to defeat the wife's claim, the wife should surely be able to set aside both dispositions. The second disposition is not a reviewable disposition for the purpose of sub-section (2) because it was not made by the husband. It could only be set aside by invoking sub-section (3) but, for my part, I can see no reason not to invoke the sub-section in those circumstances. If it cannot be invoked, there would be an easy way to defeat a wife's legitimate claim.

26 *Kremen v Agrest & Fishman* [2010] EWHC 2571 (Fam), [2011] 2 FLR 478.

27 *C v C sub nom. Christoforou v Christoforou* [2015] EWHC 2795 (Fam). Thus, in *Crowther v Crowther & Ors* [2020] EWCA Civ 762, [2020] 3 FCR 602, Males LJ noted that MCA 1973, s 37 did not apply in respect of dispositions made by third parties who were not parties to the marriage.

28 *Kemmis v Kemmis (Welland intervening)* [1988] 1 WLR 1307.

29 [2008] EWCA Civ 1456, [2010] Fam 1, [2009] 3 WLR 1092, [2009] 1 FCR 722, [2009] 1 FLR 1121.

30 [2008] EWCA Civ 1456, [2010] Fam 1, [2009] 3 WLR 1092, [2009] 1 FCR 722, [2009] 1 FLR 1121.

> 21. So I would not say that the sub-section can never be used to set aside a subsequent disposition. Eastham J merely accepted the bank's submission in *Green v Green* that the words 'consequential directions' are largely or entirely restricted to directions about repayment of monies. But I do not think the sub-section is as narrow as that.
>
> 22. I am however, clear that it should not be used in the circumstances of the present case since there is no question at all of the Bank being a party to any conspiracy or even (as I have already said) having notice of any intention on the part of the husband to defeat the wife's rights. The discretion conferred by sub-section (3), even if it can be used to set aside dispositions subsequent to the first disposition in a case where the parties acted in bad faith, should certainly not be used to set aside a subsequent disposition for valuable consideration to a person who acted in relation to it in good faith and without such notice. That is this case and HH Judge Raynor came to the correct conclusion. I would dismiss this appeal.'

Preventing a disposition

7.14 Pursuant to MCA, s 37(2)(a), provided certain conditions are satisfied, the court may make such an order as it thinks fit:

- to restrain the respondent from:
  - making a disposition of property
  - transferring property out of the jurisdiction
  - otherwise dealing with property
- or otherwise protecting the claim.

For the discretion to arise, the court must be satisfied that the respondent:

7.15 As for the exercise of its discretion:

- In some cases, it will be appropriate to freeze the asset[31] whilst in others it may be sufficient for the respondent to pay money into court or to be required give notice of any proposed dealing (sometimes referred to as a notification injunction)[32].

31 The court has the power to freeze foreign assets though it may refuse to do so where such an order would be ineffectual: *Hamlin v Hamlin* [1986] Fam. 11, [1985] 3 WLR 629, [1986] 1 FLR 61.

32 *Spencer-Churchill v Faggionato Fine Arts* [2012] EWHC 2318 (Ch).

- An application preventing a disposal should not extend beyond those assets necessary to safeguard an applicant's claim for financial relief. The court is accordingly unlikely to freeze a party's entire asset-base[33].
- An order, unless the court directs otherwise, must contain an undertaking by the applicant to pay any damages which the respondent sustains which the court considers the applicant should pay[34].

Setting aside a disposition

7.16 The court may make an order setting aside the disposition, if the court is satisfied that the respondent:

Is about to make a disposition or transfer or deal with property.

\+

Has the intention of defeating the claim for financial relief.

7.17 An order setting aside a transaction has the effect of restoring the status quo and the court shall give such consequential directions as it thinks fit for giving effect to the order (including directions requiring the making of any payments or the disposal of any property)[35]. Thus, the order may provide for the applicant to recover the reasonable costs of undoing the effect of the respondent's disposition[36]. It has been suggested that, for tax purposes, the effect of the set aside as if the transaction had never taken place[37].

Procedure

7.18 Applications under MCA 1973, s 37 may be made to a judge of District Judge level and above. The appropriate level of the tribunal will depend upon on the complexity of the case, the size of the assets and any international elements[38].

7.19 The Part 18 application procedure applies[39]. Set aside applications must be made in Form A[40] whereas freezing applications are made by Form D50G. Applications for freezing injunctions must be supported by affidavit evidence[41].

33 *Ghoth v Ghoth* [1992] 2 All ER 920, [1993] 1 FCR 177, [1992] 2 FLR 300 but the court did so in *Akhmedova v Akhmedov & Ors* [2020] EWHC 2257 (Fam), [2021] 1 FCR 458, [2021] 1 FLR 714 in light of the husband's campaign of evasion and where the court was satisfied that without the order there was a real risk the court's judgments and orders would go unsatisfied.

34 FPR 2010, PD20A, para 5.1(a).

35 MCA 1973, s 37(3).

36 *Ali v Ansar-Ali* [2016] EWCA Civ 781, [2017] 1 FCR 1.

37 *AC v DC (Financial Remedy: Effect of s.37 Avoidance Order) (No.1)* [2012] EWHC 2032 (Fam), [2013] 2 FLR 1483.

38 FPR 2010, r 9.6 read with r 2.5(2).

39 FPR 2010, Part 18.

40 FPR 2010, PD5A, para 3.1.

41 FPR 2010, PD20A, para 3.1.

7.20 Applications may be made without notice but[42]:

- The applicant must show that the matter is one of extreme urgency or that giving notice of any kind would defeat the purpose of the order sought. In any other case at least short, informal notice should be given.
- The evidence given to the court must be detailed and precise. There is a heavy duty on those presenting an application without notice to ensure that the court is directed to all the relevant facts, both favourable and unfavourable.
- There must be a return date at which the other party can be present[43] and an undertaking given by the applicant to serve on the respondent the application notice, evidence in support and any order made as soon as practicable[44].

C SENIOR COURTS ACT 1981, s 37 AND THE INHERENT JURISDICTION

Remedies not specific to financial remedy claims

Operate to prevent dispositions

Overview

7.21 In unusual cases where the provisions of the MCA 1973, s 37(2)(a) may be insufficient to deal with the case, practitioners should be aware that the court is also empowered to grant a 'freezing injunction' under the SCA 1981, s 37 which can be invoked to make freezing orders in support of financial remedy applications.

7.22 The SCA 1981, s 37 provides:

> '(1) The High Court may by order (whether interlocutory or final) grant an injunction … in all cases in which it appears to the court to be just and convenient to do so.
>
> (2) Any such order may be made either unconditionally or on such terms and conditions as the court thinks just.
>
> (3) The power of the High Court under subsection (1) to grant an interlocutory injunction restraining a party to any proceedings from removing from the jurisdiction of the High Court, or otherwise dealing with, assets located within that jurisdiction shall be exercisable in cases where that party is, as

42 *UL v BK* [2013] EWHC 1735 (Fam), [2014] Fam. 35, [2014] 2 WLR 914.
43 FPR 2010, PD20A, para 5.1(c).
44 FPR 2010, PD20A, para 5.1(b).

well as in cases where he is not, domiciled resident or present within that jurisdiction. …'

7.23 The court also has jurisdiction, under the SCA 1981, s 37 to grant an order requiring a respondent to give notice of any disposals of or dealings with assets (ie a notification injunction[45]).

7.24 Though the statutory provision refers to the High Court, the SCA 1981, s 37(6) makes clear that the remedy applies to the Family Court as it applies to the High Court. The FPR 2010, r 20.2(1)(f) further provides that the Family Court may grant an order (referred to as a 'freezing injunction') restraining a party:

- from removing assets from the jurisdiction; or
- from dealing with any assets whether located within the jurisdiction or not.

Ambit

7.25 The SCA 1981, s 37 is a general civil law remedy as opposed to a specific matrimonial tool. In *Broad Idea International Ltd v Convoy Collateral Ltd* the Privy Council reviewed in detail the development of the use of s 37 to grant freezing orders, emphasising that even if there are no ongoing proceedings in this jurisdiction the power to grant injunctions can be exercised where the court has personal jurisdiction over a party. Accordingly, the court may have jurisdiction to grant an injunction whether or not it is ancillary to pre-existing proceedings in this jurisdiction against that party. The essential purpose of a freezing order to facilitate the enforcement of a judgment which may include a judgment given in an overseas jurisdiction[46].

7.26 An order may be made at any stage, including post-judgment and as part of enforcement proceedings. It can therefore be used to freeze assets to which a financial remedy order applies. It should do no more than is necessary to protect the claim including containing limiting provisions so that they do not purport to have unintended extra-territorial operations nor affect third parties unless and to the extent required[47]. In certain circumstances a freezing order can be made against a third party where there is evidence that such a person or entity holds or controls the respondent's assets: such an order is known as a '*Chabra*' injunction, named after the decision in *TSB Private Bank International SA v Chabra*[48].

45 *Holyoake v Candy* [2017] EWCA Civ 92, [2018] Ch 297, [2017] 3 WLR 1131.

46 [2021] UKPC 24, [2022] 2 WLR 703. See also Civil Jurisdiction and Judgments Act 1982, s 25.

47 *Babanaft International Co SA v Bassatne* [1990] Ch 13; [1989] 2 WLR 232, *Ghoth v Ghoth* [1993] 1 FCR 177, [1992] 2 FLR 300, CA.

48 [1992] 1 WLR 231; see also *Mercantile Group (Europe) AG v Aiyela* [1994] QB 366, [1993] 3 WLR 1116, where the Court of Appeal confirmed the existence of the jurisdiction to grant *Chabra* injunctions.

7.27 The remedy acts *in personam* and can thus be made in respect of assets within or outside of the jurisdiction (albeit there is a high threshold in respect of the latter)[49].

7.28 An order may also be made without notice though the same conditions apply as set out above in relation to the MCA 1973, s 37.

Requirements

7.29 Relief may be granted where the court is satisfied that[50]:

The applicant had been granted, or had a good arguable case for being granted, a judgment or order that was or would be enforceable through the process of the court

+

There is a real risk of prejudice by reason of the disposal or dealing by the respondent of his assets, unless he is restrained from doing so.

+

It would be just and convenient in all the circumstances of the case to grant the relief sought.

7.30 Other than in exceptional cases, the first requirement will be easily met within enforcement proceedings. The second limb, however, requires solid evidence of a risk of unjustified dissipation[51]. Moreover, prima facie proof of a risk of dissipation requires, at least in general and broad terms, proof of *an intention* to dissipate[52]. Thus, it has been stated that there is little real difference between MCA 1973 and SCA 1981 save that the existence of the statutory presumption may make an application under MCA 1973 easier to obtain[53].

Case summary: *Les Ambassadeurs Club Ltd v Yu*[54]

Facts:

The first instance judge had refused to grant the claimant, a casino operator, a post-judgment freezing injunction against a foreign national gambling debtor in circumstances where the debtor had paid some of the money owed to the claimant but then failed to pay the balance. The judge had found that there was no real risk of dissipation.

49 *Babanaft International Co SA v Bassatne* [1990] Ch 13; [1989] 2 WLR 232.

50 *Ninemia Maritime Corp v Trave Schiffahrts GmbH & Co KG (The Niedersachsen)* [1983] 1 WLR 1412.

51 See, for instance, in a financial remedy context *Araghchinchi v Aragchinchi* [1997] 3 FCR 567, [1997] 2 FLR 142.

52 *UL v BK* [2013] EWHC 1735 (Fam); [2014] Fam. 35, [2014] 2 WLR 914.

53 *UL v BK* [2013] EWHC 1735 (Fam), [2014] Fam. 35, [2014] 2 WLR 914.

54 [2021] EWCA Civ 1310, [2022] 4 WLR 1.

Held by the Court of Appeal, Andrews LJ:

There is an important distinction to be made between a defendant who can pay but refuses to pay until he is forced to do so (ie by an order) and a defendant so determined not to pay that he would take active steps to frustrate recovery by some form of unjustified dissipation. There must be cogent evidence from which it can be at least inferred that the defendant falls into the latter category. The Court of Appeal reiterated that real risk of dissipation did not mean that the applicant was required to show that it was more likely than not that the risk would materialise. It is a lower standard.

Inherent jurisdiction

7.31 There are several older authorities recognising the High Court's inherent jurisdiction in family proceedings to make freezing orders without reference to MCA 1973, s 37 or SCA 1981, s 37. However, judges in more recent authorities have questioned this or otherwise suggested it is unlikely that the High Court has any further powers beyond those prescribed by statute[55]. Thus, the inherent jurisdiction cannot be called upon to fill any perceived deficiencies or lacunae in statute. It is suggested that, if the power does exist, it serves little practical purpose in modern financial remedy proceedings.

D INSOLVENCY ACT 1986, s 423

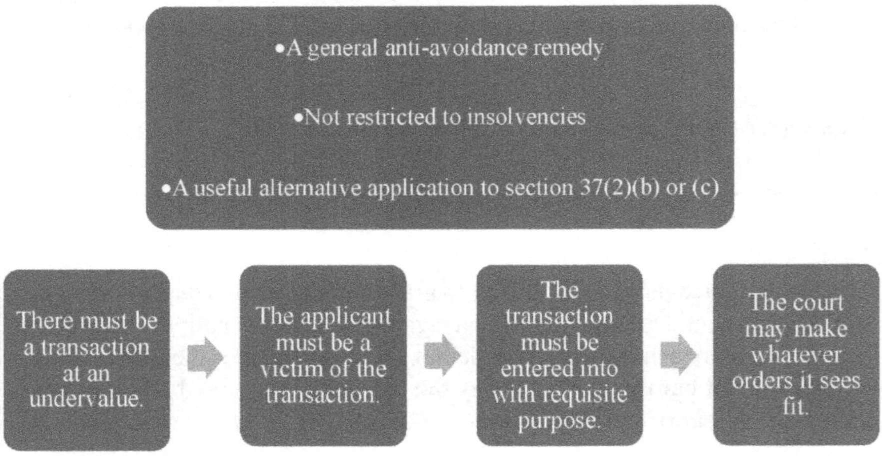

55 *ND v KP (ex parte application)* [2011] EWHC 457 (Fam), [2011] 2 FLR 662; *UL v BK* [2013] EWHC 1735 (Fam), [2014] Fam 35, [2014] 2 WLR 914; *C v C & Anor sub no. Christoforou v Christoforou* [2015] EWHC 2795 (Fam); *Goyal v Goyal* [2016] EWCA Civ 792, [2016] 4 WLR 140, [2017] 1 FCR 174, [2017] 2 FLR 223; *Tobias v Tobias* [2017] EWFC 46, [2017] 4 WLR 146, [2017] 3 FCR 399, [2018] 1 FLR 616; *Q v Q* [2021] EWHC 1757 (Fam).

Overview

7.32 An application under IA 1986, s 423 is a potential alternative to MCA 1973, s 37(2)(b) or (c). The former is an anti-avoidance remedy under the general civil law and is not restricted to cases of insolvency whereas the latter is a specific matrimonial tool. The applications can be made together in the alternative.

7.33 IA 1986, s 423 applies to disposals of property made either:[56]

Prior to the making of a final order.	/	Following the making of a final order when enforcement of that order is sought (including in relation to costs).

7.34 Claims are subject to a limitation period (see para **7.55**).

7.35 The statutory language under IA 1986, s 423 differs from that of MCA 1973, s 37. In some cases, it may be easier to obtain orders under one section than the other. However, in most cases, an application pursuant to the IA 1986 will add nothing to an application under the MCA 1973[57].

7.36 The operation of IA 1986, s 423, which has unlimited extra-territorial effect[58], requires:

A transaction at an undervalue to be entered into.	+	The transaction in question to have been entered into with the requisite purpose.

7.37 Where the two key requirements are fulfilled, the court has a wide discretion to:

Restore the position to what it would have been had the transaction not been entered into.	+	Protect the interests of persons who are victims of the transaction.

7.38 IA 1986, s 423 is intended to be a wide-ranging anti-avoidance remedy[59]. Its predecessor was Law of Property Act 1925, s 172. This means that:

56 *Trowbridge v Trowbridge* [2002] EWHC 3114 (Ch), [2004] 2 FCR 79, [2003] 2 FLR 231.
57 *Mubarak v Mubarak* [2007] EWHC 220 (Fam); [2007] 2 FLR 364.
58 See *Re Paramount Airways Ltd (in administration)* [1993] Ch. 223, [1992] 3 WLR 690 and more recently *AAZ v BBZ* [2016] EWHC 3234 (Fam), [1997] 2 FCR 415, [2018] 1 FLR 153.
59 *B v IB (Order to set aside disposition under Insolvency Act)* [2013] EWHC 3755 (Fam), [2014] 2 FLR 273: a widow was allowed to proceed with an application under s 423 to set aside a gift of shares made before the husband's death, even though he was not insolvent.

- the remedy is not confined to cases where the respondent is insolvent[60];
- there is no need for insolvency proceedings.

7.39 Nonetheless, the remedy has been scarcely used in financial remedy proceedings (it is of note that orders under IA 1986, s 423 were made as an aid to enforcement in the *Akhmedov v Ahkmedova* litigation[61] (see also para **7.8**)).

Transactions at an undervalue

7.40 IA 1986, s 423 requires the transaction to have been at an undervalue. The concept of a 'transaction' is to be construed broadly. In particular, it does not matter that the relevant transfers were made by a company owned by the person rather than by the person himself[62].

7.41 For the purposes of IA 1986, s 423[63], a person enters into a transaction at an undervalue if:

- he makes a gift to the other person or he otherwise enters into a transaction with the other on terms that provide for him to receive no consideration;
- he enters into a transaction with the other in consideration of marriage or the formation of a civil partnership; or
- he enters into a transaction with the other for a consideration the value of which, in money or money's worth, is significantly less than the value, in money or money's worth, of the consideration provided by himself.

7.42 A transfer of property at full market value will make the transaction immune from this provision, but a transfer for less than market value may be vulnerable to be set aside. In some cases it may be easier to prove that a transaction has taken place 'at an undervalue' for the purposes of IA 1986, s 423 than to prove an absence of 'valuable consideration' for the purposes of MCA, s 37(4).

Onward transactions by third parties

7.43 IA 1986, s 423 can be used to set aside transactions made from one third party to another third party so long as the statutory criteria are established[64].

60 *B v IB (Order to set aside disposition under Insolvency Act)* [2013] EWHC 3755 (Fam), [2014] 2 FLR 273.

61 Since *AAZ v BBZ* [2016] EWHC 3234 (Fam), [2017] 2 FCR 415, [2018] 1 FLR 153, the court has made further consequential orders setting aside other dispositions made by or on behalf of the husband. See for instance [2016] EWHC 3349 (Fam), [2017] 4 WLR 84; [2016] EWHC 3361 (Fam), [2017] 2 FCR 461; [2018] EWFC 23, [2018] 3 FCR 135; [2019] EWHC 2561 (Fam), [2020] 1 FCR 213; [2021] EWHC 545 (Fam), [2021] 4 WLR 88.

62 *Akhmedova v Akhmedov & Ors (Rev 1)* [2021] EWHC 545 (Fam), [2021] 4 WLR 88.

63 IA 1986, s 423(1).

64 See also para 7.13 above. In *Ansari v Ansari* [2008] EWCA Civ 1456, [2010] Fam. 1, [2009] 3 WLR 1092, [2009] 1 FCR 722, [2009] 1 FLR 1121, the Court of Appeal expressed the view that MCA 1973, s 37 was broad enough in its scope to permit subsequent disposals to be set aside.

7.44 IA 1986, s 425(5) provides that an order may affect the property of, or impose any obligation on, any person whether or not he is the person with whom the debtor entered into the transaction, but such an order:

Cannot prejudice any interest in property acquired from a person other than the debtor in good faith, for value and without notice of the relevant circumstances, or prejudice any interest deriving from such an interest.	+	Cannot require a person who received a benefit from the transaction in good faith, for value and without notice of the relevant circumstances to pay any sum unless he was a party to the transaction.

7.45 The fact that a third party no longer holds assets which were received as part of the transaction or has changed position does not provide a defence to a claim under IA 1986, s 423. It may however be relevant to the nature of the relief granted: if it is not possible to restore the property which has been subject to the transaction, the broad wording of the statute enable an applicant to pursue other remedies, including against the personal assets of the third party[65].

The requisite intention

7.46 An order may only be made if the court is satisfied that it was entered into by him for one of the following purposes:

Putting assets beyond the reach of a person who is making, or may at some time make, a claim against him.	/	Otherwise prejudicing the interests of such a person in relation to the claim which he is making or may make.

7.47 It is thus necessary to prove that the person who entered into the transaction did so with the requisite purpose. In contrast to the position under MCA 1973, s 37 there is no presumption as to the 'purpose' under IA 1986, s 423; it needs to be proved on the balance of probabilities. However, s 423 can be a useful adjunct to MCA 1973, s 37 in a case where a party cannot prove that the other intended to defeat *their* claim specifically as opposed to those of other creditors.

7.48 The applicant need not show that one of the statutory purposes was the sole or dominant purpose behind the transaction, merely it was *a* purpose. In this

65 *Akhmedova v Akhmedov & Ors (Rev 1)* [2021] EWHC 545 (Fam), [2021] 4 WLR 88. For orders which may be made under s 423 see para **7.52**.

respect, two or more purposes may co-exist[66]. 'Purpose' under IA 1986, s 423 has been held to carry the same subjective meaning as the word 'intention' under MCA 1973, s 37[67].

Who may apply and to which court

7.49 There are restrictions on who may apply. IA 1986, s 424 provides that an application under section 423 may be made by 'a victim' of the transaction[68].

7.50 A victim of the transaction is generally defined as a person who is, or is capable of being, prejudiced by the transaction[69]. The definition is therefore not to be restricted to creditors with present or actual debts. There does not have to be a connection between the purpose of the transaction and the specific prejudice caused to the victim[70]. Thus, a party will be a 'victim' of the transaction if (judged in retrospect) it adversely affects their claims, even if they were not the contemporaneous object of the other party's requisite intention.

7.51 The application may be made to the High Court or a court which has bankruptcy jurisdiction over the respondent[71].

Orders which may be made

7.52 The court has broad powers to make whatever orders it sees fit upon such an application but is not bound to do so. Without prejudice to that broad discretion, IA 1986, s 425 provides examples of orders that may be made with respect to such a transaction under s 423.

66 *IRC v Hashmi* [2002] EWCA Civ 981, [2002] 2 BCC 943. It is not even necessary to show it is a 'substantial' purpose: *JSC BTA Bank v Ablyazov* [2018] EWCA Civ 1176, [2019] BCC 96.

67 *Trowbridge v Trowbridge* [2002] EWHC 3114 (Ch), [2003] 2 FCR 79, [2003] 2 FLR 231; *Mubarak v Mubarik* [2007] EWHC 220 (Fam), [2007] 2 FLR 364.

68 It also includes provision for a variety of individuals to apply i.e. where the debtor has been made bankrupt or where the victim of the transaction is bound by an approved voluntary arrangement.

69 IA 1986, s 423(5).

70 *Hill v Spread Trustees Co Ltd and Another* [2006] EWCA Civ 542, [2007] 1 WLR 2404.

71 IA 1986, s 423(4).

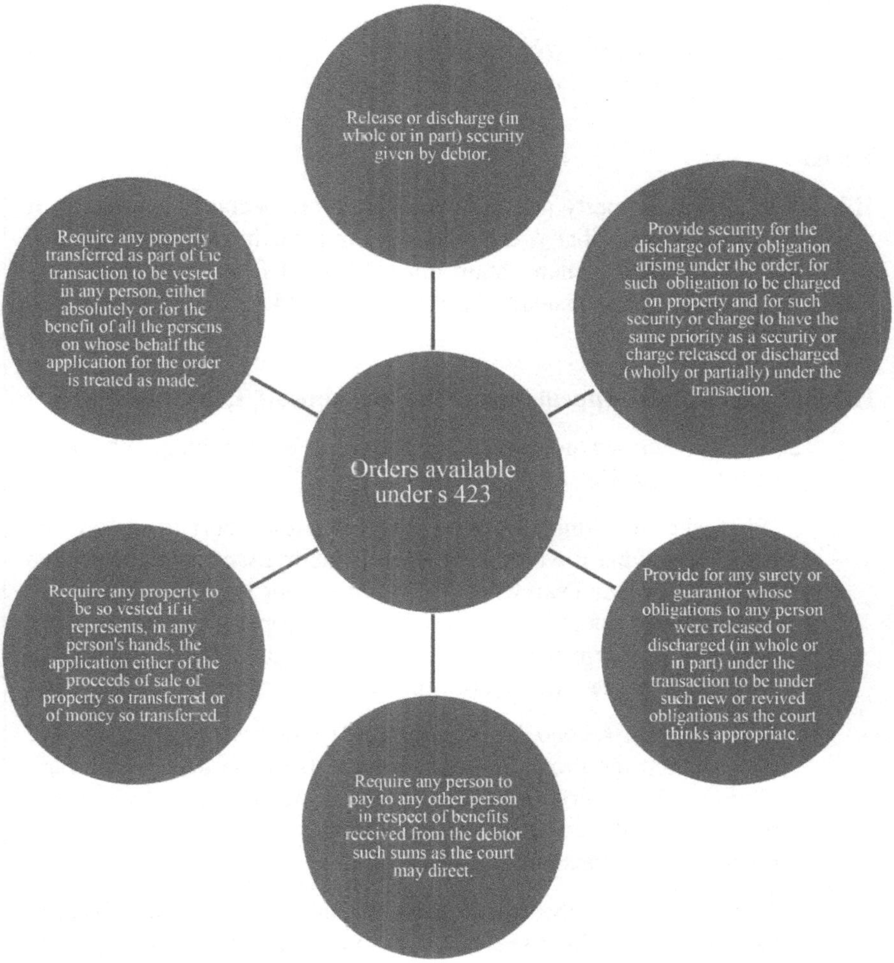

7.53 The objective of making the order is, so far as is practicable, both to restore the position to what it would have been if the transaction had not been entered into and to protect the interests of the victim(s) of it[72].

7.54 IA 1986, s 423 cannot be used to put the applicant in a better position than they would have been had the transaction not occurred.

72 IA 1986 s 423(2); *Chohan v Saggar* [1994] BCC 134, CA.

Case summary: *Ram v Ram (No 1)*[73]

Facts:

H had disposed of property at an undervalue before becoming bankrupt. It was held at first instance that W could not seek to have the property re-vested in H's name (in order to then obtain financial relief from him) as she did not have provable debts; instead, the property would vest in H's trustee in bankruptcy.

Held by the Court of Appeal (dismissing the appeal), Carnwath LJ:

> '28. …we can see no answer to the judge's reasoning, which we gratefully adopt. He said:
>
> > 'First, the first limb of s 424(2) requires the court to restore the position to what it would have been if the transaction had not been entered into. Mr Duckworth's order does not restore the position; it modifies the position. It gives the wife property to pursue in her matrimonial claim which is protected from the bankruptcy regime which affects the remainder of the husband's property.
> >
> > Secondly, the second limb of s 423(2) requires the court to take into account the protecting of the interests of the persons who are victims. Those persons are the wife and the creditors. As between the wife and the creditors the section does not require the court to reward the virtuous but to protect victims.
> >
> > Third, by making the order I propose I am putting the wife back in the position in which she would have been had the transaction not occurred, that is that she is able to make a claim against the surplus. Any other order, in particular that proposed by Mr Duckworth, would put her not in the same position but in a better position. She was at the time of the transaction, and is now, a person who may have a claim against the bankrupt. That is reflected by restoring the property to the trustee. The restoration of the property may lead to a surplus in the bankruptcy estate. It will, in any event, relieve pressure on the matrimonial home, which has hitherto been the trustee's prime target. In that way her claim is protected but to go further would do more than to restore or protect her interests but to advance them."

73 [2004] EWCA Civ 1452, [2005] 2 BCLC 476, [2004] 3 FCR 425, [2005] 2 FLR 63.

Limitation

7.55 Practitioners should also be aware that claims under IA 1986, s 423 are subject to time limits prescribed by the Limitation Act 1980 ('LA 1980')[74]. The relevant provisions state:

> '8 (1) An action upon a specialty[75] shall not be brought after the expiration of 12 years from the date on which the cause of action accrued.
>
> (2) Subsection (1) above shall not affect any action for which a shorter period of limitation is prescribed by any other provision of this Act.
>
> 9 (1) An action to recover any sum recoverable by virtue of any enactment shall not be brought after the expiration of six years from the date on which the cause of action accrued…'

7.56 Thus, the time limit is either 12 years under LA 1980, s 8(1), or 6 years under s 9(1) depending on the remedy sought. In the context of IA 1986, s 423:

- where the substance of the claim is to recover a sum of money, the period is 6 years;
- otherwise the time limit for setting aside transactions is 12 years.

However, the limitation period for such claims may be postponed by operation of LA 1980, s 32 (ie in cases of fraud, concealment or mistake).

Differences between IA 1986, s 423 and MCA 1973, s 37

7.57 The main differences between the two sections were highlighted by Knowles J in *Akhmedova v Akmedov & Ors (Rev 1)*[76] at para [113], a passage which bears setting out in full.

Case summary: *Akhmedova v Akmedov & Ors (Rev 1)*[77]

Knowles J:

> '113. It is useful to identify the differences between s.423 IA and s.37 MCA:

74 *Hill v Spread Trustee Co Ltd* [2006] EWCA Civ 542, [2007] 1 WLR 2404.
75 This applies to a contract executed as a deed and claims on a statute (though its importance has been considerably diminished by s 9).
76 [2021] EWHC 545 (Fam), [2021] 4 WLR 88.
77 [2021] EWHC 545 (Fam), [2021] 4 WLR 88.

a) S.423 is of general application whereas s.37 MCA only applies where proceedings have been brought under certain sections of the 1973 Act and the disposition is intended to defeat that claim.

b) S.37 MCA reverses the burden of proving intention in certain circumstances.

c) For s.423 to apply, there must be a transaction at an undervalue. Thus, the transferor must either receive no consideration or the consideration received by the debtor must be worth significantly less than the consideration which the debtor has provided. S.37 MCA does not require that the relevant disposition took place at an undervalue, although it will be difficult in practice to demonstrate the requisite purpose if the disposition took place for fair value (see *Trowbridge v Trowbridge*[78]).

d) Pursuant to s.37 MCA, the transferee is protected if it has given valuable consideration (even if there is an undervalue) and has acted in good faith and without notice. Under s.423 IA, a transferee cannot rely upon a bona fide purchaser defence, which is available only to a third party to the transaction under s.425(2) IA.

e) S. 37 MCA applies only where there has been a disposition by the spouse of his or her property. Accordingly, it only applies where (a) there has been a disposition of property, and (b) that property was directly owned by the spouse or his or her nominee/alter ego. On the other hand, s.423 IA adopts a much more flexible and broadly defined concept of a *'transaction'*, which can include informal arrangements and procuring acts by third parties.

f) A claim under s.423 IA is a claim brought on behalf of all victims collectively (s.424(2) IA) and the remedy granted must seek to protect the interests of all victims of the transaction (s.423(2)(b) IA). A claim under s.37 MCA is made by and for the benefit of the spouse making the financial remedies claim alone.

g) The remedies are different. Under s.37(2)(c) MCA, the primary relief is and is only *'an order setting aside the disposition'*, although the court enjoys a broad discretion to grant *'consequential directions'* pursuant to s.37(3) including against third-party recipients. Under ss. 423 to 425 IA, the court is granted a much broader discretion to *'make such order as it thinks fit'* for the purposes identified in s.423(2), which may include the wide-ranging relief set out in s.425(1) IA.'

78 [2002] EWHC 3114 (Ch), [2004] 2 FCR 79, [2003] 2 FLR 231 at para 60.

CHAPTER 8

Search orders

Content at a glance:

A INTRODUCTION

8.01 Of the many powers the court has in its arsenal to facilitate enforcement, search orders are often described as the most draconian and exceptional[1]. It is rare for such orders to be sought, even in circumstances where it would be appropriate to do so[2].

8.02 A search order is also known as an *Anton Piller* order, named after the eponymous case[3] where the Court of Appeal approved the form of order.

8.03 A search or *Anton Piller* order is a form of interim mandatory injunction. In essence, rather than requiring a respondent to provide disclosure, it requires the respondent to allow an applicant's representatives, accompanied by a supervising solicitor, to enter their home and/or premises to search for, copy and remove documents or material which might otherwise be destroyed, disposed of or concealed. Its purpose is to preserve evidence. In that way, it is conceptually and practically distinct from a disclosure order.

1 See for instance *Burgess v Burgess* [1997] 1 FCR 89, [1996] 2 FLR 34, CA; *Araghchinchi v Araghchinchi* [1997] 3 FCR 567, [1997] 2 FLR 142, CA; *Bank of Scotland v A Ltd* [2000] Lloyd's Rep Bank 271.

2 *Imerman v Tchenguiz & Ors* [2010] EWCA Civ, 908, [2011] Fam. 116, [2011] 2 WLR 592, [2010] 3 FCR 371, [2010] 2 FLR 814. Per Ward LJ at para 135: 'Of course, such orders, particularly search and seize orders, can be expensive to obtain and execute, and we accept that, particularly in cases where the amount at stake is not substantial, the cost-effectiveness, or proportionality, of seeking such an order may be questionable. But in many cases where a wife has reason to be concerned that her husband may be in the process of concealing assets or documents, or the like, seeking ex parte peremptory relief would be both appropriate and effective.'

3 *Anton Piller KG v Manufacturing Processes Ltd* [1976] Ch 55, [1976] 2 WLR 162.

8.04 Search orders can only be made by a High Court judge. Obtaining and executing the orders can be expensive. Applications are typically made without notice. Practitioners need to be aware that the court may set aside search orders at return hearings and make orders for indemnity costs and/or damages should the order have been improperly or unnecessarily obtained on a without notice basis.

B JURISDICTION

8.05 Whilst sanctioned by the Court of Appeal in *Anton Piller*[4], the court's power to make a search order is now derived from Civil Procedure Act 1997, s 7. It is available in financial remedy[5] and enforcement proceedings[6].

8.06 The court may make a search order for the purpose of securing:

- the preservation of evidence which is or may be relevant; or,
- the preservation of property which is or may be the subject-matter of the proceedings or as to which any question arises or may arise in the proceedings.

8.07 In terms of searching, the order may direct a person to permit an individual identified in the order:

- to enter premises in England and Wales; and
- while on the premises and in accordance with the terms of the order:
  - to carry out a search for or inspection of anything described in the order;
  - to make or obtain a copy, photograph, sample or other record of anything described in the order;
  - to be provided with any information or article described in the order;
  - to retain for safe keeping anything described in the order.

C REQUIREMENTS AND AMBIT

8.08 There are 'three essential pre-conditions' for the making of a search order[7]:

4 In *TBD (Owen Holland) Ltd v Simons & Ors* [2020] EWCA Civ 1182, [2021] 1 WLR 992, the Court of Appeal charted the history of the orders and concluded that the first reported reasoned decision was that of Templeman J in *EMI Ltd v Pandit* [1975] 1 WLR 302.

5 FPR 2010, r 20.2(1)(h).

6 FPR 2010, r 20.3(1)(b).

7 *Anton Piller KG v Manufacturing Processes Ltd* [1976] Ch 55. [1976] 2 WLR 162.

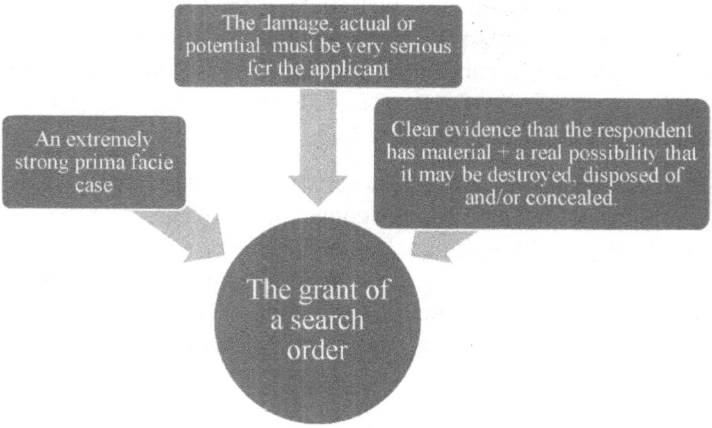

8.09 The remedy was initially utilised (and continues to be utilised) in cases involving a commercial breach of confidence, passing off or breach of intellectual property rights where a claimant believed that the defendant was concealing or destroying infringing items, incriminating material or relevant documents. It was only somewhat later that the courts were asked to make such orders in financial remedy cases[8] but thereafter there was a period when search orders were obtained too readily.

In *Burgess v Burgess* [1996] 2 FLR 34, at first instance Hale J had held that if a search order turns out to have been unjustified or unnecessary, there is a risk of incurring a substantial liability to the other side in terms of both their legal costs and their potential losses as a result of the order. Hale J set aside the search order (found to have been oppressive and without foundation) and ordered that the applicant pay indemnity costs. The Court of Appeal dismissed the appeal.

8.10 'An extremely strong prima facie [substantive] case' is a pre-condition more readily germane to civil cases, as in most family cases the parties' marriage will likely entitle a party to make an application for a financial remedy which should satisfy the condition. Moreover, the fact that a party is in breach of a financial remedy order is likely to satisfy this condition.

8.11 The requirement that *'the damage, actual or potential, must be very serious for the applicant'* is appropriate because of the Draconian nature of the remedy. It has been said that 'there must be proportionality between the perceived threat to the applicant's rights and the Draconian innovation that the remedy permits'[9]. There must be a paramount need to prevent a denial of justice which cannot be met otherwise than by a search order. Thus, a search order should not be sought where suitable alternative remedies are available to secure the

8 See for instance *Emanuel v Emanuel* [1982] 1 WLR 669 and *Kepa v Kepa* (1983) 4 FLR 515.

9 *Araghchinchi v Aragchinchi* [1997] 3 FCR 567, [1997] 2 FLR 142 per Ward LJ at p 146. See also *Imerman v Tchenguiz & Others* [2010] EWCA Civ, 908, [2011] Fam. 116, [2011] 2 WLR 592, [2010] 3 FCR 371, [2010] 2 FLR 814 at paras 134-135.

disclosure and production of documents[10]. Indeed, the very fact that the court has wide disclosure powers and is ultimately able to draw adverse inferences from a party's failure to provide full and frank disclosure means that there will be fewer cases in family proceedings where it is necessary to grant a search order than may be the case in ordinary civil proceedings[11].

8.12 A need to demonstrate a 'real possibility that material may be destroyed, disposed of and/or concealed' requires convincing evidence that the respondent will actually do any of these things. In the absence of such evidence, the order will not be granted[12]. In *Imerman v Tchenguiz & Others*[13], it was held that 'such applications should be seriously considered where there are *substantial reasons* for believing that a husband is concealing or dissipating assets, or intending to conceal or destroy documents'.

8.13 Should the three pre-conditions be satisfied, the next question which the court must address is the ambit of the order which should be made:

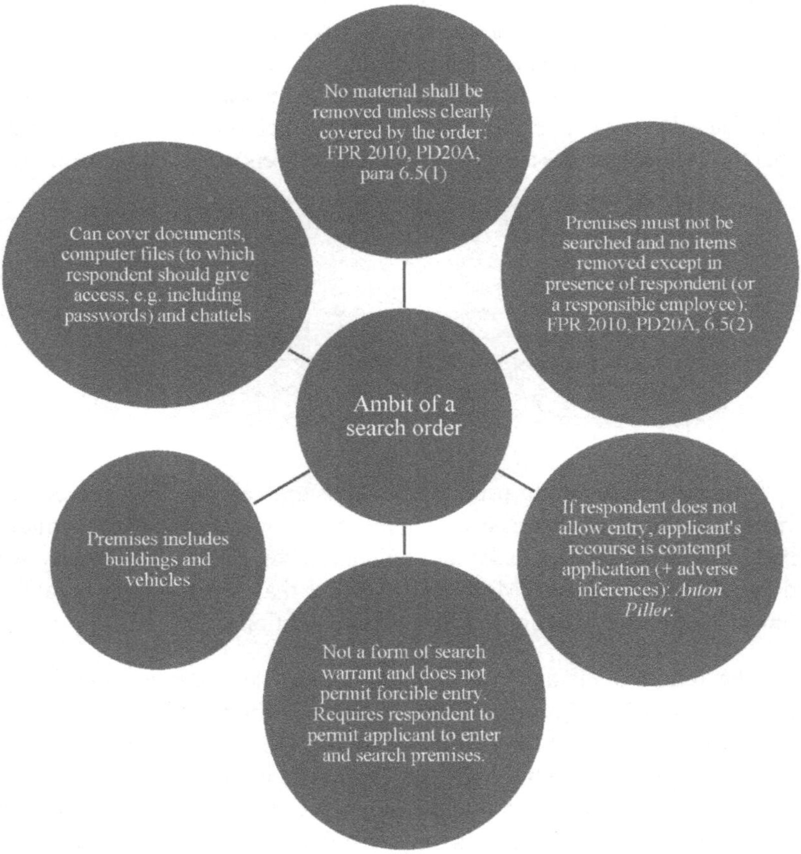

10 *Burgess v Burgess* [1996] 2 FLR 34.
11 *Araghchinchi v Araghchinchi* [1997] 3 FCR 567, [1997] 2 FLR 142.
12 *Araghchinchi v Araghchinchi* [1997] 3 FCR 567, [1997] 2 FLR 142.
13 [2010] EWCA Civ, 908, [2011] Fam. 116, [2011] 2 WLR 592, [2010] 3 FCR 371, [2010] 2 FLR 814 at para 134.

D PROCEDURE

General

8.14 In the light of their draconian nature, there are a significant number of procedural requirements which must be met to obtain a search order. These requirements can make the exercise a costly one, particularly the need for a supervising solicitor (dealt with below). Extensive guidance is set out in FPR 2010, PD20A, paras 6.1–6.9[14]. Applications must be made to a High Court judge[15].

8.15 Applications are made using the Part 18 procedure and Form D11. Any such application must be supported by affidavit evidence[16] which should very fully explain the reason(s) why the order is sought (including the probability that relevant material would disappear if the order was not made)[17]. The evidence must provide full details of the person who will act as the supervising solicitor[18].

8.16 Undertakings will be required from the applicant, the applicant's solicitor and also the supervising solicitor. The applicant must undertake to compensate the respondent for loss for which the court considers the respondent should be compensated. The applicant's solicitor must undertake[19]:

- To return retained documents (retained for the purpose of producing copies) as soon as possible and in any event within two working days of their removal;
- Where ownership of an article is in dispute, to deliver it to the respondent's solicitors within two working days of receipt of a written undertaking by them to retain the article in their safe keeping and produce it to the court when required;
- To retain all other items in their safe keeping.

Without notice applications

8.17 Applications can be (and typically are) made without notice[20]:

14 These broadly mirror those contained in Civil Procedure Rules 1998, PD25A.
15 Per the Civil Procedure Act 1997, s 7(8) and The Family Court (Composition and Distribution of Business) Rules 2014, Sch 2, Table 3, para 3. See also *Tobias v Tobias* [2017] EWFC 46, [2017] 4 WLR 146. [2017] 3 FCR 399, [2018] 1 FLR 616.
16 FPR 2010, PD20A, para 3.1.
17 FPR 2010, PD20A, para 6.3(2).
18 FPR 2010, PD20A, para 6.3(1).
19 FPR 2010, PD20A, para 6.
20 FPR 2010, r.20.4(1). For a recent example in enforcement proceedings, see *Akhmedova v Akhmedov* [2020] EWHC 3005 (Fam), [2021] 1 FCR 513 (the without notice hearing) and [2020] EWHC 3006 (Fam), [2021] 1 FCR 513 (the return hearing) at which it was recorded that devices appeared to have been 'actively concealed from the wife'.

- The reason(s) for applying without notice must be given[21] and the applicant must show that the matter is one of extreme urgency or that giving notice of any kind would defeat the purpose of the order sought. In any other case at least short, informal notice should be given.
- The facts that justify a search order being made (ie the destruction of documents) may also in appropriate cases justify the making of without notice orders but nevertheless the requirements for obtaining search orders and for obtaining without notice orders are distinct and require separate justification.
- There is a heavy duty on those presenting an application without notice to ensure that the court is directed to all the relevant facts, both favourable and unfavourable, at a without notice hearing. This is especially the case when the order sought is a draconian one, such as a search order. The order may be discharged if there has been a failure to make full and frank disclosure, or a breach of undertakings by solicitors.
- There must be a return date, which should be before the same judge, at which the other party can be present[22].

The role of the supervising solicitor

8.18 In many ways, the supervising solicitor has an unenviable task of ensuring that a significant number of procedural formalities and proper safeguards are respected during the execution of a search order. These are contained in FPR 2010, PD20A, para 6.

The supervising solicitor's role and responsibilities are as follows:

- Personally serve the search order (together with evidence and any documents capable of being copied): FPR 2010, PD20A, para 6.4(1).
- Be accompanied only by the persons mentioned in the order: FPR 2010, PD20A, para 6.4(3).
- Fully supervise entry and search.
- Explain order to the respondent in everyday language: FPR 2010, PD20A, para 6.4(4).
- Explain the respondent's rights: (i) to legal advice; (ii) to apply to vary/discharge the order; (iii) potential privilege (legal professional privilege and right against self-incrimination): FPR 2010, PD20A, para 6.4(4)(a), (b).
- Make a list of all material removed and provide a copy for the respondent; no material to be removed until the respondent has had a reasonable time to check the list: FPR 2010, PD20A, 6.5(7).

21 FPR 2010, r 20.4(3).
22 FPR 2010, PD20A, para 5.1(c).

- Produce a report on the carrying out of the order: FPR 2010, PD20A, 6.5(11).
- The solicitor cannot be an employee or member of the applicant's firm: FPR 2010, PD20A, 6.6.
- The solicitor must be experienced in the operation of search orders: FPR 2010, PD20A, para 6.2. Details may be obtained from the Law Society and, in London, the London Solicitors' Litigation Association.

CHAPTER 9

Orders against trusts

Content at a glance:

A INTRODUCTION

9.01 The English court in financial remedy proceedings has wide-reaching powers to involve and/or make orders against trusts and trustees (both English and foreign) where the assets held within a trust structure form part of a divorcing spouse's resources.

9.02 The court has the power to vary a trust which is an ante-nuptial or post-nuptial settlement: Matrimonial Causes Act 1973 ('MCA 1973'), s 24(1)(c). Theoretically, the breadth of the discretion to vary a trust that is a nuptial settlement is considerable, including even the power to exclude a beneficiary entirely from a settlement and to transfer an asset to a non-beneficiary free from the trust[1].

9.03 The court's power under MCA 1973, s 24(1)(c) is sometimes referred to in offshore jurisdictions as a 'long arm provision', which perhaps gives a flavour of how English matrimonial legislation is sometimes viewed by the courts of offshore jurisdictions.

1 *Ben Hashem v Al Shayif* [2008] EWHC 2380 (Fam), [2009] 1 FLR 115.

9.04 The steps to be taken to enforce orders that directly or indirectly affect trusts and their assets – and the likelihood of such action being successful – will depend upon:

- the precise nature of the order to be enforced;
- the location of the trust, its trustees and the trust assets; and
- the governing law applicable to the particular trust.

9.05 In general terms, it is likely to be relatively straightforward to enforce orders against a trust where the trust and/or its assets are located in England and Wales and governed by English law. Conversely, the situation will be far more complicated if the trust is offshore, its assets are offshore, and/or it is governed by the law of a foreign jurisdiction, particularly if that jurisdiction has enacted protective ('firewall') legislation aimed at protecting the trust assets from interference (see paras **9.42–9.50**).

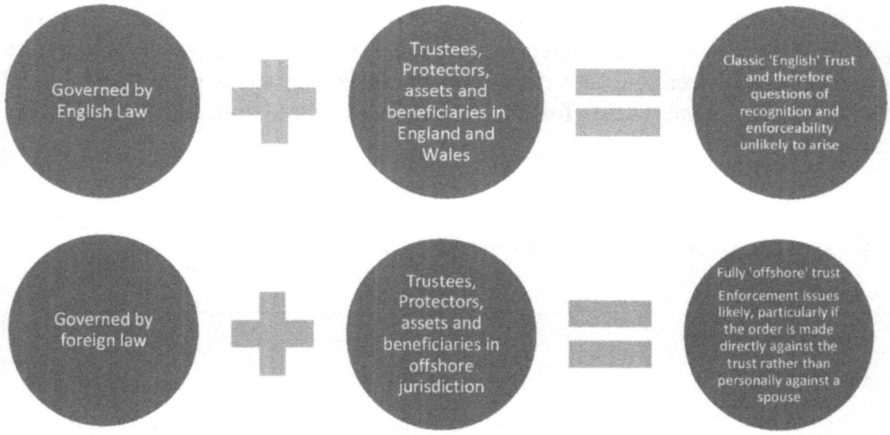

9.06 The diagrams above are an oversimplification as the categorisation of a trust as 'foreign' can be a matter of degree.

9.07 Whilst a trust governed by foreign law may be readily described as a 'foreign' trust, a trust governed by English law but containing other international elements (such as where certain of the trust assets are located outside the jurisdiction) is less easy to categorise. Enforcement issues could well arise in such cases.

9.08 It is important to consider whether a trust has international elements (location of assets, governing law, location of trustees) that will have a bearing on issues of enforcement. The greater the number of those international elements, the harder enforcement is likely to be. If the assets and the trustees are located away from the reach of the English court's enforcement mechanisms and protected by local legislation, then there may be very real practical difficulties in enforcing the order.

9.09 Practitioners acting for applicants should identify at an early stage (ie well in advance of final orders being obtained):

- the nature of the order that will be sought against the respondent;
- whether there is likely to be a need to enforce any part of that order against a trustee or trust assets; and, if so,
- in *which* jurisdiction any enforcement action would take place.

This will enable an assessment to be made about the applicant's likely prospects of recovery.

9.10 Future enforcement considerations should influence the trajectory of the case. They will be relevant to decisions about the orders that should be sought and how these should be framed.

9.11 A robust cost-benefit analysis will need to be undertaken at the outset. In cases where the trust or its assets are offshore it may be necessary to obtain foreign legal advice and representation. A decision should also be taken as to whether the trustees and any third-party adult beneficiaries need to be joined to the proceedings, either for the purposes of disclosure or to aid future enforcement.

Case summary: *Tchenguiz-Imerman v Imerman*[2]

Facts:

In financial remedy proceedings W sought assets worth £120 million including a variation of certain trusts on the basis they were post-nuptial settlements. The beneficiaries were H's three adult children from a previous relationship, H's parents, the ten-year old child of the marriage and one of H's grandchildren. The trust held assets of approximately £130 million including businesses for which the three adult children worked. The trustees were joined as parties but then applied to the Royal Court of Jersey and the Eastern Caribbean Supreme Court and were granted approval not to take part. That was supported by the beneficiaries. H's adult children then applied to be joined as parties.

Held by Moylan J (joining the beneficiaries):

The English family court must consider the interests of beneficiaries when deciding whether, and if so how, to exercise its powers to vary settlements.

2 [2012] EWHC 4277 (Fam), [2014] 1 FLR 865.

The trustees would be in the best position, from the court's perspective, to assist the court but the beneficiaries are not bound by the trustees' decision not to participate, though they supported that course of action.

It was desirable for the adult beneficiaries to participate directly, as this would assist with the investigation and resolution of the matters, would be consistent with the overriding objective and would be likely to assist with enforcement. The beneficiaries would be bound by the court's decision.

9.12 Where enforcement against a trust is likely to be difficult, costly or protracted, it is worth considering whether to focus on obtaining orders against any visible, non-trust assets on the basis that the respondent will retain the benefit of trust assets. Such an approach may avoid enforcement difficulties altogether.

9.13 This chapter will provide an overview of the main issues to consider when a party needs to enforce a financial order in a variety of different circumstances where the relevant assets are held within a trust structure. In a case involving an overseas trust it is likely that specialist advice will be required, as to the laws of the relevant jurisdiction and their application to the trust in question.

B IDENTIFYING AND ANALYSING THE NATURE OF THE TRUST ISSUE

9.14 There are a number of common scenarios in which issues of trust law arise in family proceedings. The following examples raise very different legal issues and practical concerns:

NON-DISCLOSURE	If there is a lack of information about a trust or its assets, the court may need to make third party disclosure orders directly against trustees or issue 'letters of request'[3] to a foreign court to assist the court and parties to obtain missing information.
RISK OF DISSIPATION	A party may invite the English court to make an interim freezing injunction against the assets of a trust where there is a risk that the other party will take steps to dissipate assets[4].
'SHAM' TRUSTS	The court may be invited to declare that an alleged trust is a 'sham' set up to disguise the fact that the 'beneficiary' spouse continues to be the true legal owner of the asset(s).

3 See **Chapter 10**.
4 For freezing injunctions see **Chapter 7**.

REAL OWNERSHIP	A court may find that on a proper construction of the trust deed the trustees hold all the trust assets on trust for the beneficiary spouse such that the trust structure – though not a 'sham' – is nonetheless illusory as the spouse continues to be the true owner of the assets.
THOMAS v THOMAS CASES	The court may conclude, in the context of a discretionary trust, that the trustees are likely to satisfy any request made by the beneficiary spouse for provision of assets from the trust and make orders designed to give effect to this conclusion, with or without extra 'encouragement' from the court.
NUPTIAL SETTLEMENTS	The court might decide to vary a trust (if it is a nuptial settlement[5]) to ensure that the divorcing spouses receive a fair division of matrimonial property and resources.

9.15 Depending on the nature of the trust issue, the court at a final hearing may or may not be asked to make orders directly against a trustee or trust.

If orders are made personally against a spouse (for example requiring the spouse to transfer non-trust assets located in England to the other spouse in lieu of resources available to the former from a discretionary trust) then issues of enforcement against a trust and international enforcement difficulties may not arise at all.

9.16 Practitioners should therefore first identify whether the financial orders will need to be enforced *directly* against third party trustees. If such enforcement is likely to prove necessary, the following may need to be joined to the proceedings:

- the trustees;
- minor beneficiaries; and/or
- potentially, other adult beneficiaries.

9.17 Joinder may increase the chances of the orders later being enforceable[6]. The involvement of third parties, however, will invariably increase the costs.

9.18 In *Behbehani v Behbehani*[7] the Court of Appeal stated that in financial remedy proceedings where there was a dispute as to the beneficial ownership of an asset, it would be disproportionate to insist that all potential owners be joined so as to determine the issue of ownership where a party was not seeking transfer of that asset. For enforcement purposes, the Court of Appeal concluded that where a judge had found that assets were beneficially owned by a party to proceedings (but legally held by a third party) the other party was not precluded from seeking to enforce a lump sum order *against* those assets simply because

5 For the purposes of MCA 1973, s 24(1)(c).
6 FPR 2010, r 9.26B. See also *TM v AH* [2016] EWHC 572 (Fam), [2016] 4 WLR 78 for joinder in the context of an application involving a nuptial settlement.
7 [2019] EWCA Civ 2301, [2020] 1 FCR 603.

the third party had not been joined to proceedings. In such circumstances the legal owners could be joined to the enforcement proceedings and the claimant spouse was not precluded from seeking to enforce against those assets.

9.19 Where there will be a need to enforce orders against trustees the English court will need to be satisfied at the outset of the litigation that everything possible has been done to assert jurisdiction over the trustees. For example:

(i) Ensuring that the appropriate rules have been complied with in respect of service of court documents on the trustees (including compliance with rules for service out of the jurisdiction, where relevant);

(ii) Although joinder of trustees is not strictly a pre-requisite for the court exercising its powers against a trust, it is hard to see how trustees (particularly offshore trustees) will be bound by findings of fact about a trust if they have not been joined to the proceedings and afforded the opportunity to participate[8];

(iii) Considering whether the trustees have submitted to the jurisdiction of the English court. If the trustees have submitted to the jurisdiction then this increases the likelihood the court of the trust jurisdiction will recognise and enforce the English court order[9];

(iv) Considering the terms of the trust deed itself and whether there are any express terms within the deed that give the English court jurisdiction over the trustees or whether, conversely, there is legislation that expressly prohibits recognition of the foreign judgment in the offshore jurisdiction.

Applicable law

9.20 Irrespective of the location of the trust or the law governing the trust, the law that the *English family court* will apply when deciding whether to make orders that directly or indirectly affect the trust is the law of England and Wales. This was emphasised by Baroness Hale in *Radmacher v Granatino*[10]:

8 There are conflicting High Court authorities on this point. In *DR v GR (Financial Remedy: Variation of Overseas Trust)* [2013] EWHC 1196 (Fam), [2013] 2 FLR 1534, Mostyn J stated that there was no requirement for trustees to be joined in an application to vary a settlement, although in accordance with FPR 2010, r 9.13, notice was required to be given to the trustees and the settlor (if living). He stated that if they had been served in accordance with those rules and did not seek to be joined, it was clear that any variation order would be valid and binding. Mostyn J also queried whether enforcement would be better achieved if trustees were joined, relying on *Mubarak v Mubarik* [2008] JRC 136. By contrast, in *TM v AH* [2015] EWHC 572 (Fam), [2016] 4 WLR 78, the wife sought to join the trustees (who had made clear they were not submitting to the jurisdiction and needed to apply to the supervisory courts in Switzerland and the British Virgin Islands for guidance). Moor J stated that in general, trustees should be joined, as it was hard to see that a court could make an order for variation without them being parties, let alone say it was binding.

9 In *Minwalla v Minwalla* [2004] EWHC 2823 (Fam), [2005] 1 FLR 771 the trustees' submission to the jurisdiction was relied upon by the Jersey Court in subsequent enforcement proceedings, see *Re the Fountain Trust* [2005] JLR 359.

10 [2010] UKSC 42, [2011] 1 AC 534, [2010] 3 WLR 1367, [2010] 3 FCR 583, [2010] 2 FLR 1900. See also Lord Phillips at para [103].

Key citation: *Radmacher v Granatino*[11]

'In strict legal terms the so-called 'foreign element' is irrelevant. If the proceedings take place in England and Wales, the applicable law is that of England and Wales, irrespective of where the parties come from, how long they have been here, or how close their connection is with this jurisdiction… Anyone who chooses to divorce here must be advised that the court will apply English law and not the law of the country which the parties have chosen or with which the marriage has the closest connection.'

9.21 Despite this apparent simplicity, practitioners should bear in mind:

(i) The fact that the English court has made orders does not mean that the foreign court will assist with enforcement of those orders;

(ii) The English court may decline to make orders against overseas trusts in the first place where it considers that those orders are not capable of being enforced in the overseas jurisdiction[12].

Case summary: *BJ v MJ (Financial Order: Overseas Trust)*[13]

Facts:

H and W were married for over 30 years and had one child, aged 25 at the time of trial. W sought financial relief. The family wealth was largely derived from H's 1/3 shareholding in the company in which he had worked. His share of a public flotation of the company was placed in an offshore company, controlled by two Jersey trusts. This was primarily to avoid capital gains tax, but also intended to provide collateral benefit to the family including future generations.

The terms of the first trust provided that the trustees were to give the income to H for life, with power to appoint capital to him, and thereafter to W, with the same power, thereafter to their child, H's siblings and siblings-in-law and the Charities Aid Foundation. The beneficiaries of the second trust were any grandchildren, remoter issue, the Charities Aid Foundation, siblings and siblings-in-law and employees of the original company – H, W and their son were specifically excluded as beneficiaries.

11 [2010] UKSC 42, [2011] 1 AC 534, [2010] 3 WLR 1367, [2010] 3 FCR 583, [2010] 2 FLR 1900. See also Lord Phillips at para [103].

12 *Hamlin v Hamlin* [1986] Fam 11, [1985] 3 WLR 629, [1986] 1 FLR 61.

13 [2011] EWHC 2708 (Fam), [2012] 1 FLR 667.

The overall trust assets totalled £4.31 million, with £1.87 million invested in two English properties. W also sought to add back gifts of c£140,000 made by H to their son shortly after separation.

The trustees were joined but declined to submit to the jurisdiction, though they did partially comply with disclosure orders and made it clear they would provide reasonable support to H and W as beneficiaries. The parties' adult son was also contacted, as a beneficiary of the trust, to give him the opportunity to take legal advice and make written submissions. It was not known whether any order made concerning assets out of the jurisdiction would be enforced by the Jersey court.

Held by Mostyn J:

The court could make an effective order for variation in respect of a nuptial trust where it was satisfied that the order would be enforced by an overseas court *or* where the trust assets fell within the court's jurisdiction and therefore subject to its enforcement powers. It would be unlikely that the court would make a variation order where both the trust and its assets are overseas unless satisfied that the order would be implemented by the court exercising effective control over the trust. If, however, the court is satisfied that any variation would be effective against the husband (or beneficiary spouse) *in personam*, the order would be more likely to be made.

C *THOMAS v THOMAS* 'JUDICIOUS ENCOURAGEMENT' CASES

9.22 Where a spouse is a beneficiary of a trust and there is a track record of that spouse being financially supported by the trust, the court may conclude that the assets of the trust or the potential for future distributions are a 'resource' of the spouse to be taken into account when deciding what financial remedy order to make.

9.23 In such cases, unless the trust is 'a nuptial settlement', a court cannot make orders directly against the trust; rather, any order would be made against the spouse personally (on the basis the spouse is expected to fulfil his or her obligations by continuing to rely on distributions from the trust or by making a request to the trustees that is likely to be met by them).

9.24 Such orders may be said to give what is termed 'judicious encouragement' to trustees to act in a way that enables the court's award to be satisfied (see *Thomas v Thomas*[14]; *TL v ML (Ancillary Relief: Claim against Assets of Extended Family)*[15]). The authorities make it clear that while it may be appropriate for the court to give a strong 'steer' to trustees to act in a certain way, this must fall short of placing them under improper pressure[16]

14 [1996] 2 FCR 544, [1995] 2 FLR 668.

15 [2005] EWHC 2860 (Fam), [2006] 1 FCR 465, [2006] 1 FLR 1263.

16 *Thomas v Thomas* [1996] 2 FCR 544, [1995] 2 FLR 668; *TL v ML (Ancillary Relief: Claim against Assets of Extended Family)* [2005] EWHC 2860 (Fam), [2006] 1 FCR 465, [2006] 1 FLR 1263.

Case summary: *Thomas v Thomas*[17]

Facts:

H was joint managing director of a successful family business and became a name at Lloyds during the marriage. His resources included the family home, which secured a mortgage to the bank, a bank guarantee covering his contingent liabilities to Lloyds and a Lloyds losses loan, a pension fund and his shareholding in the company. His income from the company was relatively low, in line with company policy. W had no capital and no independent source of income.

The judge held that H had failed to satisfy the court that it was beyond his power to free the equity in the family home by providing the bank with alternative security. He ordered the sale of the family home and payment to the wife of the majority of the equity and periodical payments of over half of H's monthly salary plus the children's school fees. He expressed the view that the deficiency of income was one H would make good by procuring changes in company policy.

H appealed both in regard to the lump sum order and the income award.

Held by the Court of Appeal (dismissing the appeal):

Under the wide discretion of the MCA 1973, ss 23–25A the court was not obliged to have regard exclusively to capital or income which were shown to exist but might infer the availability of unidentified resources. Moreover, where a spouse enjoyed *access* to wealth, but no absolute entitlement to it, the court would not act in direct invasion of a third party's rights, nor put a third party under pressure to act in a way which would enhance the means of the maintaining spouse, but nevertheless did not need to act in total disregard of that potential wealth.

Although the order involved a 'powerful inducement' to the extended family to come to H's assistance, it fell far short of the kind of the order which was contrary to authority in that it placed 'improper pressure' on third parties.

9.25 In this category of cases, there is unlikely to be a need to join the trustees to the proceedings[18] as there would be no power to directly enforce any resulting orders against them in any event.

17 [1996] 2 FCR 544, [1995] 2 FLR 668.

18 Although if disclosure orders are sought directly against trustees they would need to be parties to that specific application and would be entitled to be represented on that application.

9.26 In 'judicious encouragement' cases it is helpful to consider whether the future financial order against the spouse falls into the category of a 'fresh money' case[19] or a backfill case[20].

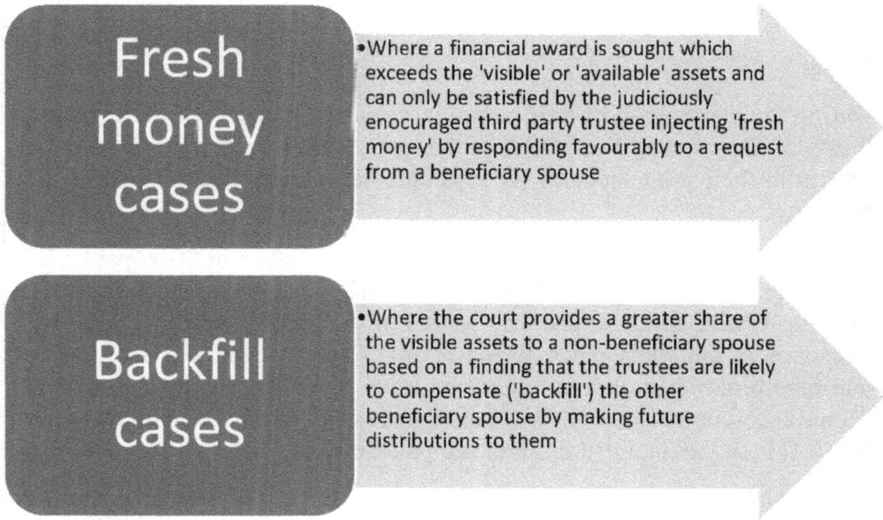

9.27 In a 'fresh money' case, enforcement is likely to be much more problematic. If – despite the court's findings – the trustees do *not* in fact provide the respondent with the anticipated injection of trust capital, the order may prove impossible to enforce, as:

- the order will be framed as a lump sum order against the other spouse and will not involve the sale or transfer of any visible asset owned by either spouse; and
- the third party trustees can be encouraged – but not compelled – to satisfy the terms of an order made against a spouse.

9.28 Whether the trustees are likely to exercise their discretion so as to give effect to any order, and whether an order encouraging them to do so should be made in the first place, are interconnected questions as MCA 1973, s 25(2)(a) requires the court to have regard to the financial resources a spouse either has or is 'likely' to have in the foreseeable future.

9.29 A spouse is only 'likely' to have future resources from a trust if the trustees are likely to exercise their discretion to provide those resources to the spouse. If the trustees are unlikely so to act, then the assets are not a likely future resource and should not be taken into account. Thus, the court is required to consider the issue of future enforcement in judicious encouragement cases as part and parcel of whether the substantive order should be made.

19 See Coleridge J in *AM v SS* [2014] EWHC 2887 (Fam).
20 *AM v SS* [2014] EWHC 2887 (Fam) at para 39.

Case summary: *Daga v Bangur*[21]

Facts:

During the marriage, both parties had professional careers but led a modest lifestyle. They rented homes rather than purchasing property and paid the rent from their joint incomes. W's parents had always disapproved of the marriage.

W created two discretionary trusts in 2015; W's father in 2016 paid £2.7 million into a bank account of the wife and substantial sums into the trusts, totalling US$23 million. The true source of the money was uncertain, but it was clear the sums never formed part of the matrimonial assets. The marriage broke down around the same time. H petitioned for divorce and decree absolute was granted. W repaid the majority of the £2.7 million to her father, it being maintained this had been a loan.

In financial remedy proceedings H W was the settlor and beneficiary of the discretionary trusts, so had assets of around £17.5 million. No distribution had ever been made, but H argued that a lump sum order should be made directed against the trusts and 'judicious encouragement' given to the trustees to distribute to W the funds with which to pay it.

W submitted that she did not have access to nor was a beneficiary of the trusts and relied on her father's evidence, which was that no funds could be paid, no sums had been paid and he did not see any distribution in the foreseeable future. He further stated that no-one, not W or his grandson, would receive sums from the funds and there would be no distribution in his lifetime.

Held by Holman J (dismissing the claims of both parties):

It was not possible to make an order in reliance upon the trust funds. The father's evidence was clear that, even if a lump sum order was made against the wife, the father would advise the trustees that they should not distribute funds to her with which to pay it.

Before a court made an order relying upon judicious encouragement it had to be satisfied that the trustees would be likely to respond to that encouragement. This stemmed from the language of MCA 1973, s 25(2)(a). Unless trustees are likely to make the funds available, there is no room for an order based on judicious encouragement.

21 [2018] EWFC 91, [2019] 2 FCR 646, [2019] 1 FLR 1340.

9.30 For the reasons summarised by Holman J in *Daga v Bangur*[22], it will be unusual for the court to make an order, the satisfaction of which will depend upon a third party trustee providing fresh money to meet an award.

D ENFORCING ORDERS DIRECTLY AGAINST TRUSTS – VARYING A NUPTIAL SETTLEMENT

9.31 Where the court exercises its powers under MCA 1973, s 24(1)(c) to vary a nuptial settlement and distribute trust assets to the parties, future enforcement of the order is likely to involve action taken directly against the trustees.

9.32 If the trust is governed by English law and the assets, trustees and beneficiaries are located in England, enforcement may not present any difficulty as the court's approach to making orders against the trust will generally involve the same or similar considerations to those relevant to a fair outcome in the financial remedy proceedings[23].

9.33 Where the court proposes to vary an offshore settlement, practitioners need to consider how the offshore jurisdiction will receive any order for variation and, in particular, whether the offshore trust has enacted protective or 'firewall' legislation which will prevent enforcement of the English order. If the proposed variation of the trust contravenes the relevant statutory provisions in the offshore jurisdiction it may be impossible to enforce.

9.34 Practitioners should obtain advice as to the law of the jurisdiction in which enforcement may be required in relation to the following matters in particular:

- whether the concept of a 'nuptial' settlement in recognised under the law of the offshore jurisdiction and if so, how that concept is interpreted;
- whether any legislation would preclude variation of the offshore settlement in question.

9.35 The following diagram summarises the steps that should be taken or, at least, considered in cases involving the enforcement of variation orders against overseas trusts:

22 [2018] EWFC 91, [2019] 2 FCR 646, [2019] 1 FLR 1340 paras 59-60.
23 See, for example, *AB v CB (Financial Remedies: Variation of Trust)* [2014] EWHC 2998 (Fam), [2015] 3 FCR 135, [2015] 2 FLR 25, Mostyn J and [2015] EWCA Civ 447, [2016] 1 FLR 437, CA (upheld on appeal to the Court of Appeal).

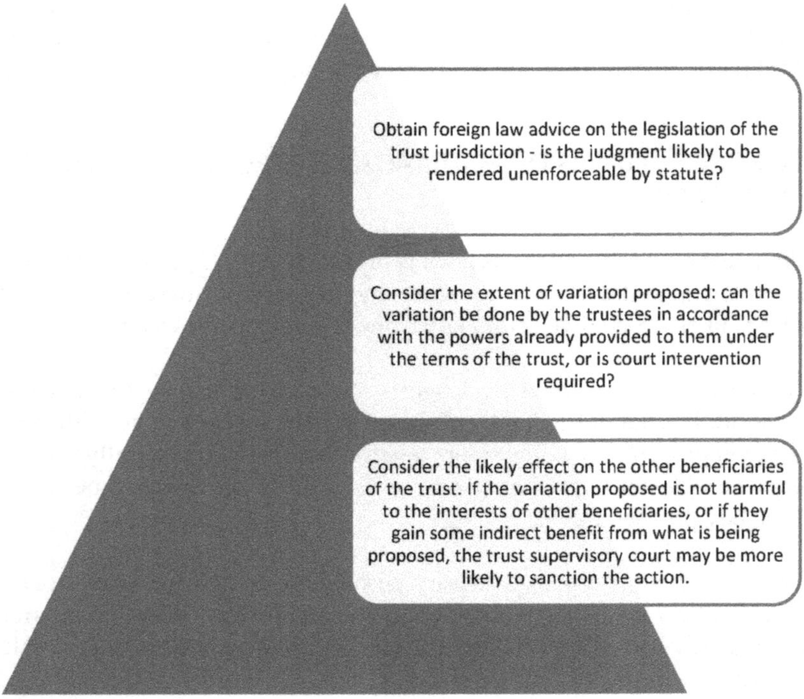

9.36 *Mubarak v Mubarik*[24] is an example of an exceptional case in which the court varied a trust under MCA 1973, s 24(1)(c) as an option of last resort to enforce an order that had been made against the husband personally. That option was only available, however, as the trust was a 'nuptial settlement'.

Case summary: *Mubarak v Mubarik*[25]

Facts:

W applied for all forms of financial relief. H conceded at the final hearing that assets held by a Jersey trust could be treated as being his personal assets of H. H and W had been the trust settlors and W had been one of the original beneficiaries, but shortly after separation H had signed an instrument of exclusion, revocably declaring that W was an excluded beneficiary. W was awarded a lump sum of £4,875,000 to be paid forthwith, with periodical payments until this was paid.

Seven years later, W sought to enforce the lump sum and arrears of periodical payments. She applied, inter alia, to vary the terms of the trust as a post-nuptial

24 [2007] EWHC 220 (Fam), [2007] 2 FLR 364.
25 [2007] EWHC 220 (Fam), [2007] 2 FLR 364.

settlement under MCA 1973, s 24(1)(c). All of the trust beneficiaries other than H (ie the children) supported W's application to vary the settlement.

At an earlier hearing[26], a *Hadkinson* order[27] had been made which, as a condition of H's participation in the proceedings, required H to sign a letter to the trustees accepting irrevocably that he would be bound by any decision of the English court and that he wished them to assist him in meeting his obligations under the order. H had signed the letter.

Held by Holman J:

Order made varying the terms of the trust to require the trustees to pay W the sum owed to her.

The original order would have become a comprehensive capital order if and when the lump sum was paid in full, but pending payment W's claim for variation of settlement remained open.

The discretion to vary the post-nuptial settlement was then exercised, notwithstanding the delay. W had repeatedly sought to enforce and H had not made any realistic attempt to pay. Although the Jersey courts considered that foreign courts ought not to purport to vary terms of Jersey trusts, this was an exceptional case and the expert opinion suggested a sufficient prospect of success. Moreover, the court took account of H's concession that the trust was in reality and on his own evidence an alter ego of H himself.

> '[159]…I do appreciate the very rare and exceptional nature of the course I am asked to take, namely, to make a further property adjustment order years after the 'main' order and essentially as a method of enforcement. I deeply appreciate that 'as a general rule it will be an exorbitant exercise of jurisdiction for this court to purport to vary the terms of a Jersey settlement'. But, as Bodey J said many years ago, this is, or has become, a wholly exceptional case. It no longer attracts general rules.'

The variation would cover not just the lump sum, but the other sums owed to W even though there would've been no power to do this if the lump sum were paid in full.

9.37 When the proceedings in *Mubarak* then went before the Jersey court, it found that the English order had the effect of 'altering' (rather than 'varying') the trust, a direction to which the court could not ordinarily give effect as it went beyond the trustees' powers. However, that course could be adopted as all of the adult beneficiaries (including H, by virtue of the letter he had signed) had consented to the English judgment being given effect in Jersey.

26 *Mubarak v Mubarik (No 2)* [2006] EWHC 1260 (Fam), [2007] 1 WLR 271, [2007] 1 FLR 722
27 For *Hadkinson* orders see **Chapter 5**.

9.38 Where an order is made against a spouse personally in a 'judicious encouragement' case involving a trust which is also a nuptial settlement, it is good practice to make clear on the face of any order that:

- the ability of the creditor spouse to apply for a variation of the trust for the purpose of enforcement remains available; and
- the spouse's claims under MCA 1973, s 24(1)(c) are not to be dismissed until the substantive order has been fully complied with.

E TRUSTEES SEEKING GUIDANCE FROM THE FOREIGN COURT

9.39 It is important to bear in mind that – whatever the English court may order – the trustees are likely to approach their supervisory court in order to obtain approval from that court before exercising any dispositive powers. The reason for this is to insulate the trustees (particularly when they are paid, professional trustees) from potential civil claims brought by other beneficiaries of the trust. Aggrieved beneficiaries might assert that in providing benefit to one discretionary beneficiary (ie the spouse) over and above the interests of the beneficiaries as a whole, the trustees have acted in breach of their fiduciary duties.

Case summary: *Re the X Trust*[28]

Facts:

The case concerned financial remedy proceedings in Jersey. H was a discretionary beneficiary of a Jersey trust which owned the parties' family home and other assets. The court held that the trust was not a post-nuptial settlement and there was therefore no power to vary it. However, the court took into account the fact of the trust and made personal orders against H, requiring him to procure the transfer to W of the family home and its contents, a lump sum of £1.8 million and the transfer of a half interest in a company. These orders could only be fulfilled if the trustees chose to exercise their discretion to make distributions enabling H to make those payments and to transfer the property to W.

Before deciding whether to exercise their discretion in this way, the trustees applied to the supervisory court in Jersey to approve this course of action (to protect them from the risk of claims being made against them by any other beneficiaries). The husband and the minor and unborn beneficiaries were also represented at the hearing.

28 (2002) 5 ITELR 119

Held by the Deputy Bailiff of the Royal Court:

It was recorded that the trustees had not surrendered their discretion to the court, but sought the court's approval: this meant the court had to be satisfied whether the decision was formed in good faith, whether it was a reasonable decision and whether it was vitiated by a conflict of interest. As W was the ultimate recipient and beneficiary, the court also had to consider whether such distributions would constitute a fraud on a power.

As to the lump sum, the court considered that it was for H's benefit that the trust made a distribution to him to meet his obligation, as W was effectively his creditor and could take action to enforce it if not paid. The same reasoning was applied to the cancellation of loan accounts to enable the company shareholding to be transferred.

Although the transfer of the family home and its contents was ultimately to W, the trust (supported by H and the minor beneficiaries) submitted this would be for the benefit of H and his daughters, as it was in H's interests for it to be done and for litigation to be brought to an end. It was also noted that it was proper for the trustees to consider that an appointment made to comply with a moral obligation on a beneficiary, with their consent, is for their benefit.

The course of action was therefore approved.

9.40 In *Re the X Trust* the financial remedy proceedings were taking place in the same jurisdiction (Jersey) as the location of the trust, the trustees and the assets. Enforcement may be more difficult where the supervisory court is in a different jurisdiction from the court that has made the original financial remedy order. It is also important to note that the trustees were supported by the husband and the minor and unborn beneficiaries in their application.

9.41 It is prudent to obtain specialist trust advice as to how the trust supervisory court is likely to view future requests by the spouse beneficiary in order to assess how likely it is that any such request will be granted. If the supervisory court is unlikely to approve the proposed course of action then it is most unlikely that the trustees will exercise their discretion in following that course because to do so would expose them to the risk of civil claims.

9.42 A relevant consideration will be the extent to which the order which needs to be enforced departs from the terms of the trust deed itself. In general, if the order made by the English court requires the trustees to use a power that they already have by virtue of the existing terms of the trust, and to exercise it in a way which is broadly harmonious with the nature of the trust[29], it is more likely that the supervisory court will sanction the action.

29 An example might be to pay the children's school fees out of a discretionary trust where payment of school fees is specifically permitted by the terms of the trust.

F FIREWALLS

9.43 A number of jurisdictions in which trusts are commonly located (Jersey, for example) have a strong private wealth economy that relies upon wealthy individuals and companies being reassured that their wealth will be adequately protected by the offshore structure. If there is a perception that the trusts of that jurisdiction are at risk of being varied or set aside by the court of another jurisdiction then, understandably, the use of trust structures in that jurisdiction will be far less attractive to those individuals and this will have a detrimental impact on the financial services sector of that country.

9.44 Many offshore jurisdictions have enacted defensive legislation (often termed 'firewall' legislation) to protect their local trusts. Such legislation may either:

- modify the choice-of-law rules which would otherwise apply, so that any challenges to the validity or the effect of the trusts are to be governed solely by the local law[30]; or
- prohibit challenges to the trust based on rights arising under a foreign law[31].

9.45 A key objective of firewall legislation is to ensure that any challenges to the validity of a trust are governed in the local law of the trust and in accordance with local law.

9.46 In addition, firewalls often expressly prevent the enforcement of foreign judgments concerning trusts if the order of the foreign court is considered to be inconsistent with the domestic law of the local court.

9.47 At the time of writing, jurisdictions with firewall legislation now include:

- The Bahamas;
- Bermuda;
- The British Virgin Islands;
- The Cayman Islands;
- Dubai;
- Guernsey;
- Hong Kong;
- The Isle of Man;
- Jersey; and

30 The Trusts (Guernsey) Law 2007, s 14 makes clear that any questions arising in relation to a Guernsey trust including its validity, administration and distribution of property '*are to be determined according to the law of Guernsey without reference to the law of any other jurisdiction*'.

31 Section 91 of the Trusts Law (2011 revision) of the Cayman Islands provides, *inter alia*, that trusts governed by Cayman law are not void, voidable or liable to be set aside or defective by reason that the trust avoids or defeats rights, claims or interests conferred by foreign law.

- Singapore.

9.48 England and Wales does not have firewall legislation; nor does Australia, New Zealand or Canada.

9.49 Firewalls are highly relevant to whether orders of the English court in relation to a trust are capable of enforcement in the offshore jurisdiction.

9.50 Whilst a detailed analysis of the nature and effect of specific firewall legislation in each offshore jurisdiction is beyond the scope of this work (and would require case-specific advice from the local jurisdiction as discussed above), there are a number of common features of firewall legislation in general about which practitioners should be aware. These broadly fall into three categories, which are summarised in the following diagram:

Requirement for ocal law

- The firewall legislation often only applies if the applicable law of the trust is expressed to be local law - eg a trust governed by Cayman Islands law can rely on Cayman Islands firewall legislation.
- Firewalls typically contain both positive and negative provisions in favour of the local law of the trust - e.g. questions of validity are to be determined solely in accordance with local law - or expressly require foreign law to be disregarded if it would prejudice the trust.

Time limits and location of trustees

- Some firewall legislation requires trusts to be created on or after a certain date.
- Some countries (e.g. Hong Kong) additionally require trustees to be based in the jurisdiction at the relevant date in order for firewall legislation to be available to them.

Prohibitions on reognition and enforcement of foreign law

- Firewalls often prevent recognition or enforcement of a foreign judgment which is considered to be inconsistent with the firewall provisions.
- It is common to see express prohibition on the setting aside of any trust by a foreign court order.
- In some jurisdictions, legislation prohibits any obligation being imposed on the trustees, settlor and sometimes even the beneficiaries themselves by foreign law concepts. This might include where the foreign law does not recognise the trust as valid, for example.

9.51 When dealing with a jurisdiction that has firewall legislation designed to defend trusts against orders made in financial remedy proceedings practitioners will need to gain a clear understanding as to the operation of the legislation: what it is designed to do or prevent and how that relates to the trust in question and the financial order that has been or will be made. Advice should be sought as to the following issues:

- what the firewall is aiming to protect against;
- what is it *not* concerned with; and
- how it will affect the order which requires enforcement.

G ENFORCEABILITY WHERE THERE ARE ALLEGATIONS OF SHAM

9.52 Cases of 'sham trust' in this context usually entail a finding that assets which purport to be held under the terms of a discretionary trust are in reality held on bare trust for benefit of the settlor absolutely. Typically, the genuine owner will be one of the parties to the proceedings who has claimed that assets are held in trust in order to hide their true ownership.

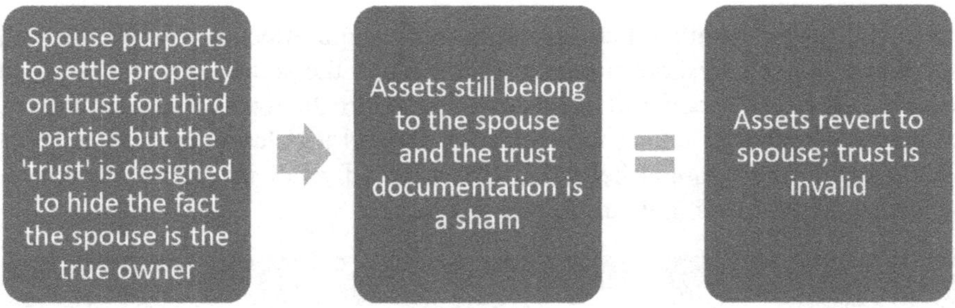

9.53 In such a case, the trust documentation is in fact a 'sham' as it does not reflect the true beneficial ownership of the assets, such that the trust documents '...are not intended to create the legal rights and obligations which they give the appearance of creating'[32]. Accordingly, if the trust is an invalid/sham trust, then the trust's assets revert to the ownership of the settlor. The court can then make orders directly against that spouse to transfer the assets which they own. In order to enforce the order, however, the trust assets may need to be transferred by the trustees to the spouse.

9.54 Where the trustees are located in an overseas jurisdiction, they are highly likely to seek guidance from their supervisory court as to whether to comply with an order to transfer the assets out of the 'trust' found to be a sham. It may be impossible to obtain compliance if the trust is governed by foreign law containing firewall provisions that require questions of the validity of the trust to be determined by that foreign law and not by English law. Moreover, in a case where sham is alleged, it is likely that the foreign trustees will have refused to submit to the jurisdiction of the English court or play any part in the English proceedings (often with the sanction of the supervisory court).

9.55 As a finding of sham necessarily attacks the very heart of the trust, in *Re Fountain Trust*[33] the Jersey Royal Court held that an assumption of jurisdiction by a judge of the English High Court to declare a Jersey trust to be a sham would generally be considered an exorbitant exercise of jurisdiction by the English court, a principle approved by the Court of Appeal in *Charman v Charman (No 4)*[34], although the Court of Appeal there were *not* in fact declaring that the relevant trust was a sham nor was she seeking variation of it.

32 *Snook v London and West Riding Investments Ltd* [1967] 2 QB 786 per Diplock LJ.
33 [2005] JLR 359.
34 [2007] EWCA Civ 503, [2007] 2 FCR 217, [2007] 1 FLR 1246 para 58.

Case summary: *Re the Fountain Trust*[35]

Facts:

This involved an application to enforce the order of the English Court in *Minwalla v Minwalla*[36] in which Singer J had held that a Jersey trust was a sham set up by H to try to shelter his assets offshore. He found that H was in fact the beneficial owner of the trust assets and they were held on bare trust. On that basis, it was ordered that the trust should be set aside (as a post-nuptial settlement) and W was awarded £4,185,000. H was found to have been uncooperative and obstructive, and to have failed to make full and frank disclosure.

The trustees had participated, to a limited extent, in the English proceedings. They were aware of the relief sought by W and submitted to the jurisdiction, having asserted they would abide by any order or declaration made.

The trustees applied to the Jersey court for directions as to how they should respond to the judgment. W submitted the judgment should be recognised and enforced as a matter of comity; H by contrast submitted it would be contrary to public policy to enforce it or, alternatively, the order was unenforceable because it was declaratory.

Held by the Royal Court of Jersey:

The English court had erred by applying English law in finding that the trust was a sham; the law of what constitutes a 'sham' trust is different in Jersey to that in England. Further the assumption by a foreign court of the power to vary a Jersey trust or declare it to be a sham would generally be considered an 'exorbitant exercise of jurisdiction' and a Jersey court would be reluctant to enforce such a judgment.

However, on the facts of this case, the court did decide to enforce the order. Parties to matrimonial proceedings should not be permitted to inhibit a proper assessment of their financial positions, so it would not be contrary to public policy to enforce a judgment which sought to do justice in circumstances where H had been obstructive and failed to disclose his assets.

Moreover, the trustees had submitted to the jurisdiction knowing the nature of the relief sought by W and had been participants in the proceedings, such that there was no prejudice to them in enforcing the findings. H had had every opportunity to participate in the English proceedings and raise defences.

35 [2005] JLR 359.
36 [2004] EWHC 2823 (Fam), [2005] 1 FLR 771.

9.56 In light of the above and to avoid the risk of problems enforcing a finding of the English court, a course open to litigants is to initiate preliminary trust litigation in the offshore jurisdiction in order that findings of sham can be made by the foreign court in accordance with the applicable foreign law as this may well make it far easier to enforce the finding against the trustees in the foreign court.

H CHECKLIST TO AID ENFORCEMENT AGAINST TRUSTS

9.57 By way of summary, when dealing with orders involving overseas trust assets:

Specialist advice on enforcement

- Obtain the earliest possible specialist local advice including considering whether applications should be made to the foreign trust court to gain assistance and/or guidance on what the trust court may or may not be able to order.

Specialist advice on statutes

- Obtain specialist local advice on the relevant statute sof the trust jurisdiction, including any firewall legislation. The local statutes may contain provisions that make it desirable to litigate some aspects of the case in that foreign court, for example the issue of whether the trust is a valid one. Litigation in the trust jurisdiction also has the advantage that the trustees will be resident and present and cannot avoid enforcement by refusing to submit to the jurisdiction.

Provision of information

- Consider the extent to which offshore trustees and foreign trust courts may be prepared to help the English court with the provision of information at an early stage, including obtaining advice about how such requests would be looked on by a trust supervisory court.

Undertakings against dissipation

- Consider seeking undertakings regarding the dissipation of assets. If undertakings are not forthcoming, a freezing injunction may be required and thought will need to be given to whether the injunction will be given effect by the foreign court if the assets are located outside of the jurisdiction.

Joinder

- Consider whether the trustees and any adult beneficiaries need to be joined to the proceedings.

Leave claims open

- As a precaution, if possible, leave claims open until compliance with the order by a debtor spouse (e.g. the ability to make a future application to vary a nuptial settlement) as an aid to enforcement.

CHAPTER 10

Practical issues in international enforcement

Content at a glance:

A INTRODUCTION

10.01 The enforcement of financial remedy orders between different jurisdictions is a highly complex area involving myriad conventions, regulations, statutes and statutory instruments. Family practitioners must additionally grapple with the significant legal and procedural changes brought about as a consequence of Brexit and the end of the transitional arrangements at 11pm on 31 December 2020 (which is referred to as 'Implementation Period Completion Day' – shortened to 'IP' day).

10.02 The following is intended to provide an overview to point practitioners in the right direction, with a focus on practical tips and suggestions: specialist legal advice in respect of the law of the particular jurisdiction in which enforcement action is envisaged is likely to be required.

For a more detailed look at international enforcement of maintenance, see **Chapter 11**.

Identifying the issues

10.03 As a starting point when dealing with issues of reciprocal enforcement between jurisdictions, the following checklist of information to gather and issues to consider is suggested:

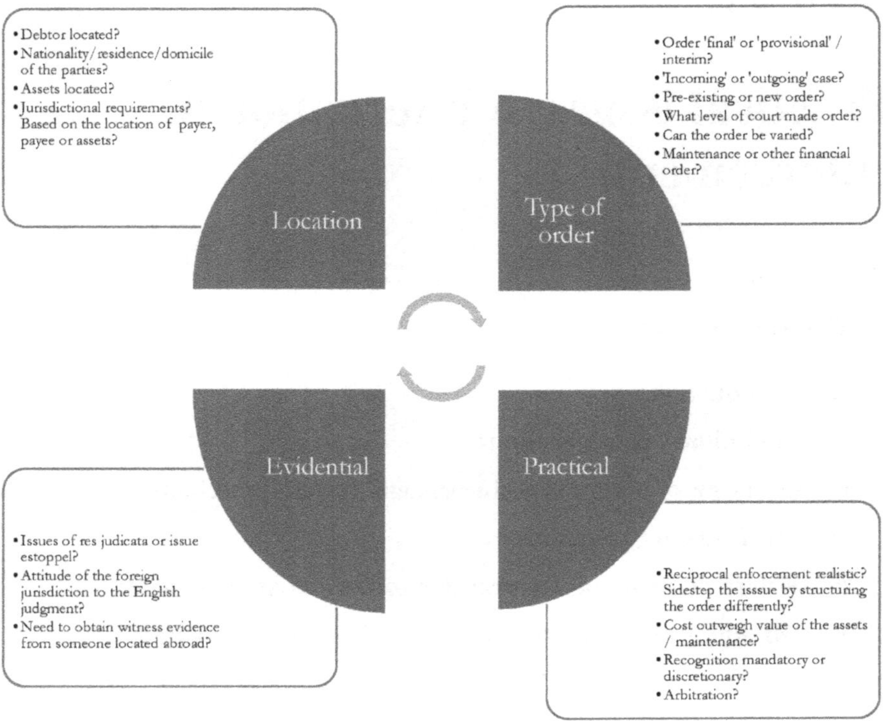

B PRELIMINARY CONSIDERATIONS

10.04 Because of the significant complexities and costs involved (especially where more than one route is available) careful consideration should be given to international enforcement issues and the practical realities well before the final order is made.

10.05 The following is a checklist of practical issues which practitioners may wish to consider:

- Can the order be structured to avoid international enforcement by ensuring that the creditor receives their award through onshore assets?
- Is it better to limit the claim to onshore assets or those which are more susceptible to enforcement?
- Is a freezing injunction necessary to preserve onshore assets?
- Will exchange controls impede or delay enforcement?
- Will delay reduce the value of an asset through inflation?
- Will the costs of enforcement be disproportionate to the assets?
- Is it necessary or desirable to include specific language in an order to facilitate enforcement (eg characterising a lump sum as 'needs-based' or 'maintenance')?

10.06 Where it is advantageous for a client to receive their award or maintenance from onshore assets practitioners should consider whether steps need to be taken to secure assets, including:

- Seeking a freezing injunction to prevent assets being moved offshore;
- Obtaining security in respect of the UK assets: eg agreeing that a sum of money is held in an account that cannot be accessed unilaterally by the parties.

10.07 In the case of unpaid child maintenance pursuant to a CMS calculation, Child Support Act 1991 ('CSA 1991'), s 39B enables the Secretary of State for Work and Pensions to apply to disqualify a debtor from holding or obtaining a UK travel authorisation (eg a UK passport) if:

- they have already taken specified enforcement action[1] against the debtor,
- all or part of the sum remains unpaid, and
- the SoS is of the opinion there has been a 'wilful refusal or culpable neglect' to pay.

This may be a useful tool to prevent the payer from leaving the jurisdiction whilst child maintenance remains unpaid, although only the Secretary of State can apply for the order. The remedy will be of little use if the payer has a non-UK passport.

10.08 Practitioners should check whether any other creditors (eg HMRC, a bank or a former spouse) have already taken enforcement action against the spouse in the applicable foreign jurisdiction and whether that action was successful.

What sort of order are you dealing with?

10.09 The availability of enforcement and the route or routes to be taken often depends on the subject matter of the order you are seeking to enforce. The following should be considered in relation to different categories of order:

- Transfer of real property in a foreign country:
  - Advice will be needed about the applicable property law of the foreign jurisdiction and its effect.
  - Unless the transfer of property is made for the purposes of maintenance (in the broader sense of a needs-based award), such an order is not likely to be covered by conventions and treaties. The ability to enforce such an order will vary widely dependent upon local property laws.
- Maintenance order:
  - It may be easy to identify that an order can be classified for the purposes of international enforcement as 'a maintenance order' (eg a child maintenance assessment); other orders, such as a lump sum, may be more difficult to classify as maintenance and practitioners will need to focus on the purpose for which the order was made.
  - Under CJEU case law, orders which are intended to meet the 'needs' of the recipient are classified as 'maintenance orders' (see *Van den Boogaard v Lauman*[2]), as does the EU Maintenance Regulation.

1 Pursuant to CSA 1991, ss 35 or 38 or by way of a third party debt order or charging order under CSA 1991, s 36.

2 27 February 1997, Case C220/95 [1997] QB 759, [1997] 3 WLR 284, [1997] 2 FLR 399, [1997] 3 FCR 493.

- Pension sharing order:
  - It will be sensible to make early contact with the pension provider for advice about their requirements of a UK pension sharing order.
- Trust or company
  - If enforcement is required directly against a trust or company, local advice in respect of both local trust or company legislation will be needed as well as regards the involvement of the trustees or company in any English proceedings.
  - This is covered in more detail in **Chapter 9.**

10.10 The potential costs and difficulties of international enforcement mean that practitioners should seek advice from a local lawyer in the offshore jurisdiction at the outset in order to understand what would be involved if international enforcement measures have to be taken, whether effective enforcement options are even available to a party, as well as a realistic estimate of the likely costs and time involved in the process. It should not be assumed that the foreign jurisdiction will have the same enforcement mechanisms as England and Wales.

10.11 An inability to enforce an order overseas may lead the court to refuse to make an order against foreign property in the first place[3].

Particular problems with enforcing undertakings in international cases

10.12 Undertakings, whilst very familiar to English practitioners (and commonly used to secure promises by a spouse to do or not do something, including the payment of money), are often an alien concept to foreign courts and foreign lawyers.

10.13 The English court has the power to deal with a breach of undertaking (with sanctions including a fine, seizure of assets or, in serious cases, imprisonment) both at common law and under the Contempt of Court Act 1981. The relevant procedure rules are contained in the Civil Procedure Rules 1998 ('CPR 1998'), Part 81 and the Family Procedure Rules 2010 ('FPR 2010'), Part 37. This power is unlikely to be of any real use if the person in breach is outside the jurisdiction and there is no extradition procedure with the relevant overseas jurisdiction in order to physically bring the defaulting party back to England.

10.14 Where an extradition treaty *is* in force, breach of an undertaking is likely to be considered a civil contempt rather than a criminal matter, such that there may be no basis upon which an extradition order can be made[4].

3 *Hamlin v Hamlin* [1986] Fam. 11, [1985] 3 WLR 629, [1986] 1 FLR 61.
4 *R v O'Brien* [2014] UKSC 23. [2014] AC 1246, [2014] 2 WLR 902.

10.15 An undertaking is unlikely to be enforceable by committal in a foreign court as:

(i) breach of an undertaking involves a party breaking its promise to an *English* court (it does not involve contempt of an overseas court); and

(ii) the concept of an undertaking may be completely unfamiliar to the foreign court.

There may, however, be contractual remedies available arising from a person's failure to comply with their agreement to take the steps which they have undertaken to perform.

C OVERVIEW OF POTENTIAL RECIPROCAL ENFORCEMENT MECHANISMS

10.16 International enforcement is highly procedural and technical, with very little in the way of case law guidance. Practitioners will need to identify the relevant statutory provisions for each country. Many of the provisions overlap and there can be a choice of route to take for which the advantages and disadvantages have to be considered. When dealing with the enforcement of maintenance the REMO Unit[5] is a helpful resource which may be able to highlight issues and avenues to consider (although the Unit cannot give legal advice). The REMO Unit website has a list of the countries that have reciprocal maintenance enforcement arrangements with the UK.

Enforcement of maintenance in international cases is dealt with in **Chapter 11**.

10.17 Where registration of an outgoing order depends on the order being made by a 'superior' court, practitioners will need to ensure the English order has been made in the High Court as an order of the Family Court order will be insufficient: see *Goyal v Goyal*[6], at para [19] for an example of the difficulties that can be encountered.

10.18 The following table is a summary of the statutory routes to enforcement potentially available at the time of writing. In respect of the statutes or statutory instruments dealing with the enforcement of maintenance, see **Chapter 11** for a more detailed discussion of these routes. In the table, 'outgoing' order means an order made by the courts of England and Wales that a party seeks to enforce abroad; 'incoming' order means an order made in a foreign jurisdiction that a party seeks to enforce in England.

5 REMO Unit, Official Solicitor and Public Trustee, Victory House, Post Point 0.53, 102 Petty France, London SW1H 9AJ, and https://www.gov.uk/child-maintenance-if-one-parent-lives-abroad. The REMO Unit is the Central Authority for England and Wales for international maintenance claims.

6 [2016] EWCA Civ 792, [2017] 1 FCR 174, [2017] 2 FLR 223.

Jurisdiction of original order	Statute or SI	Nature of order this applies to	Points to note
Within UK	Maintenance Orders Act 1950	Periodical payments; Lump sums.	Once registered, the order is enforced under the law of the country of enforcement (eg English order enforced in Scotland under Scottish law). Payer must reside in country of registration + it must be 'convenient' that the order is enforceable there – MOA 1950 s 17(2) Considered at paras **11.07–11.13**.
Within UK	Civil Jurisdiction and Judgments Act 1982, Schs 6 and 7	Orders **other than** periodical payments or lump sum	Governed by CPR 1998, rr 74.14–74.18 and PD 74A10. Time for appealing order must have expired or appeals disposed of and no stays of enforcement in force. 6 months to register the certificate. Certificate acts as a local order and can be enforced locally. Enforcement can be stayed or set aside.
Common-wealth Countries that are not included within the FJ(RE)A 1933 (see below)	Administration of Justice Act 1920	Periodical payments; Lump sums	Governed by CPR 1998, Parts 23 and 74 and PD 74A and 74B Order does not need to be 'final' –variable maintenance orders and lump sum orders *are* included. For **outgoing** High Court judgments the application for certification is made under CPR 1998, Part 23 (country for enforcement). **Incoming** superior court orders are registered by application to a Master of the QBD under CPR 1998, Part 23 Considered at paras **11.65–11.68**.
Contracting states inc Australia, Canada (apart from Quebec), Isle of Man, India (certain territories only), Pakistan, Israel, Jersey, Guernsey, Suriname and Tonga	Foreign Judgments (Reciprocal Enforcement) Act 1933	Lump sums only	Governed by CPR 1998, Parts 23 and 74 and PD74A Once registered, a prohibition on other routes of enforcement exists and the order becomes enforceable as if it had been made in the country of registration. Registration of incoming orders is in the High Court and only outgoing High Court orders can be enforced overseas Considered at paras **11.69–11.75**.

Certain Common-wealth Countries and the USA	Maintenance Orders (Reciprocal Enforce-ment) Act 1972, Part I	Periodical payments and lump sums for maintenance	Debtor has to be resident in the country of enforcement or have assets located there (the latter point only if *not* a 1973 Hague Convention country) Registration administrative and all levels of court are included. Considered at paras **11.14–11.42**.
Reciprocating countries[7]	Maintenance Orders (Reciprocal Enforce-ment) Act 1972, Part II	Periodical payments + lump sum for maintenance of any person whom the debtor liable to maintain under law of 'original court'	Not a means of enforcement of an existing order, but enable the finalisation of a maintenance order in one country where the debtor is residing where the process has begun in another. Once made, maintenance order can be enforced by registration in the country where order was made. Where an order already exists and a claim is transmitted to a reciprocating country, the courts of that country may not exceed the scope of the original order – Maintenance Orders (Reciprocal Enforcement) Act 1972, s 28A(4)–(5). See *Bhura v Bhura*[8]. Considered at paras **11.43–11.50**.
Common-wealth Countries not covered by the MO(RE) Act 1972	Maintenance Orders (Facilities for Enforcement) Act 1920	Periodical payments only	Only if one party lives in the UK and the other in a participating Commonwealth country or territory. Considered at paras **11.52–11.64**.
Australia, Denmark, Switzerland[9]	Reciprocal Enforcement of Maintenance Orders (Hague Convention Countries) Order 1993	Periodical payments only	Registration abroad of an existing maintenance order. Debtor must reside in the reciprocal country (not sufficient to have assets there). Only applies to periodical payment orders for the maintenance of a person whom the debtor is liable to maintain *under the law of the original country*.

7 Algeria, Australia, Austria, Barbados, Belgium, Bosnia and Herzegovina, Brazil, Burkina Faso, Cape Verde, Central African Republic, Chile, Czech Republic, Croatia, Cyprus, Ecuador, Finland, France (including overseas departments), Germany, Greece, Guatemala, Haiti, Holy See, Hungary, Ireland, Israel, Italy, Luxembourg, Mexico, Monaco, Morocco, Netherlands, New Zealand, Niger, Norway, North Macedonia, Pakistan, Philippines, Portugal, Romania, Slovakia, Slovenia, Spain, Sri Lanka, Suriname, Sweden, Switzerland, Tunisia, Turkey, Uruguay

8 [2012] EWHC 3633 (Fam), [2013] 3 FCR 142, [2013] 2 FLR 44

9 Although the list, as amended, is contained in Schedule 1 of the Reciprocal Enforcement of Maintenance Orders (Hague Convention Countries) Order 1993, Norway and Turkey are contracting states to the 2007 Hague Convention so the Convention takes precedence and Denmark is now included following IP day.

USA (enforceable on a Federal basis)	Reciprocal Enforcement of Maintenance Orders (USA) Order 2007	Periodical payments and lump sums for maintenance.	Provision is now largely superseded by the USA becoming a signatory to the 2007 Hague Convention (on 1 January 2017) – see below.
Signatories to the 2007 Hague Convention UK became a member in its own right on 1 January 2021. EU member states (except Denmark) are members	Hague Convention on the International Recovery of Child Support and other forms of Family Maintenance 2007	Maintenance including lump sums for maintenance	The physical presence of child or applicant is not required in proceedings in the receiving state – Art 29. There are different categories of application available to a creditor and a debtor. Considered at paras **11.8711.105**.
Contracting states to New York Convention 1958 inc all EU Member States)	New York Convention 1958	Arbitral awards	An arbitral award is capable of enforcement under the New York Convention when it has become binding on the parties – see Arbitration Act 1996, s 101. In a family law context, a subsequent court order in the terms of the arbitral award must have been obtained.

D THE LUGANO CONVENTION

The UK ceasing to be a party to the Lugano Convention

10.19 The Civil Jurisdiction and Judgments Act 1982 ('CJJA 1982'), as amended, and the Civil Jurisdiction and Judgments Act 1991, incorporate the Lugano Conventions into domestic law. They apply to countries that are parties to the Lugano Convention on Jurisdiction and Judgments and Civil and Commercial Matters 1988, namely Switzerland, Norway and Iceland and the EU.

10.20 The 1988 Lugano Convention was replaced by a revised 2007 Lugano Convention. The UK was a party to the 2007 Lugano Convention by virtue of its EU membership, which ceased on 31 December 2020.

10.21 The Lugano Convention is not a designated 'family law' convention; its reach crosses a number of areas of legal practice. However it is significant in the sphere of international family law because it contains provisions clarifying which national courts have jurisdiction in cross-border family disputes about maintenance as well as important provisions on enforcement of maintenance orders.

10.22 On 8 April 2020, the UK applied to become a member of the 2007 Lugano Convention in its own right after it ceased to be a member of the EU. The European Commission has published a communication stating that the EU should not permit the UK's accession to the Convention. In June 2021, the EU informed the convention Depository that it was 'not in a position to give its consent to invite the United Kingdom to accede to the Lugano Convention'. At the time of writing, there has been no further progress on this issue and the UK therefore is not currently a member.

10.23 The Lugano Convention provides Contracting States with a common set of rules for jurisdiction. Without membership of Lugano, there does not exist a uniform basis for resolving issues of jurisdiction between the UK and the other Lugano states. Issues of jurisdiction fall to be determined under the domestic law of each state where a dispute may arise. The relevant law will vary, depending upon the state in question and the type of claim being made.

10.24 The Lugano Convention contains 'lis pendens' provisions designed to avoid competing claims proceeding in parallel jurisdictions. As was the case under the Maintenance Regulation pre-Brexit, the Lugano provisions state that proceedings initiated first in time prevail and later proceedings must be stayed pending resolution of the first proceedings.

10.25 If there are no rules in place governing which proceedings have priority, the English courts have to decide whether to allow the English proceedings to continue or whether to stay them so that the case in the other country may continue.

The statutory rules for stays are set out in the Domicile and Matrimonial Proceedings Act 1973, ('DMPA 1973'), s 5(6) and Sch 1 .The rules are primarily based on *where* the other proceedings are taking place:

In a related jurisdiction

- Scotland, Northern Ireland, Jersey, Guernsey and the Isle of Man (defined in paragraph 8 of Sch 1 DMPA 1973)
- Where there are concurrent proceedings in a related jurisdiction, and the parties have lived together since the marriage, and the placed where they lived together when proceedings begun or where they last lived together is that related jurisdiction, and either was habitually resident in that related jurisdiction throughout the year ending with the date of the petition or the date they last lived together, the court **must** stay the English proceedings.

In all other countries

- Governed by paragraph 9 of Sch 1 DMPA 1973
- The court **may** grant a stay if proceedings in respect of the marriage or capable of affecting its validity/subsistence are continuing outside England and Wales and the balance of fairness (including convenience) as between the parties is such that it is appropriate for the proceedings in that foreign jurisdiction to be disposed of before further steps are taken in English proceedings

The court also has jurisdiction to order a stay pursuant to the inherent jurisdiction. The House of Lords in *de Dampierre v de Dampierre*[10] made clear that the authorities dealing with stays under the inherent jurisdiction should be referred to when determining an application for a stay pursuant to DMPA 1973; the test is, accordingly, essentially the same.

There is a two-stage test to be applied:

1 The most natural forum for the dispute: the forum with which the case has the most real and substantial connections. The burden of proving this is on the party seeking the stay.

2 If another forum is more appropriate, then the court should consider whether the party opposing the stay can show that justice requires that the trial should take place in England. This is not a question of where the party would receive more money, but whether substantial justice will be done.

The court has a wide discretion and each case is to be decided on its own facts. Some relevant factors the court has considered include:

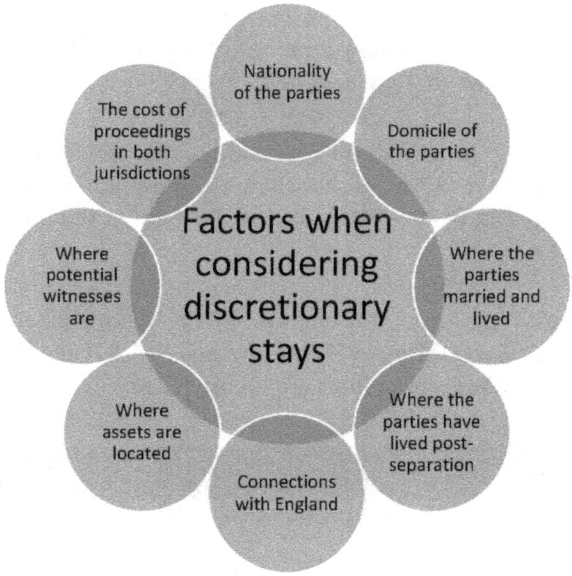

10.26 If the English Court refuses a stay and allows proceedings to continue in this jurisdiction, such a decision will not bind the overseas court. Thus, without a uniform set of rules governing jurisdiction, there may be risk of conflicting decisions English proceedings and foreign proceedings both carry on independently of each other. The English order may be very difficult to enforce in the foreign jurisdiction if the latter is engaged in substantive proceedings in respect of the same dispute or has made orders which conflict with the English orders.

10 [1988] AC 92, [1987] 2 WLR 1006, [1987] 2 FLR 300.

10.27 The Lugano Convention provides that where an order is made by the courts of one member country, other member countries must automatically recognise and enforce the order, subject only to limited exceptions. For so long as the UK is precluded from acceding to the Convention, litigants seeking the recognition and enforcement of UK maintenance orders will need to rely upon:

- other international conventions (eg the 2007 Hague Convention[11] to which the EU is a signatory); or
- the domestic law of the jurisdiction in which recognition and enforcement is sought.

Under the Hague Convention, there is an increased risk that recognition and enforcement will be refused as it is based on a discretionary exercise whereas the Lugano Convention is designed to provide for automatic recognition and enforcement. See **Chapter 11**, section G for more detail on the 2007 Hague Convention.

E WHERE THERE ARE NO RECIPROCAL ENFORCEMENT ARRANGEMENTS

10.28 A number of jurisdictions have no reciprocal arrangements for recognition and enforcement of maintenance or other financial orders. Non-exhaustively, these include China, Russia, Japan, Ukraine, Serbia and South American jurisdictions.

Incoming orders

10.29 Where there are no reciprocal enforcement arrangements a party will have to rely for enforcement on English common law principles. These provide that, in order to be enforced, the judgment of the foreign court must be:

(i) final and conclusive; and

(ii) for a definite sum of money (which can include costs).

10.30 Ongoing maintenance is not a 'final and conclusive' order and therefore is not enforceable at common law[12]. Arrears of maintenance in a defined sum might, however, be provided they cannot be remitted abroad[13].

11 Convention of 23 November 2007 on the International Recovery of Child Support and Other Forms of Family Maintenance; see contracting states on HCCH website.

12 *Cartwright v Cartwright* [2002] EWCA Civ 931, [2002] 2 FCR 760, [2002] 2 FLR 610.

13 *B v R* [2009] EWHC 2026 (Fam), [2010] 1 FLR 563 (albeit there was no expert evidence in that case about the ability of the French court to remit arrears, and the case was decided on the basis of a jurisdictional error)

10.31

Case summary: *B v R*[14]

Facts:

M and child went to live in France following the breakdown of the parents' relationship. M obtained a French order for child maintenance when the child was around five, which required F to pay 3,000 francs until the child finished her studies. M asserted that F had not paid anything under the order; F claimed he had paid some money.

When the child was 15, shortly after F was declared bankrupt, M issued an application under Children Act 1989, Sch 1 seeking a 'lump sum and periodical payments order'. F failed to take party in the English proceedings and did not attend the final hearing, despite an order requiring him to do so.

The judge ordered F to pay a lump sum of £42,219 – equivalent to the total arrears under the French order – and thereafter periodical payments of €767 per month until the child ceased full-time education. F failed to make any of the payments, though a charging order was made against his London property in respect of the lump sum and the mother's costs almost two years after the making of the English order, M applied to increase the periodical payments and to restore her secured periodical payments and property adjustment orders applications. F appealed the original order.

Held by Hogg J:

There was no power to make a lump sum or property adjustment order under Children Act 1989, Sch 1 where the mother and child lived outside of the jurisdiction of England and Wales.

Moreover, the common law had not provided the English court with jurisdiction to make a lump sum or property adjustment order by way of enforcement of the French order. The mother should have sought recognition and enforcement of the French order; the French court remained seised and the English court should have declined jurisdiction.

10.32 The English court will not entertain an action under the common law for the enforcement – either directly or indirectly – of a penal law of a foreign country (eg taxes payable under a foreign country's revenue system) and will not enforce a foreign judgment ordering the payment of taxes or penalties[15].

14 [2009] EWHC 2026 (Fam), [2010] 1 FLR 563.

15 *Government of India, Ministry of Finance (Revenue Division) v Taylor* [1955] AC 491 at §514; *Huntingdon v Attrill* [1893] AC 150.

10.33

Case summary: *United States of America v Inkley*[16]

Facts:

The defendant, a British subject, was arrested in the USA and charged with fraud offences. He was released on bail by a US district court, having entered into an 'appearance bond' to secure his appearance back before the court. He later obtained permission from the same court to attend his father's funeral in England, but failed to return to the US and so breached bail.

The US government obtained a US judgment for the amount of the appearance bond plus interest and then attempted to enforce it in England by issuing a writ in the High Court and obtaining a default judgment.

A High Court Master set aside the judgment and struck out the claim by the US. Though the bond required the defendant to pay a sum of money, its true nature was as an aid to the criminal law of the foreign state – it was an enforcement mechanism designed to ensure the attendance of those charged with criminal offences before criminal courts in that jurisdiction. As such, it was held that it could not be enforced in England.

Held by the Court of Appeal:

Purchas J set out the relevant principles as follows:

- The consideration of whether the claim sought to be enforced in the English courts involves the assertion of foreign sovereignty, whether it be penal, revenue or other public law, is to be determined according to English law;
- Regard will be had to the attitude adopted by the courts in the foreign jurisdiction, which will always receive serious attention and may on occasions be decisive;
- The category of the right of action – ie whether public or private – will depend on the party in whose favour it is created, on the purpose of the law or enactment in the foreign state on which it is based and on the general context of the case as a whole;
- The fact that the right, statutory or otherwise, is penal in nature will not deprive a person who asserts a personal claim depending on that right from having recourse to the courts of England and Wales; on the other hand, if the

16 [1989] QB 255, [1988] 3 WLR 304.

purpose of the action is the enforcement of a sanction, power or right at the instance of the state in its sovereign capacity, it will not be entertained;

- The fact that in the foreign jurisdiction recourse may be had in a civil forum to enforce the right will not necessarily affect the true nature of the right being enforced in this country.

10.34 Enforcement at common law is a civil claim and so CPR 1998 applies (although the application may be transferred to be heard by the Family Division).

Outgoing orders

10.35 Where there are no formal international agreements, the issue of whether or not an English order will be enforced in a foreign jurisdiction requires advice from a foreign lawyer. An example of the difficulties that can encountered where there are no bilateral treaties in place is *Akhmedova* litigation (see *AZ v BBZ (Financial Remedies: Sharing Principle: Special Contribution)*[17]) where after obtaining from the English court an award of £453 million the wife faced difficulties in enforcing the award in overseas jurisdictions.

F OBTAINING EVIDENCE FROM ABROAD AND LETTERS OF REQUEST

10.36 Witnesses residing outside the jurisdiction cannot be compelled to give evidence or attend a hearing in this country. The ability to obtain evidence for use in the English court from a person based overseas will depend upon:

- the jurisdiction in question;
- the nature and form of the evidence sought; and
- whether any relevant international agreements are in force.

10.37 The Hague Convention on the Taking of Evidence Abroad in Civil or Commercial Matters 1970 ('Hague Evidence Convention') is the main international instrument for obtaining evidence from other jurisdictions. It operates through Central Authorities[18].

17 [2016] EWHC 3234 (Fam), [2017] 2 FCR 415, [2018] 1 FLR 153. There have been extensive and lengthy proceedings since the original judgment: *Akhmedova v Akhmedov & Ors (Injunctive Relief)* [2019] EWHC 1705 (Fam), *Akhmedova v Akhmedov & Ors* [2019] EHWC 2561 (Fam), *Akhmedova v Akhmedov & Ors* [2019] EWHC 2732 (Fam), *Akhmedova v Akhmedov* [2019] EWHC 3140 (Fam), *Akhmedova v Akhmedov & Ors (Litigation Funding)* [2020] EWHC 1526 (Fam), *Akhmedova v Akhmedov & Ors* [2020] EWHC 2235 (Fam), *Akhmedova v Akhmedov & Ors* [2020] EWHC 2257 (Fam), *Akhmedova v Akmedov & Ors* [2020] EWHC 3005 (Fam), *Akhmedova v Akhmedov & Ors* [2020] EWHC 3006 (Fam) and Akhmedova v Akhmedov & Ors [2021] EWHC 545 (Fam).

18 In England and Wales, the Central Authority is The Senior Master, For the attention of the Foreign Process Section, Room E16, Royal Courts of Justice, Strand, London, WC2A 2LL; telephone +44 207 947 7772 (option 2); email: foreignprocess.rcj@justice.gov.uk.

10.38 The EU Regulation on Taking of Evidence in Civil Matters ceased to have effect at 11pm on 31 December 2020, save in relation to requests made prior to that date. That being said, the Withdrawal Agreement and its implementing regulations permit the English court to treat a request made under the Regulation as being a request under the Hague Evidence Convention. With the exception of Austria, Belgium and the Republic of Ireland, however, all EU member states are also signatories to the Hague Evidence Convention.

Letters of request

10.39 In civil proceedings, including family proceedings, a party may ask the High Court[19] for judicial 'assistance' by way of a 'letter of request'. These are addressed to a foreign court. They comprise a request to the foreign court to provide assistance in relation to the English proceedings by compelling a witness to attend before the foreign court for oral evidence and cross-examination, or to produce documents or respond to written questions.

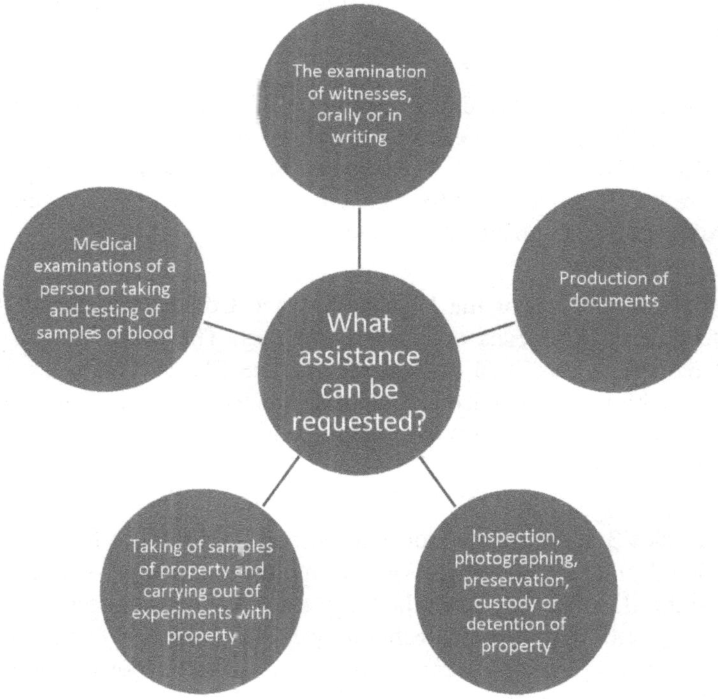

10.40 A letter of request can be helpful tool for understanding the nature and location of assets held outside the jurisdiction or for obtaining other information that may prove valuable for enforcement purposes. It is important to note, however, that a letter of request is not an 'order' requiring a witness to comply; it

19 Per FPR 2010, r 24.12 this is a power which applies to the High Court only.

is a request for assistance. The English court may be reluctant to issue the request unless the foreign court is likely to be receptive to it.

10.41 The English courts, in dealing with incoming letters of request have emphasised in this context the importance of affording respect to the laws and procedures of foreign jurisdictions and the mutual benefits of international judicial cooperation. In *Seyfang v Searle (GD) & Co*[20], Cook J held that:

> 'Any request by a foreign court should be treated with sympathy and respect and complied with so far as practicable…'.

10.42 In *Minwalla v Minwalla*[21], where Singer J used a letter of request as an aid to enforcement, he expressed himself in diplomatic terms, stating:

> 'I repose confidence in the courts of Jersey and of Guernsey that they will do their best, of course always in accordance with their domestic law and procedures, to ensure the speedy and efficient implementation of the orders that I will make to reflect the findings and the award contained in this judgment'.

10.43 The principles governing the granting of letters of request abroad are taken from the Evidence (Proceedings in Other Jurisdictions) Act 1975, which introduced the Hague Evidence Convention into English law. At the time of writing there are 63 signatories to the Convention[22]. It operates through designated Central Authorities in each signatory state.

10.44 Articles 1 to 14 of the Hague Evidence Convention provide for the taking of evidence by means of letters of request. The procedure for issuing letters of request is contained in FPR r 24.12 and PD 24A. Articles 15 to 22 provide for taking of evidence by commissioners and Consular officers of the state in which proceedings are in train, but in the territory of another contracting state.

10.45 Articles 3 and 4 of the Convention, require a request to be in writing and translated into the language of the requesting country. A number of Central Authorities have a specific template letter of request which they prefer to be used[23]. The use of technology to facilitate the operation of the taking of evidence, including email and video links, is consistent with the framework of the Convention and particularly useful now that remote working

20 [1973] 1 QB 148, at 151.

21 [2004] EWHC 2823 (Fam), [2005] 1 FLR 771, at para 99.

22 A list of signatories can be found on the HCCH website: https://www.hcch.net/en/instruments/conventions/status-table/?cid=82

23 The HCCH website contains a model for Letters of Request at https://www.hcch.net/en/publications-and-studies/details4.

is commonplace[24]. However, the Convention does not provide for the taking of evidence by video-conferencing[25], although a willing witness would likely co-operate with this even absent a formal request. However, an unwilling witness cannot be compelled to give evidence save by the mechanisms outlined in the convention.

10.46 The importance of following the specified procedures for taking of evidence from abroad was emphasised by the Court of Appeal in the below case; though not a case involving financial remedies or enforcement of the same, it provides a useful warning of the procedural rigours of these applications.

Case summary: *Re M (BIIa Article 19: Court First Seised)*[26]

Facts:

F had issued Children Act 1989 proceedings in England in the context of a jurisdiction dispute and alleged abduction involving England and Poland. M was a litigant in person based in Poland and had requested her evidence be heard by video link 'by way of assistance by the Polish court'. The English court's directions simply provided for M's evidence to be given by video link if she informed the English court and F's solicitors in advance, and the order required her to be personally responsible for setting up and testing the video-link. The final hearing ultimately proceeded in her absence and she sought to apply to set these aside. This was refused, and M appealed that refusal.

Held by the Court of Appeal:

The Court of Appeal allowed M's appeal (albeit not *solely* because of the failure to comply with the Taking of Evidence Regulation). It was held that the taking of evidence from another EU member state was governed by the Taking of Evidence Regulation, so that procedure should have been followed. The court noted that the Regulation was less commonly used in international family proceedings, but highlighted that judges should be aware that other States and their nationals may expect that it would be used and this should be taken account of when determining the appropriate arrangements.

24 This was permitted by the High Court in *Kimathi v FCO* [2015] EWHC 3684 (QB), although the Convention is not referenced there.

25 By contrast to the Taking of Evidence Regulation, which in Article 10.4 specifically provided for this.

26 [2018] EWCA Civ 1637, [2018] 3 FCR 405, [2019] 1 FLR 741. Whilst this case considered the EU Taking of Evidence Regulation, which is no longer applicable post Brexit, it is suggested that then principles expressed in this decision are relevant when dealing with the Hague Evidence Convention.

10.47 The taking of evidence by diplomatic officers or consular agents is dealt with in Articles 15–22 of the Evidence Convention. Where this is to be done without compulsion, Article 17 applies. It provides that a person appointed as a commissioner for the purpose may take evidence in the territory of a Contracting State for proceedings commenced in another Contracting State if:

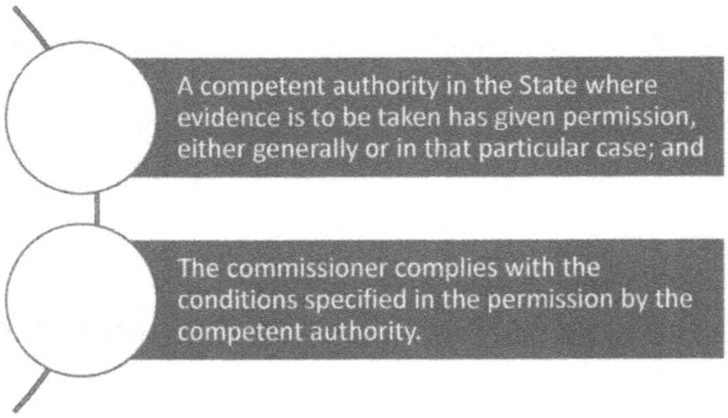

10.48 Article 18 applies where compulsion is required. That places the burden on the diplomatic officer, consular agent or commissioner to apply to the competent authority for assistance to obtain the evidence by compulsion. The declaring state can impose such conditions as it sees fits and the measures of compulsion are to be appropriate and as prescribed by the domestic law.

10.49 Other important features of the taking of evidence under these Articles are:

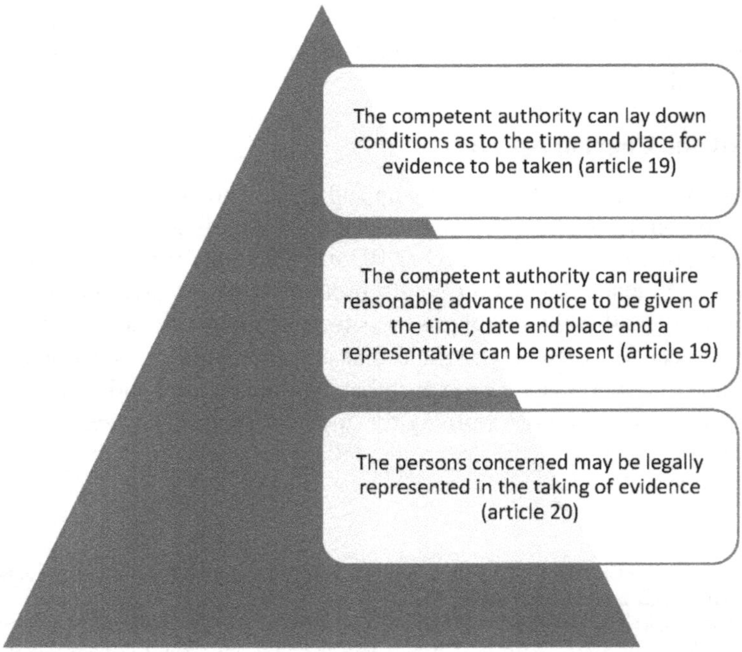

CHAPTER 11

Enforcement of overseas maintenance orders

Content at a glance:

A INTRODUCTION

11.01 The most difficult part of enforcing in this country a maintenance order made by a court overseas is identifying which one of a number of available jurisdictional routes is applicable to a particular maintenance order. In some instances, more than one route will be available. In others, there may be no prescribed enforcement route at all.

Brexit

11.02 The UK ceased to be a Member State of the European Union ('EU') as of 31 January 2020. From that date, there was a transition period which ended at 11pm on 31 December 2020. This has had great implications for recognition and enforcement of orders between other Member States of the EU and the UK. Most obvious is the revocation of the EU Maintenance Regulation[1], which provided for the direct enforcement in the UK of all EU maintenance orders (*inter alia*).

1 Council Regulation (EC) No.4/2009 on Jurisdiction, Applicable law, Recognition and Enforcement of Decisions and Co-Operation in Matters Relating to Maintenance Obligations.

The EU Maintenance Regulation continues to apply to enforcement of orders made in proceedings instituted prior to the end of the transition period. It is thus essential to note that the critical date is *not* when the maintenance order was made, or when the application to enforce was issued; under the Withdrawal Agreement[2] the critical date is *the date on which the substantive proceedings were instituted*, ie those proceedings which subsequently gave rise (for the purposes of this chapter) to a maintenance order that now needs to be enforced[3]. The 'Notice to Stakeholders' issued by the European Commission[4] said this[5]:

> '**Regulation (EC) No 4/2009 (Maintenance Regulation)**[25] shall apply to recognition and enforcement of decisions given in legal proceedings instituted before the end of the transition period and to court settlements approved or concluded and authentic instruments established[26] before the end of the transition period.'

11.03 As it is likely that practitioners will still encounter cases in which a party seeks to enforce a maintenance order made by a court of an EU Member State arising from proceedings instituted prior to 31 December 2020, this chapter contains a discussion on the EU Maintenance Regulation below[6]. However, as time passes, the relevance of those paragraphs will diminish. If the underlying proceedings were instituted *after* the end of the transition period, as explained below, the most likely route to enforce a maintenance order made by an EU court will be the 2007 Hague Convention[7].

11.04 Upon leaving the EU, the UK had to re-apply to join the Lugano Convention[8]. On 1 July 2021 the European Commission formally rejected the application by the UK to accede to the Convention[9]. Thus the Lugano Convention offers no route for the enforcement of orders of any form made in a court of a Member State of the EU.

Definition of maintenance

11.05 The definition of a maintenance order differs depending upon the enforcement route being used and, in some instances, the country which made the original order[10]. Thus, under each enforcement route below, a heading is devoted to the meaning of a maintenance order in that context.

2 the Agreement on the Withdrawal of the United Kingdom of Great Britain and Northern Ireland from the European Union and the European Atomic Energy Community, OJ L 29, 31.1.2020, p 7 ('Withdrawal Agreement').

3 at Article 67(2).

4 27 August 2020, Notice to Stakeholders on the Withdrawal of the UK and UU Rules in the Field of Civil Justice and Private International Law.

5 Section 3.1.

6 At **11.76ff**.

7 2007 Hague Convention on the International Recovery of Child Support and other Forms of Family Maintenance. See section G below.

8 Convention on Jurisdiction and the Recognition and Enforcement of Judgments in Civil and Commercial Matters concluded at Lugano on 30 October 2007.

9 Notification to the Parties of the [Lugano Convention] by the Swiss Federal Council dated 1 July 2021.

10 See the different definitions of maintenance order within the Maintenance Orders (Reciprocal Enforcement) Act 1972 below as regards to the USA, reciprocating countries and 1973 Hague Convention countries, discussed below at **11.21** and **11.22**.

Which route should I use?

11.06 The following graphic may assist with navigating the numerous enforcement routes available and which are discussed in turn below[11]:

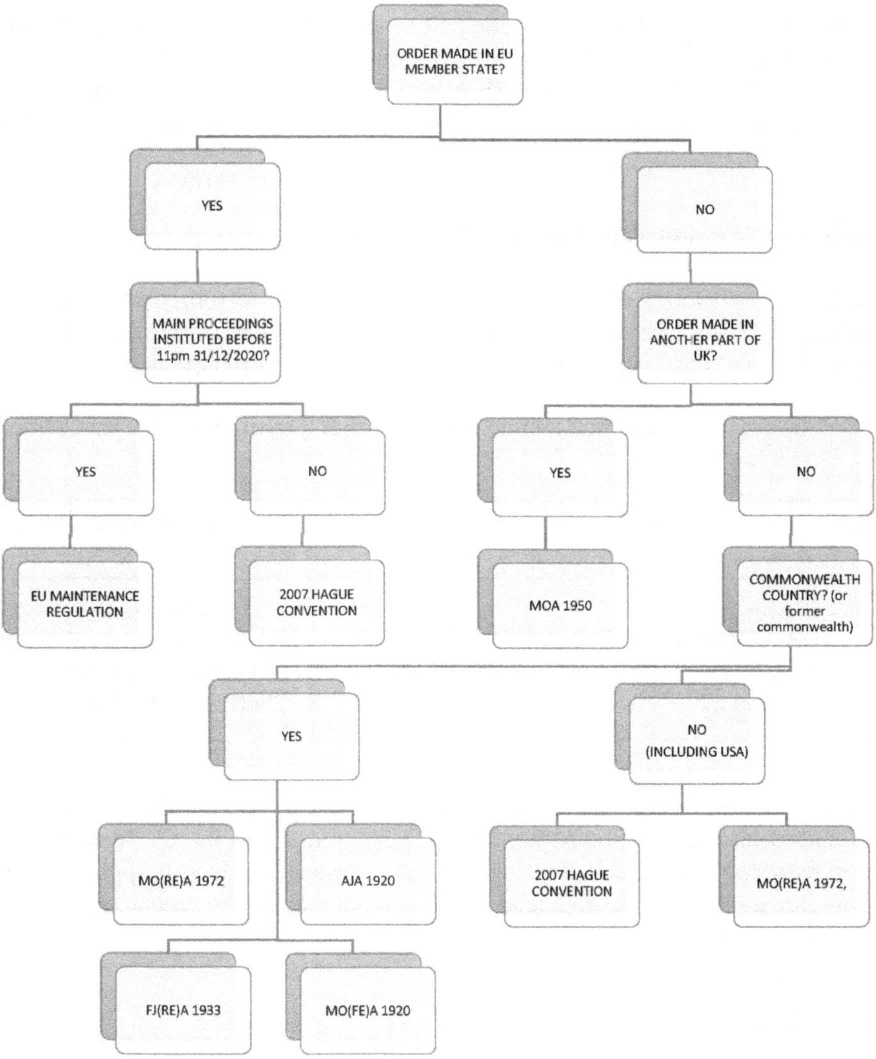

11 The abbreviations for the statutory instruments used in the graphic below mean as follows: 'EU Maintenance Regulation' means Council Regulation (EC) No 4/2009 on jurisdiction, applicable law, recognition and enforcement of decisions and cooperation in matters relating to maintenance obligations; '2007 Hague Convention' means the Convention of 23 November 2007 on the International recovery of Child Support and Other Forms of Family Maintenance; 'MOA 1950' means the Maintenance Orders Act 1950; 'MO(RE)A 1972' means the Maintenance Orders (Reciprocal Enforcement) Act 1972; 'AJA 1920' means the Administration of Justice Act 1920; 'FJ(RE)A 1933' means the Foreign Judgments (Reciprocal Enforcement Act 1933; 'MO(FE)A 1920' means the Maintenance Orders (Facilities for Enforcement) Act 1920.

B ENFORCEMENT WITHIN THE UK: MAINTENANCE ORDERS ACT 1950

11.07 Maintenance Orders Act 1950 ('MOA 1950'), Part II provides for the reciprocal enforcement of maintenance orders made within the UK. The central premise is that any order made in one part of the UK must be registered with the original court in accordance with the provisions of the Act[12]. It is then transmitted to the court of another part of the UK in which the paying party lives. It can then be enforced in in all respects as if it was an order that had been made by that other court[13].

Which orders can be registered and enforced?

11.08 MOA 1950, s 16(2)(a) contains a full list of the statutory provisions (in England and Wales, Scotland and Northern Ireland) which can be the subject of registration and enforcement under the Act, including (emphasis added):

> 'An order for alimony, maintenance or **other payments** made or deemed to be made.'

The section then goes on to list a full spectrum of financial orders, for example:

All orders under Matrimonial Causes Act 1973, ss 22, 23 and 27	All orders under Children Act 1989, sch 1	Orders under Matrimonial and Family Proceedings Act 1984, ss 14 and 17

Alongside the reference to 'other payments' in MOA 1950, s 16(2)(a) above, this makes it clear that the MOA 1950 is not, contrary to its title, confined to the registration and enforcement only of 'maintenance' orders; it applies to the whole range of orders for financial relief available under the numerous statutes in force in the UK[14].

Procedure

11.09 MOA 1950, s 17(1) provides that an application to register a maintenance order

> '…shall be made in the prescribed manner to the appropriate authority, that is to say –

12 MOA 1950, S 17(1)(C).

13 MOA 1950, S 18(1).

14 FPR 2010 r 32.2 also defines a 'maintenance order' as a 'maintenance order to which s 16 of the 1950 Act applies'.

(a) […]

(b) Where the maintenance order was made by a court of summary jurisdiction in Northern Ireland, a resident magistrate…

(c) In every other case, **the prescribed officer of the court which made the order.**'

11.10

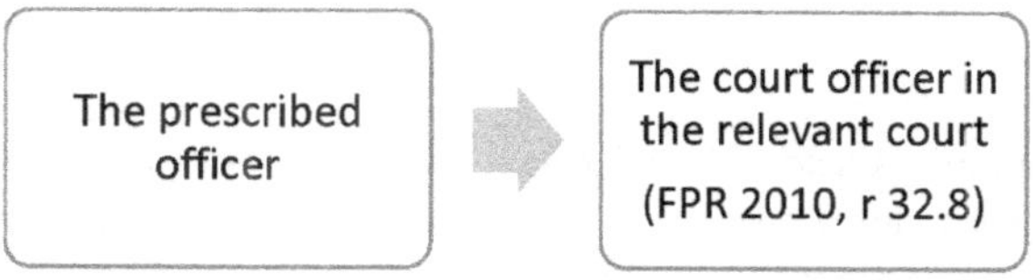

11.11 Family Procedure Rules 2010 ('FPR 2010'), Part 32, Chapter II contains the procedural rules relating to the registration and enforcement of orders under MOA 1950[15]. For an outgoing order (i.e an order made in England to be enforced elsewhere) the process under FPR 2010, r 32.3 is straightforward:

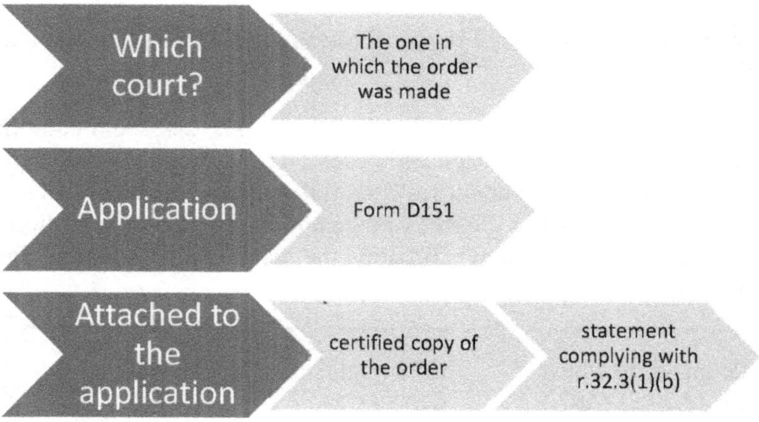

11.12 In respect of an incoming order (ie an order made and registered in another court of the UK and transmitted to England for enforcement), if the order is transmitted to the Family Court, then the court *can* vary or discharge orders on an application made by the payer[16].

11.13 If the order is transmitted to the High Court because the order was made by a 'superior court' in Scotland or Northern Ireland[17] then the order cannot be

15 Rules 32.3 to 32.5A, which refer to the registration of a 'High Court order', are applicable to Family Court orders (FPR 2010, r 32.6).

16 MOA 1950, s 22. The application would be made as if making an application for the variation of an order made in England.

17 On account of having been made in a 'superior court' in Scotland or Northern Ireland, defined in Maintenance Orders Act 1950, s 17(3)(a).

varied or discharged[18]. Once registered and transmitted, an application can be made by the recipient party under the Maintenance Act 1958 ('MA 1958'), s 2 for the order to be registered in the Family Court[19].

C RECIPROCAL ENFORCEMENT OF MAINTENANCE ORDERS: MAINTENANCE ORDERS (RECIPROCAL ENFORCEMENT) ACT 1972, PART I

Introduction

11.14 Maintenance Orders (Reciprocal Enforcement) Act 1972 ('MO(RE)A 1972'), Part I provides a mechanism for enforcement in the UK of maintenance orders made in a 'reciprocating country'[20].

MO(RE)A 1972, Part I also provides a route for a maintenance order made in the UK to be transmitted to a reciprocating country for enforcement[21].

FPR 2010, rr 34.12–34.28ZF contain the relevant procedural rules.

Reciprocating Countries, 'Hague Convention 1973' Countries and the USA

11.15 The use and interpretation of MO(RE)A 1972 can seem complicated. Although the text of the Act itself only prescribes a single regime applicable to orders of 'reciprocating countries', several subsequent Orders of Council have broadened the scope of the Act's range and modified its application (most notably to the USA – see below). Broadly, the reciprocating countries fall into three sub-categories[22]:

Countries to which the MO(RE)A 1972 applies unamended	1973 Hague Convention countries	United States of America

The effect of MO(RE)A 1972, Part I is slightly different in relation to these sub-categories. Each of them has different:

- jurisdictional bases (albeit the differences are subtle);
- definitions of maintenance;
- procedures.

18 Maintenance Orders Act 1950, s 21(1).
19 Maintenance Act 1958, s 2. See the procedure set out in FPR 2010, Part 34.
20 Sections 6 to 11.
21 MO(RE)A 1972, ss 2 to 5.
22 Reference to the 1973 Hague Convention means the Convention on the Recognition and Enforcement of Decisions Relating to Maintenance Obligations signed at the Hague on 2 October 1973.

11.16 The complexity has been somewhat lessened by the Hague Convention 2007[23], which came into force in the UK in August 2014 and in the USA in January 2017. The Hague Convention 2007 is discussed below (see **11.87** onwards)[24]. It is important to note that this development had two key consequences for the purposes of reciprocal enforcement of maintenance orders under MO(RE)A 1972[25]:

'1. For all contracting states to the 2007 Hague Convention, the 1973 Hague Convention was replaced[26]. That means that the **only** 1973 Hague Convention countries to which MO(RE)A 1972 now applies are[27]:

- Australia
- Denmark
- Switzerland

2. The 2007 Hague Convention now applies to reciprocal enforcement of maintenance orders between the USA and the UK. So the modified MO(RE)A 1972, Part I as applicable to the USA[28] is no longer needed.'

Reciprocating countries which are not 1973 Hague Convention countries

11.17 The following countries / territories are reciprocating countries under MO(RE) 1972, Part I but are **not** 1973 Hague Convention countries[29]:

Anguilla	Jersey
Barbados	Kenya
Bermuda	Nauru
Brunei	Papua New Guinea
Falkland Islands	South Africa
Fiji	St Helena
Ghana	Singapore

23 The Hague Convention on the International Recovery of Child Support and Other Forms of Family Maintenance dated 23 October 2007, which came into force in the UK on 1 August 2014 and was ratified by the UK (independently of the European Union) on 28 September 2020.

24 The Hague Convention 2007 is now the only route to enforce maintenance orders as between the UK and EU Member States following Brexit.

25 Article 48 of the 2007 Hague Convention replaced the 1973 Hague Convention, subject to some 'transitional provisions' in Article 56 of the 2007 Hague Convention which are beyond the scope of this book (it being unlikely in 2022 that a case would fall under those transitional provisions).

26 Article 48 of the 2007 Hague Convention.

27 List as amended is contained in Reciprocal Enforcement of Maintenance Orders (Hague Convention Countries) Order 1993/593, sch 1. Note that (1) Denmark has been added following Brexit completion day, but (2) Norway & Turkey, while still on the list, are contracting states to the 2007 Hague Convention.

28 Reciprocal Enforcement of Maintenance Orders (United States of America) Order 2007.

29 The following are no longer included this list, as they are contracting states under the 2007 Hague Convention: Canada and New Zealand.

Gibraltar	Turks and Caicos Islands
Hong Kong	Tanzania (except Zanzibar)
India	Zimbabwe
Isle of Man	

What are the 1973 Hague Convention Countries?

11.18 The only 1973 Hague Convention countries for the purposes of reciprocal enforcement under MO(RE)A 1972, Part I are now:

Australia
Denmark
Switzerland

Why does it matter?

11.19 Whether a reciprocating country is or is not a 1973 Hague Convention country matters for three main reasons:

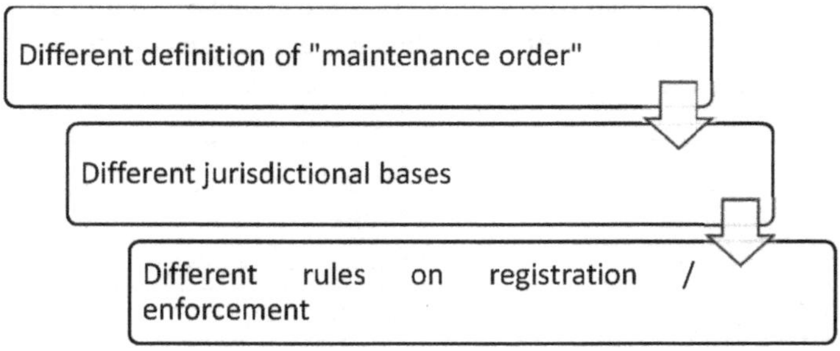

These differences will be addressed in turn below.

Definition of a 'maintenance order'

11.20 MO(RE)A 1972 allows for reciprocal enforcement of a 'maintenance order'. Unhelpfully, there are two different definitions, depending upon whether the order was made in a 1973 Hague Convention country or not[30].

11.21 For those reciprocating countries which are *not* 1973 Hague Convention countries listed in **11.17**, a maintenance order is **broadly** defined[31] in MO(RE) A 1972, s 21 as follows:

30 As per para 11.16 above and the discussion at 11.87 below, enforcement as between the USA and the UK is now covered by the 2007 Hague Convention.

31 The definition applies equally to MO(RE) 1972, Part II (s 39).

'(1)(a) An order[32]... which provides for the payment of a lump sum or the making of periodical payments towards the maintenance of any person, being a person whom the person liable to make payments under the order is, according to the law applied in the place where the order was made, liable to maintain...

(2) ...an order shall be taken to be a maintenance order so far (but only so far) as it relates to the payment of a lump sum or the making of periodical payments as mentioned in [(1)(a) above]...

(3) Any reference...to the payment of money for the maintenance of a child shall be construed as including a reference to the payment of money for the child's education.'

11.22 For *1973 Hague Convention countries* listed in **11.18**, a maintenance order is more **narrowly** defined[33]:

> 'maintenance order' means an order (however described), including any settlement made by or before a competent court in a Hague Convention country, of any of the following descriptions, and, in the case of an order which is not limited to the following descriptions, the part of the order which is so limited, that is to say–
>
> '(a) an order ... which provides for the periodical payment of sums of money towards the maintenance of any person, being a person whom the person liable to make payments under the order is, according to the law applied in the place where the order was made, liable to maintain...'

11.23 The practical difference in the definition is obvious: the broad definition permits enforcement of capital orders for maintenance, the narrow definition is confined to periodical payments.

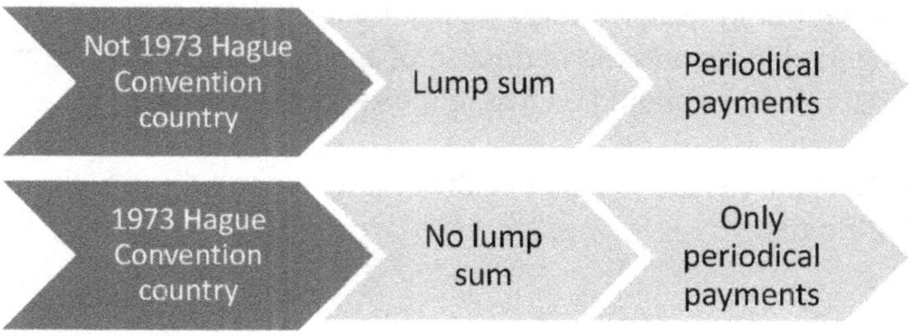

32 This includes an 'affiliation order or order consequent upon an affiliation order'. An affiliation order is defined in MO(RE) 1972, s 21(1) as '*an order (however described) adjudging, finding or declaring a person to be the father of a child, whether or not it also provides for the maintenance of the child*'.

33 Reciprocal Enforcement of Maintenance Orders (Hague Convention Countries) Order 1993/593, sch 2, para 21(2)(e).

Jurisdiction

11.24 MO(RE)A 1972, s 6(2)[34] provides that the jurisdiction to register a maintenance order from a reciprocal country under Part I may be founded on two bases:

- the payer is resident in the UK, or
- the payer has assets in the UK[35].

For 1973 Hague Convention countries (see above), the existence of assets in this country is not relevant; jurisdiction can only be based on the payer under the order residing in the UK[36].

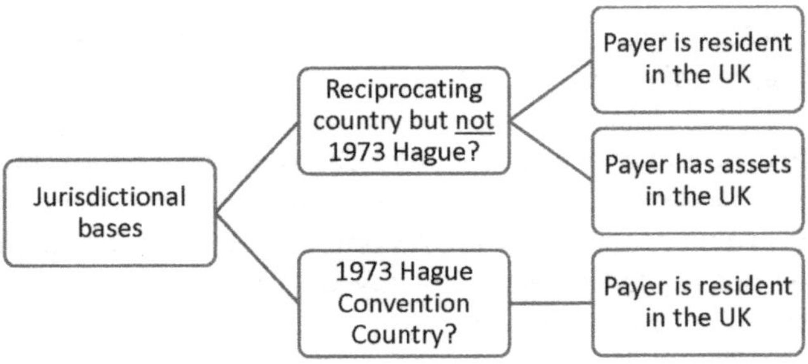

Registration and enforcement of maintenance orders made in reciprocating countries which are not 1973 Hague countries

11.25 The following paragraphs relate to registration and enforcement of orders made in reciprocating countries which are not 1973 Hague Convention countries (ie not Australia, Denmark or Switzerland). There are a number of modifications to MO(RE)A 1972, Part I in respect of 1973 Hague Convention countries, all of which are set out in the secondary legislation in painstaking detail[37]. The key differences (jurisdiction and the definition of maintenance order) have been set out above, but reference should be had to the secondary legislation.

11.26 MO(RE)A 1972, s 6 sets out the staged process by which an order is registered in England[38]:

34 See also MO(RE)A, s 6(4), which imposes on the officer of the court an obligation to 'take such steps as he thinks fit' to ascertain whether one of the jurisdictional bases is satisfied before registering the foreign maintenance order. If he is satisfied neither is made out, he 'shall return' the order to the Secretary of State.

35 If neither of these criteria are satisfied, the court officer will cancel the registration of the order and notify the secretary of state (MO(RE)A 1972, s10(2)).

36 Reciprocal Enforcement of Maintenance Orders (Hague Convention Countries) Order 1993/593, Sch 2, para 6(2) and (4).

37 Reciprocal Enforcement of Maintenance Orders (Hague Convention Countries) Order 1993/593, Sch 2.

38 Reciprocal Enforcement of Maintenance Orders (Hague Convention Countries) Order 1993/593.

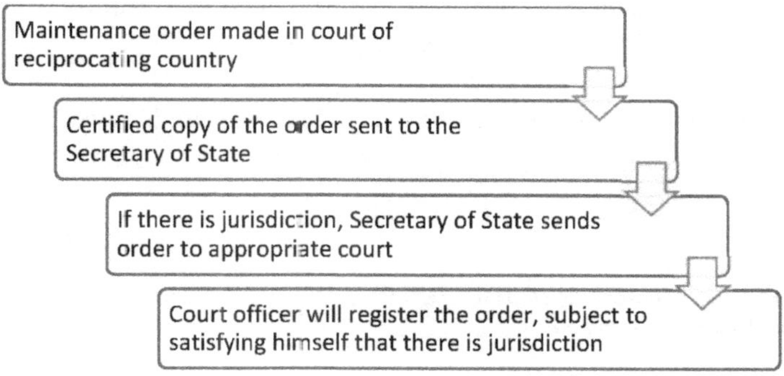

11.27 The 'appropriate court' in England and Wales under the process above is the Family Court[39]. Once the order has been registered by the Family Court for enforcement, MO(RE)A 1972, s 8 provides that:

> '(1) …a registered order **may be enforced in the United Kingdom as if it had been made by the registering court** and as if that court had had jurisdiction to make it; and proceedings for or with respect to the enforcement of any such order may be taken accordingly.'

AND

> '(7) …sums of money payable under a registered order shall be payable in accordance with the order as from the date on which they are required to be paid under the provisions of the order.'

In other words, once the order has been registered under the process above, for enforcement purposes it is treated as if it were an order made in the Family Court.

11.28 There is, however, a practical difference between a registered order and an order which was actually made in the Family Court. FPR 2010, r 34.23 provide that where an order has been registered in the Family Court for enforcement under MO(RE)A 1972:

r 34.23(1) …the court **must order** that the payment of sums due under the order be made

- to the registering court, and
- at such time/place as the court officer directs

r 34.23(2) where the registering court [makes the order for payment above], the court officer **must send** the payments

- by post, to either (i) the court which made the order, or (ii) such other person/authority as [is directed], or
- through Crown Agents for Overseas Governments and Territories [specific countries listed in PD34A para 8.1]

39 MO(RE)A 1972, s 21(1)(a).

In other words, payments will be ordered to be made to the Family Court (not to the payee) which will then forward on the payments.

11.29 In respect of an order for periodical payments under a registered order, FPR 2010, r 34.24 provides that the *court officer* (ie not the payee):

Must take reasonable steps to notify the payee of the means of enforcement available

If the periodical payments are in arrears:

(a) May, or

(b) Must (if arrears > 4 weeks)

Proceed in the officer's own name to recover the sums due, unless unreasonable to do so.

Provisional orders: confirmation, registration and enforcement

11.30 Several sections of MO(RE)A 1972 refer to what are termed 'provisional' maintenance orders. For the purposes of this chapter, this term is particularly relevant to the court's power to vary or revoke a maintenance order which is made in a reciprocating country that is not a 1973 Hague country (see table at **11.17**) and then registered in the Family Court (variation/revocation is discussed at **11.34–11.38**).

11.31 A provisional order is defined in MO(RE)A 1972, s 21(1) as follows (emphasis added):

> (a) an order made by a court in the United Kingdom which is provisional only **and has no effect unless and until confirmed…by a competent court in a reciprocating country**; or
>
> (b) an order made by a court in a reciprocating country which is provisional only and has no effect unless and until confirmed…by a court in the United Kingdom having power under this Part of this Act to confirm it.

Generally speaking (and subject to what is set out below) a provisional order is likely to be one of two types of order:

(1) An outgoing order: an order made in the UK which provisionally varies or revokes a maintenance order originally made in a reciprocating country which has been transmitted here for registration and enforcement.

(2) An incoming order: either

(a) a maintenance order made in a reciprocating country against a paying party who resides in the UK and did not take part in the proceedings in the reciprocating country, or

(b) a provisional order varying / revoking a maintenance order which was originally made by the UK court.

11.32 MO(RE)A 1972, s 21(1)(b) provides that an incoming provisional order of Type (2) above has *no effect* unless and until the Family Court has 'confirmed' the order. Similarly, an outgoing provisional order of Type (1) above has *no effect* unless and until it is 'confirmed' in the courts of the reciprocating country (s 21(1)(a)).

The approach of foreign courts to the confirmation of provisional orders is necessarily outside the scope of this book, but it is important to consider how the Family Court in this jurisdiction confirms a provisional order from another reciprocating country.

The answer lies in MO(RE)A 1972, s 7 *and* FPR 2010, r 34.16, which together provide for the following procedure for confirmation and, assuming confirmation is successful, registration of an overseas provisional order[40]:

(1) Provisional maintenance order made in the reciprocating country.

(2) A certified copy of the order is sent to the Secretary of State, with:

   (a) document summarising the evidence given to the originating court; and

   (b) a statement of the grounds on which the making of the order might have been opposed by the payer.

(3) If the payer resides in the UK, the Secretary of State will send the order and documents to the court officer of the appropriate court (Family Court).

(4) On receipt of the documents, the court must fix a date, time and place for a hearing or a directions appointment.

(5) The court must give the payer notice of the hearing and a copy of the documents received. The hearing must be within 21 days of sending the documents to the payer.

(6) At a substantive hearing the court shall:

   (a) if the payer establishes any grounds on which they might have opposed the making of the order, refuse to confirm it; or

   (b) in any other case, confirm the order without alteration, or with such alteration(s) as it thinks reasonable.

(7) If the court confirms the order, the officer registers the order in that court and may exercise 1 of the following 3 powers:

40 Note that the jurisdiction to confirm a provisional order depends upon whether the payer **resides** in the UK (i.e. it matters not whether they have assets in the UK): MO(RE)A 1972, s 7(2).

(1) payments to be made directly to the court;

(2) payments to be made by standing order; or

(3) attachment of earnings order.

(8) The court officer sends written notice of the confirmation to the relevant court of the reciprocating country (FPR 2010, r 34.19(2)).

11.33 If the provisional order from a reciprocating country is one which seeks to vary or revoke a UK maintenance order (ie a Type (2)(b) order in **11.31**), the process of confirming that provisional variation/revocation (or not, as the case may be) is identical to that set out in the diagram above:

> MO(RE)A 1972, s 9(6)[41]
>
> Where a certified copy of a provisional order made by a court in a reciprocating country, being an order varying a registered order, together with a document, duly authenticated, setting out or summarising the evidence given in the proceedings in which the provisional order was made, is received by the registering court, that court may confirm the order either without alteration or with such alterations as it thinks reasonable or refuse to confirm the order

Variation or revocation of registered orders

11.34 Once the Family Court has registered an order (whether provisional or not), its powers are not limited to enforcement; the court is given the '*like power*' to vary and to revoke a registered order as if it had been made originally in the English court[42].

However, that general power to vary / revoke is made expressly subject to a number of caveats contained in the later sub-sections of MO(RE)A 1972, s 9[43], the most important of which are set out below.

11.35 There are **two absolute prohibitions** on variation/revocation of a registered maintenance order[44]:

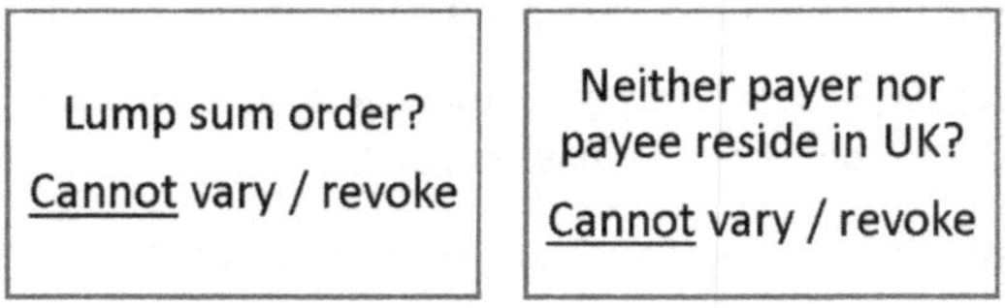

41 MO(RE)A 1972, s 9(6).

42 MO(RE)A 1972, s 9(1). The substantive law on variation of maintenance orders is outside the scope of this book.

43 MO(RE)A 1972, s 9(1A)-(10).

44 MO(RE)A 1972, s 9(1A)-(1B).

11.36 The power to vary a registered order is qualified by the general rule that any order varying a registered maintenance order is only a 'provisional' order and thus dependent on subsequent confirmation by the courts of the reciprocating country. This is made subject to some limited exceptions[45]:

> 'The court shall not vary a registered order **otherwise than by a provisional order** unless:
>
> (a) Both payer and payee are residing in the UK 'for the time being'; or
>
> (b) The application to vary is made by the payee; or
>
> (c) The variation is for a reduction in the rate of payments under the order and is made solely on the ground that there has been a change in the financial circumstances of the payer since the order was made or (if a provisional order) confirmed.'

11.37 The power to revoke a registered order is also heavily qualified:

> The court shall not revoke a registered order otherwise than by a provisional order **unless both payer and payee are residing in the UK**[46]
>
> On an application to revoke an order, the court shall (unless both payer and payee reside in the UK) 'apply the law applied by the reciprocating country'[47]

11.38 If the UK court does vary or revoke a registered order, the court officer will send the following to the court of the reciprocating country, depending on whether the order is provisional or not:

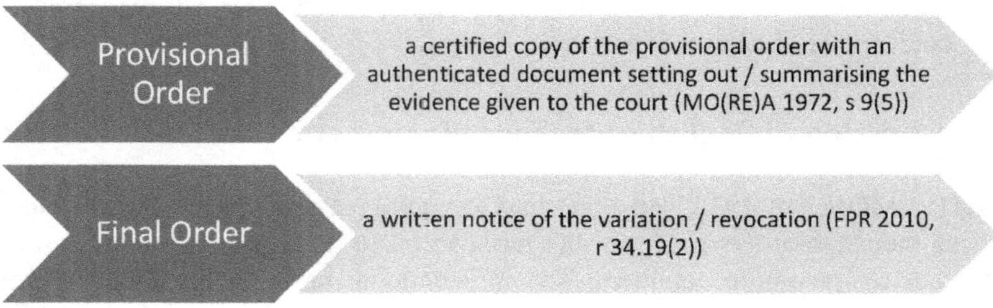

The variation/revocation will take effect **from the date on which the variation/ revocation is to take effect under the provisions of the order**. That applies equally to a provisional order which has subsequently been confirmed by the

45 MO(RE)A 1972, s 9(2).
46 MO(RE)A 1972, s 9(3).
47 MO(RE)A 1972, s 9(4). The section permits the court to make a provisional order on the basis that it 'has reason to believe' there is ground for a revocation under the foreign law even though it '*has not been established*'.

court of the reciprocating country, which is then treated 'as if it had never been a provisional order'[48].

Appeals

11.39 MO(RE)A 1972, s 12 provides as follows (in summary)[49]:

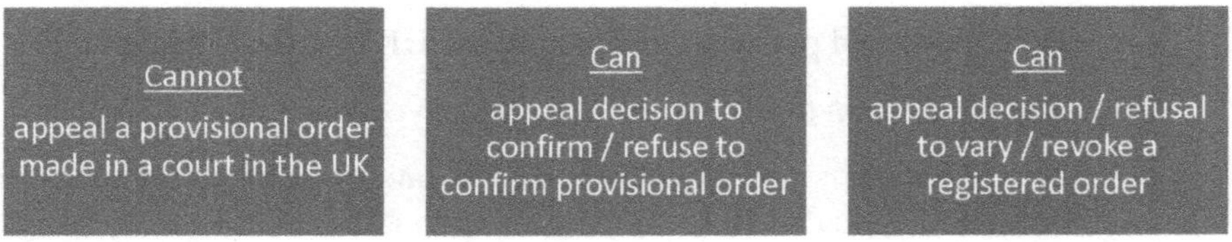

Currency conversion

11.40 MO(RE)A 1972, s 16(2) explicitly addresses the situation where a registered order is expressed in a currency other than Pounds Sterling:

> 'From the relevant date, the order shall be treated as if it were an order requiring the payment of such sums in the currency of the United Kingdom as, on the basis of the rate of exchange prevailing at that date, are equivalent to the sums so required to be paid.'

The 'relevant date' is (as appropriate):

(1) the date on which the order was registered or confirmed (whichever is earlier)

(2) the date on which the last order varying a registered order was registered or confirmed (whichever is earlier)

Transmission of English order for enforcement

11.41 MO(RE)A 1972, Part I provides a statutory scheme for the transmission of maintenance orders made in this jurisdiction to be registered and enforced in other reciprocating countries. The jurisdictional basis is the same[50] as for registration and enforcement of foreign orders (para 11.24 above), under MO(RE)A 1972, s 2:

> The payer is residing in a reciprocating country.

OR

> The payer has assets in a reciprocating country.

48 MO(RE)A 1972, s 9(8)-(9).
49 MO(RE)A 1972, s 12(1)-(3).
50 MO(RE)A 1972, s 2(1).

11.42 FPR 2010, r 34.14 provides that an application to transmit a maintenance order to another country under MO(RE)A 1972, s 2 must be made in accordance with PD 34A. PD 34A, paras 4.1–4.11 set out in detail the application which must be made and the documents which must accompany the application[51]:

D RECOVERY OF MAINTENANCE: MAINTENANCE ORDERS (RECIPROCAL ENFORCEMENT) ACT 1972, PART II

11.43 MO(RE)A 1972, Part I, addressed in **11.14–11.43**, is concerned with the reciprocal **enforcement of maintenance orders** as between reciprocating countries.

In contrast, MO(RE)A 1972, Part II, s 26(1) and (2) enables an applicant to apply to transmit to another country two types of **maintenance claim**[52]:

An application to 'recover' maintenance from a payer (i.e. an application for maintenance to be paid).

An application to vary the amount of maintenance payable to the payee.

The only jurisdictional criteria are that:

51 See also MO(RE)A 1972, s 2(4). If the country in question is a 1973 Hague Convention country, PD34A paras 4.6 and 4.7 contain extra information which must accompany the application to transmit.

52 MO(RE)A 1972, s (26)(1) and (2).

The other country is a 'Maintenance Convention' country.

AND

The payer is for the time being subject to the jurisdiction of that country.

'Maintenance Convention Country'

11.44 The reference to the 'Maintenance Convention' in MO(RE)A 1972, Part II is a reference to the 1956 United Nations Convention on the Recovery Abroad of Maintenance[53].

The 2007 Hague Convention[54] has replaced the Maintenance Convention (save for transitional provisions)[55]. Where the 2007 Hague Convention applies, MO(RE) A 1972, Part II does not. Most notably the 2007 Convention applies as between the UK and the USA.

11.45 Following the 2007 Hague Convention coming into force, the Maintenance Convention Countries for the purposes of MO(RE)A 1972, Part II are now as follows[56]:

Algeria	Macedonia
Australia	Mexico
Barbados	Monaco
Burkina Faso[57]	Morocco
Cape Verde	Niger
Central African Republic	Pakistan
Chile	Philippines
Ecuador	Sri Lanka
Guatemala	Suriname
Haiti	Switzerland
Holy See	Tunisia
Israel	Uruguay

53 The United Nations Convention on the Recovery Abroad of Maintenance done at New York on 20th June 1956: MO(RE)A 1972, s 25(2).

54 The Hague Convention on the International Recovery of Child Support and Other Forms of Family Maintenance dated 23 October 2007, which came into force in the UK on 1 August 2014 and in the USA in January 2017.

55 Article 49 of 2007 Hague Convention.

56 The Recovery Abroad of Maintenance (Convention Countries) Order 1975, SI 1975/423, without duplication of those countries which have ratified the 2007 Hague Convention.

57 Burkina Faso signed the 2007 Hague Convention on 7 January 2009, but it has not yet been ratified and/or entered into force (HCCH Website – Status Table).

Outgoing application

11.46 Where an application is made in this jurisdiction for the recovery of maintenance in a Maintenance Convention Country, an officer of the Family Court[58] will send the application to the Secretary of State, who then transmits it, with any accompanying documents, to the appropriate authority in the relevant country[59]. The application will then proceed in that country.

Incoming application to recover maintenance

11.47 An applicant can make an application in a Maintenance Convention Country for their claim for the recovery of maintenance to be determined in the courts of England and Wales[60]. The process is as follows[61]:

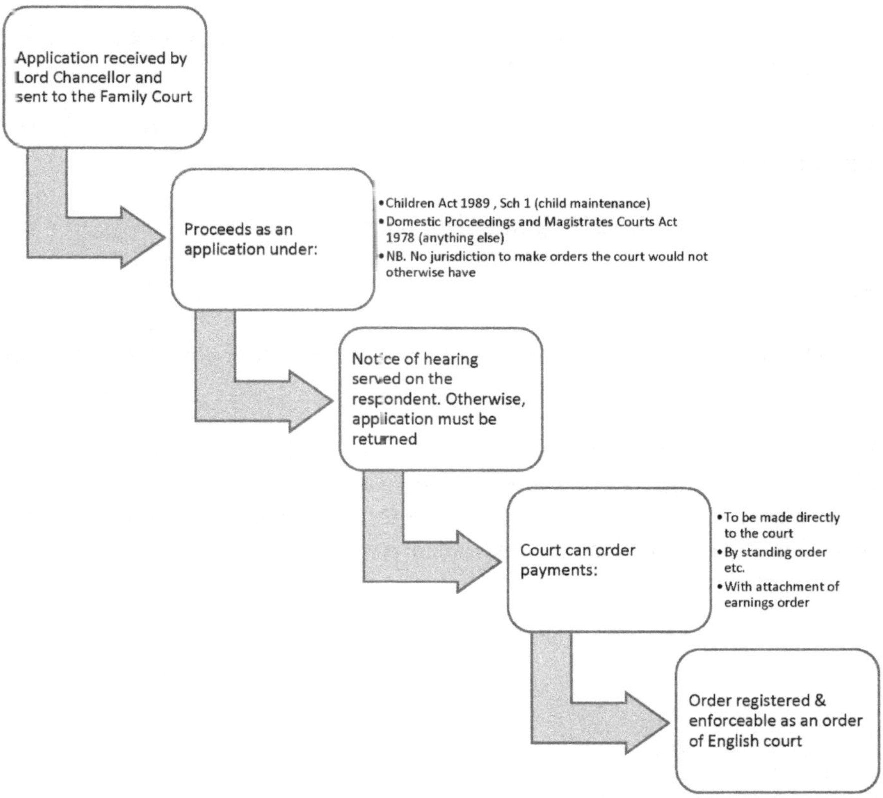

58 MO(RE)A 1972, s 26(6)(a).
59 MO(RE)A 1972, s 26(4) and (5).
60 Section 27A MO(RE)A 1972, s 27A.
61 MO(RE)A 1972, ss 27A-27C and, for enforcement, s 33.

Variation/revocation

11.48 A variation application is treated as an application to vary an English maintenance order made in the Family Court[62]. The application can either be made directly to the court which registered the maintenance order[63] or through the Lord Chancellor[64] who, as in the process set out in the graphic above, will transmit the application to be issued and heard in the Family Court[65].

11.49 No limitations are imposed on the court's power to vary or revoke[66], save that the court must order (as under MO(RE)A 1972, Part I) that the payments be made to the court, as opposed to directly to the payee[67].

11.50 MO(RE)A 1972, s 35 gives the Family Court jurisdiction to determine an application to vary/revoke a maintenance order even when the respondent is residing outside of the jurisdiction of England and Wales[68]. However, it can only do so where[69]:

> The application is made by the person against whom or on whose application the registered order was made.

The court can also hear and determine that application in the **absence of the respondent**, as long as the court is *satisfied* of two conditions[70]:

> The respondent is residing outside England and Wales.

And

> The prescribed notice of hearing has been given to the respondent in the prescribed manner.

The 'prescribed notice of hearing' and 'prescribed manner' are set out in FPR 2010, r 34.38ZJ, and the notice to be used is contained in PD 34D. The notice is sent *by post* to the Lord Chancellor for onward transmission to the convention country in which the respondent resides[71].

62 MO(RE)A 1972, s 34(1).
63 FPR 2010, r 34.28ZI(2).
64 For which read the UK Central Authority.
65 MO(RE)A 1972, s 34(3)(a).
66 MO(RE)A 1972, ss 34 and 34A.
67 MO(RE)A 1972, s 34A(3).
68 MO(RE)A 1972, s 35(1A).
69 MO(RE)A 1972, s 35(1)(a).
70 MO(RE)A 1972, s 35(3).
71 FPR 2010, r 34.28ZJ(3). The hearing must not be listed earlier than 6 weeks after the date on which the notice is sent to the Lord Chancellor (Central Authority) (r 34.28ZJ(4)).

E THE COMMONWEALTH

11.51 Where a Commonwealth (or former Commonwealth) country or territory is not a reciprocating country under MO(RE)A 1972, Part I, there are three other possible avenues available to enforce a maintenance order:

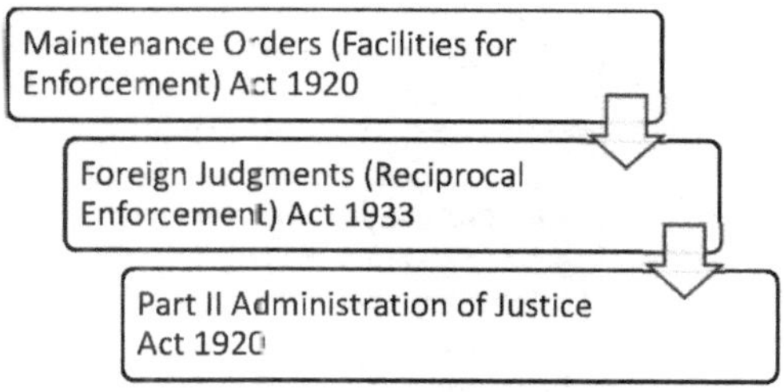

Maintenance Orders (Facilities for Enforcement) Act 1920

11.52 The Maintenance Orders (Facilities for Enforcement) Act 1920 ('MO(FE)A 1920') provides for reciprocal enforcement of maintenance orders in countries of the Commonwealth which have ***not*** been designated as 'reciprocating countries' under MO(RE)A 1972[72].

Practically, there is very little difference between enforcing a maintenance order under MO(FE)A 1920 and enforcing a maintenance order under MO(RE) A 1972 as the schemes are very similar: an order (whether final or provisional) is transmitted from the relevant country for registration and enforcement.

11.53 The countries to which the MO(FE)A 1920 extends are set out in the Maintenance Orders (Facilities for Enforcement) Order 1959[73].

'Maintenance order'

11.54 Under MO(FE)A 1920 the definition of a 'maintenance order' is limited to **periodical payments** for a spouse or dependant[74]:

> '"maintenance order" means an order ...for the periodical payment of sums of money towards the maintenance of the wife or other dependants of the person against whom the order is made, and the expression 'dependants' means such persons as that person is, according to the law in force in the part of His Majesty's dominions in which the maintenance order was made, liable to maintain.'

72 Section 22(2) of the Maintenance Orders (Reciprocal Enforcement) Act 1972 repealed the entirety of the MO(FE) 1920, but s 22(2) has only been brought into force in respect of countries designated as 'reciprocating countries' under the MO(RE) 1972, see **11.16–11.18**.

73 SI 1959/377, Sch 1.

74 MO(FE)A 1920, s 10.

Registration and enforcement of final overseas maintenance orders

11.55 A final (i.e. not provisional) maintenance order made overseas is transmitted for registration under MO(FE)A 1920, s 1. The process of registration is simple[75]:

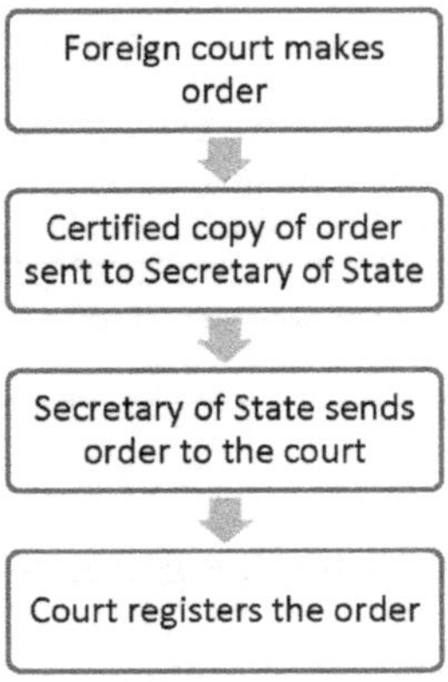

The court in which the order will be registered in the UK[76] depends upon the level of court in which the order was made in the overseas jurisdiction:

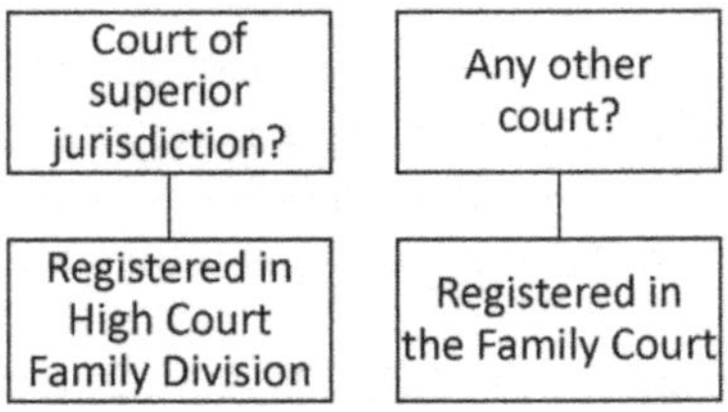

11.56 Once registered, the order[77]:

> 'shall, from the date of such registration, be of the same force and effect, and…all proceedings may be taken on such order as if it had been an order originally obtained in the court in which it is so registered, and that court shall have power to enforce the order accordingly.'

11.57 From an enforcement perspective[78]:

> 'A court…in which an order has been registered under this Act…shall take all such steps for enforcing the order as may be prescribed.'

75 MO(FE)A 1920, s 1(1).
76 MO(FE)A 1920, s 1(2).
77 MO(FE)A 1920, s 1(1).
78 MO(FE)A 1920, s 6(1).

Since a registered order is treated as an order of the Family Court, the order can be enforced by any means available to enforce a Family Court order for the payment of maintenance. The only exception is that where an order has been registered for enforcement under MO(FE)A 1920:

> The court must order payments due to be made to the court[79]

FPR 2010, r 34.7(2)[80] provides that a court officer:

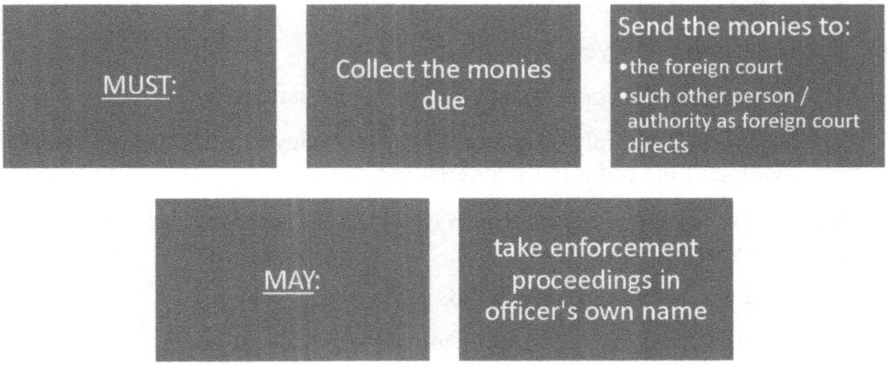

11.58 Practitioners should note that there is no power in the MO(FE)A 1920 to vary or to revoke an overseas maintenance order which has been registered here for enforcement.

Provisional overseas maintenance orders: confirmation, enforcement and variation

11.59 The meaning of '**provisional order**' is discussed above at **11.31** as regards MO(RE)A 1972. The meaning is the same under MO(FE)A 1920: an order which has *no effect* unless and until it has been *confirmed.*

When an application is made to enforce a provisional order made in a reciprocating country, the following will be transmitted to the Family Court via the Secretary of State:[81]

1. A certified copy of the order
2. The depositions of any witnesses
3. Statement of the grounds on which the order might have been opposed

11.60 When the court receives the order[82]:

79 FPR 2010, r 34.6.

80 This rule applies both to (a) a final order which has been registered in the Family Court AND (b) a provisional order which has been confirmed by the Family Court.

81 MO(FE)A 1920, s 4(1).

82 MO(FE)A 1920, s 4(1)-(5) and FPR 2010, r 34.5.

- The court officer must serve on the payer:
  - A notice.
  - Certified copies of the provisional order and accompanying documents.
- The notice of hearing must:
  - Contain the time and date of the hearing.
  - State that the payer may attend to show cause why the order should not be confirmed.
- At the hearing the payer:
  - Can oppose the confirmation of the provisional order.
  - But, can ONLY rely on grounds on which they might have opposed the making of the order in the originating court.
- If the payer does not appear, or fails to satisfy the court that the order should not be confirmed, the court can:
  - Confirm the order without modifications.
  - Confirm the order with modifications as may seem just.
- The court can adjourn and remit the case to the originating court to take more evifence.

11.61 If the Family Court confirms the provisional order, it *may* exercise one of a number of powers relating to how the payments are to be made, but payments must be made directly to the court (ie not to the payee)[83]. The court will take into account any representations made by the payer[84].

11.62 The Family Court is expressly given the power **to vary or to revoke** a provisional order which has been confirmed, in '*like manner*' as if it had originally been made in the Family Court[85].

That power to vary is made subject to one proviso[86]:

IF

> The respondent to a variation /revocation application is **residing in a Commonwealth country to which MO(FE)A 1920 applies.**

THEN

> The Family Court has jurisdiction to hear the application (if it would not otherwise have jurisdiction) if it **would have had jurisdiction to hear it had the respondent been habitually resident in England and Wales.**

83 MO(FE)A 1920, s 4(5A)-(5B).
84 MO(FE)A 1920, s 4(5C).
85 MO(FE)A 1920, s 4(6).
86 MO(FE)A 1920, s 4A(2).

Transmission overseas of English maintenance orders

11.63 MO(FE)A 1920 provides also for the transmission overseas (to the relevant Commonwealth countries) of maintenance orders (provisional or otherwise) made in this jurisdiction. The process is the reverse of that discussed above[87].

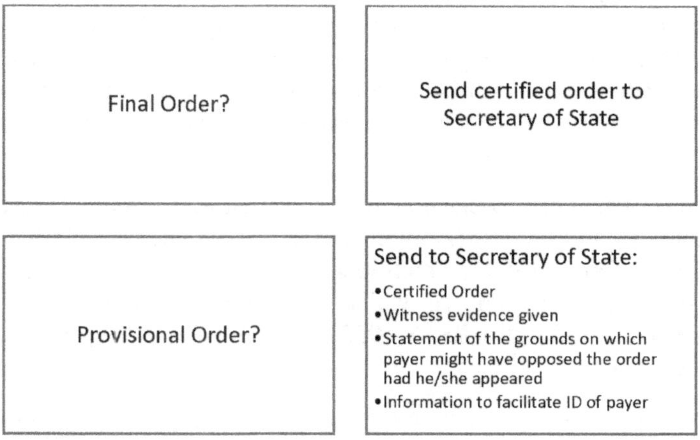

11.64 The following should be noted about provisional maintenance orders made in the Family Court[88]:

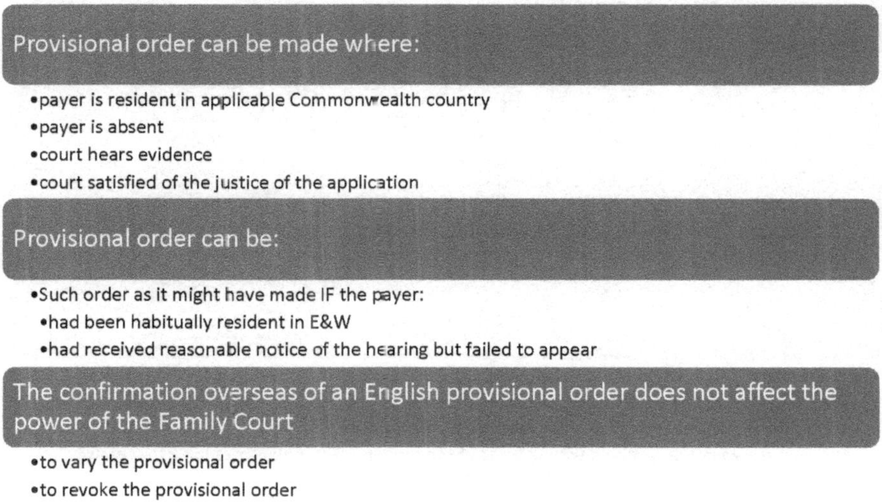

87 Note that FPR 2010, r 34.10 sets out a slightly different procedure for making such an application in respect of a maintenance order made in the High Court. Essentially it is the same, but an application has to be made to a District Judge in the Principal Registry of the Family Division.

88 MO(FE)A 1920, s 3.

Administration of Justice Act 1920, Part II

11.65 Part II of the Administration of Justice Act 1920 ('AJA 1920') is another statutory regime that provides for reciprocal enforcement between Commonwealth countries and the UK. AJA 1920 is not limited to maintenance orders, but applies to a 'judgment' defined as follows[89]:

> '...any **judgment or order** given or made by a court in any civil proceedings, whether before or after the passing of this Act, whereby **any sum of money is made payable**, and includes an award in proceedings on an arbitration if the award has, in pursuance of the law in force in the place where it was made, become enforceable in the same manner as a judgment given by a court in that place.'

11.66 AJA 1920 applies to the countries and territories listed in the Reciprocal Enforcement of Judgments (Administration of Justice Act 1920, Part II) (Consolidation) Order 1984[90]. Practitioners should, however, note that should the relevant country be one to which the Foreign Judgments (Reciprocal Enforcement) Act 1933 ('FJ(RE)A 1933') applies (see **11.75**), then AJA 1920 ceases to have effect[91].

11.67 AJA 1920, s 9 provides a mechanism to make an application for the judgment to be registered in the UK court. There are a number of hoops through which an applicant must jump[92]:

Judgment must have been obtained in a superior court in the foreign country

An application under s 9 must be made within 12 months of the date of the judgment (unless the court allows longer)

The court may register the judgment if:

- In all the circumstances of the case it is just and convenient to enforce in the UK

A judgment cannot be registered if

- The foreign court acted without jurisdiction
- The debtor did not voluntarily appear or submit ot the jurisdiction of foreign court & was neither ordinarily resident nor carrying on business in that jurisdiction
- The debtor was not duly served with process of the foreign court, notwithstanding that he was orindarily resident or carrying on business in that jurisdiction
- Judgment was obtained by fraud
- Debtor satisfies UK court that an appeal is pending, or that he is entitled to and intends to appeal
- Other public policy reason

89 AJA 1920, s 12(1).
90 SI 1984/129.
91 FJ(RE)A 1933, s 7(1).
92 AJA 1920, s 9(1)-(2).

11.68 If the order is registered, then from the date of registration:

> 'It shall be of the same force and effect, and proceedings may be taken thereon, as if it had been a judgment originally obtained or entered up on the date of registration in the registering court.'

Additionally, the reasonable costs of and incidental to the registration of the judgment are recoverable as if they were sums payable under the judgment itself[93].

Foreign Judgments (Reciprocal Enforcement) Act 1933

11.69 FJ(RE)A 1933 provides a mechanism for enforcing in this jurisdiction a judgment for the payment of money originating from a 'recognised court' in another country. The foreign courts to which the FJ(RE)A 1933 applies are those which provide for reciprocity of enforcement of equivalent judgments made here (see **11.75**).

11.70 FJ(RE)A 1933 only applies if the judgment fulfils three conditions[94]:

> It is final and conclusive as between the debtor and creditor.

OR

> It requires the debtor to make an interim payment to the creditor.

AND

> It is for the payment of a sum of money (not taxes, a fine or other penalty).

AND

> It is given after the relevant Order in Council which made the foreign court a recognised court.

A judgment is final and conclusive even if there is an appeal pending in the court of origin[95].

11.71 The procedure is simple[96]:

93 AJA 1920, s 9(3)(c).
94 FJ(RE)A 1933, s 1(2).
95 FJ(RE)A 1933, s 1(3).
96 FJ(RE)A 1933, s 2(1).

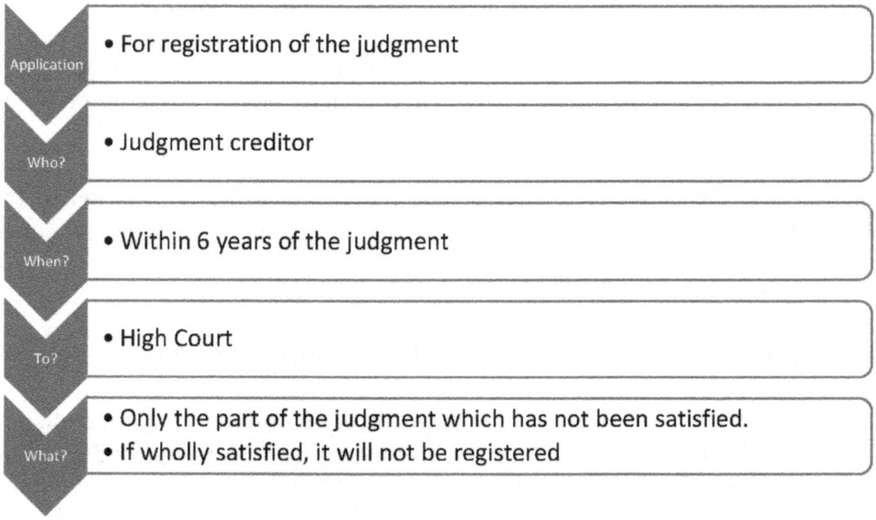

11.72 Once the judgment has been registered it is as if the judgment was originally given in the registering court as at the date of registration[97], and:

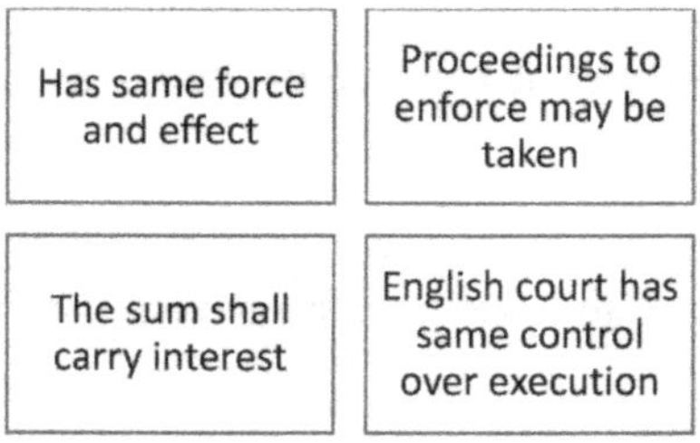

11.73 However, the court can set aside the registration of the judgment on an application if[98]:

> 'The applicant satisfies the registering court either that an appeal is pending, or that he is entitled and intends to appeal against the judgment…'

The court then has a discretion ('if it thinks fit') to set aside the registration or adjourn the application until the expiry of such period as is reasonably sufficient to enable the applicant to have the appeal heard[99].

11.74 FJ(RE)A 1933, s 4 also contains detailed provisions as to the circumstances where the court **must** set aside the registered judgment or **may** set it aside, on an application by the person against whom the judgment is to be enforced[100]:

97 FJ(RE)A 1933, s 2(2).
98 FJ(RE)A 1933, s 5(1).
99 FJ(RE)A 1933, s 5(1).
100 FJ(RE)A 1933, s 4(1)(a)-9b).

MUST set aside

- judgment is not one to which the FJ(RE)A 1933 applies
- original court had no jurisdiction (see s 4(2) & (3))
- judgment debtor did not receive notice of original proceedings
- judgment obtained by fraud
- enforcement contrary to public policy
- rights under judgment not vested in person who applied to register

MAY set aside

- If court satisfied that matter in dispute in the original court had previously been the subject of a final and conclusive judgment by another court with jurisdiction.

11.75 There is no list of 'recognised courts' for the purpose of FJ(RE)A 1933. Instead there are a number of Orders in Council, extending its reach. If the FJ(RE)A 1933 applies to a country, then AJA1920, Part II, is disapplied[101].

The countries with recognised courts to which FJ(RE)A 1933 applies are as follows[102]:

Australia	India	Norway
Austria	Isle of Man	Pakistan
Canada	Israel	Suriname
France	Italy	Tonga
Germany	Jersey	
Guernsey	Netherlands	

F EU MAINTENANCE REGULATION

11.76 Reference should be had to the introduction to this Chapter. The UK ceased to be a Member State of the EU as of 31 January 2020. From that date, there was a transition period which ended at 11pm on 31 December 2020.

The Maintenance Regulation[103], which provided for the direct enforcement in the UK of all maintenance orders made in EU Member States, now has no effect as

101 FJ(RE)A 1933, s 7(1).

102 Reciprocal Enforcement of Foreign Judgments – Orders 1958/141, 1958/425, 1961/119, 1962/636, 1962/1339, 1969/1063, 1971/1039, 1973/612, 1973/611, 1973/1894, 1977/2149, 1980/1523, 1981/735, 1986/2027, 1987/468, 1987/2211, 1988/1853, 1989/987, 1991/1724, 1992/1731, 1994/1091, 1995/2708, 2003/2618, 2020/1338.

103 Council Regulation (EC) No. 4/2009 on Jurisdiction, Applicable law, Recognition and Enforcement of Decisions and Co-Operation in Matters Relating to Maintenance Obligations.

regards proceedings which were initiated *after* the transition period. As noted in the introduction, the key question is when the substantive proceedings were issued.

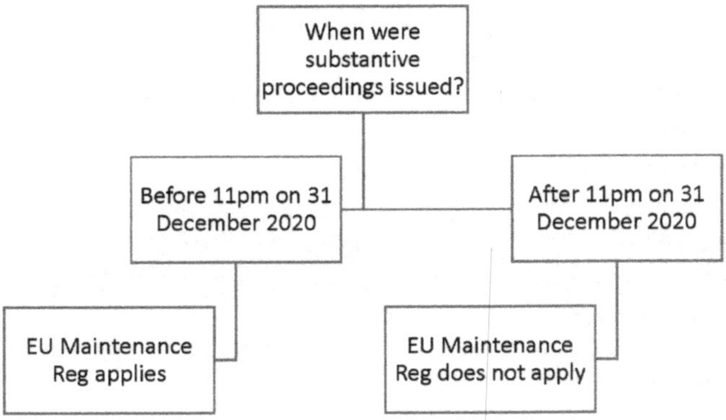

The meaning of 'maintenance'

11.77 The Maintenance Regulation only applies to 'maintenance obligations arising from a family relationship, parentage, marriage or affinity'. However, 'maintenance' is nowhere defined within the text of the Regulation.

Although it is a decision which applied to a different EU Regulation, the seminal case on the autonomous meaning of 'maintenance' as a matter of European law is *Van den Boogaard v Laumen*[104]

Case summary: *Van den Boogaard v Laumen*[105]

Facts:

H and W were married in the Netherlands under a separation of property regime / contract. They moved to live in England. In July 1990 they were divorced and the High Court in England made orders for financial relief (and disregarded the separation of property contract). In order to achieve a 'clean break' the court awarded W a capital sum in lieu of periodical payments.

W sought to enforce the order against H in the Netherlands. She was successful. H appealed. The appellate court in the Netherlands was uncertain as to the extent to which the High Court's decision was a 'decision in respect of maintenance obligations'.

The court was also unsure about the correct interpretation to be given to the applicable EU Regulation[106] and the interplay between 'maintenance' on the

104 (ECJ Case C-220/95) [1997] QB 759, [1997] 3 WLR 284, [1997] 3 FCR 493, [1997] 2 FLR 399.
105 (ECJ Case C-220/95) [1997] QB 759, [1997] 3 WLR 284, [1997] 3 FCR 493, [1997] 2 FLR 399.
106 Council Regulation (EC) No.44/2001 on jurisdiction and the recognition and enforcement of judgments in civil and commercial matters ('Brussels I').

one hand (which was enforceable) and 'rights in property arising out of a matrimonial relationship' on the other (which was not enforceable).

A reference was made to the European Court of Justice

Decision of the ECJ (with emphasis added):

> '[22] It should be possible to deduce that aim from the reasoning of the decision in question If this shows that **a provision awarded is designed to enable one spouse to provide for himself or herself or if the needs and resources of each of the spouses are taken into consideration in the determination of its amount, the decision will be concerned with maintenance**. On the other hand, where the provision awarded is solely concerned with dividing property between the spouses, the decision will be concerned with rights in property arising out of a matrimonial relationship and will not therefore be enforceable…
>
> [23] **It makes no difference in this regard that payment of maintenance is provided for in the form of a lump sum**. This form of payment may also be in the nature of maintenance where the capital sum set is designed to ensure a predetermined level of income.
>
> [24] In the present case, … the court of origin was under an obligation to consider whether it had to impose a clean break between the spouses and to order payment of a lump sum instead of periodical payments. It is clear that **the choice of method of payment made by the court of origin cannot alter the nature of the aim pursued by the decision**.
>
> [25] Likewise, the fact that the decision of which enforcement is sought also orders ownership in certain property to be transferred between the former spouses cannot call in question the nature of that decision as an order for the provision of maintenance. **The aim is still to make provision, by means of a capital sum, for the maintenance of one of the former spouses**.
>
> [26] … the English court's statement that it did not consider itself bound by the separation of goods agreement should be read in its context and in any event is not relevant for the purposes of defining the nature of the decision in question.
>
> [27] Consequently, the answer to be given must be that **a decision rendered in divorce proceedings ordering payment of a lump sum and transfer of ownership in certain property by one party to his or her former spouse must be regarded as relating to maintenance and therefore as falling within the scope of [the Regulation] if its purpose is to ensure the former spouse's maintenance**. The fact that in its decision the court of origin disregarded a marriage contract is of no account in this regard.'

In other words, maintenance is not confined to periodical payments. In subsequent authorities, this decision has been followed and further analysed. A full analysis is beyond the scope of this Chapter, but some of the relevant authorities are set out below[107]. In broad terms, where an award (capital or income) is based on meeting a spouse or dependant's 'needs', it can without difficulty be categorised as being for the purpose of 'maintenance'.

Originating State not bound by the Hague Protocol: declaration of enforceability

11.78 The UK and Denmark are not bound by the 2007 Hague Protocol on the Law Applicable to Maintenance Obligations ('the Hague Protocol').

The Maintenance Regulation applies slightly differently in respect of decisions made in a Member State that is not bound by the Hague Protocol, in that it retains a system akin to registration prior to enforcement (known as exequatur)[108].

11.79 For a decision made in England or Denmark to be enforced in another Member State under the Maintenance Regulation, an application must be made for **a declaration of enforceability**.

11.80 The procedure for making an application for a declaration of enforceability in another Member State is contained in Article 28 of the Maintenance Regulation. An applicant seeking such a declaration will need:

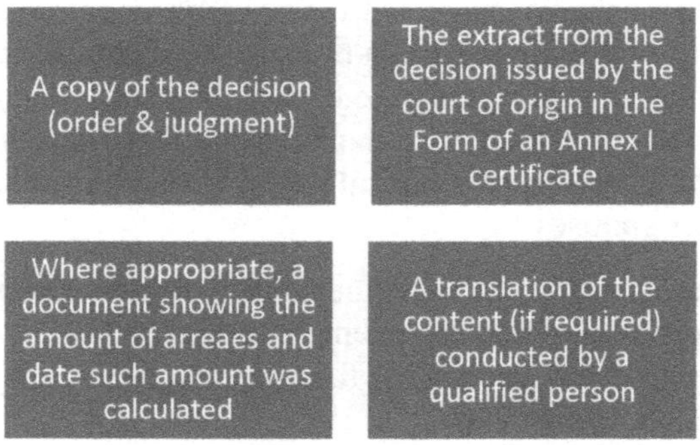

107 See: *Moore v Moore* [2007] EWCA Civ 361, [2007] 2 FLR 339; *Traversa v Freddi* [2011] EWCA Civ 81, [2011] 2 FLR 272; *Agbaje v Agbaje* [2010] UKSC 13, [2010] 1 AC 628, [2010] 1 FLR 1813; *Ramadani v Ramadani* [2015] EWCA Civ 1138, [2016] 2 FLR 1233; *Johnson v Takieddine* [2016] EWHC 1895 (Fam); *DB v PB* [2016] EWHC 3431 (Fam), [2017] 4 WLR 44, Francis J, overturned on appeal (different point) in *Brack v Brack* [2018] EWCA Civ 2862, [2019] 1 WLR 3438; *Potanina v Potanin* [2021] EWCA Civ 702, [2022] Fam. 23, [2021] 3 WLR 967, [2021] 2 FLR 1457.

108 Maintenance Regulation, Art 26.

Once these formalities have been complied with, the decision will be declared enforceable 'without any review' **immediately**[109] unless one of the very limited grounds for refusal of recognition are made out[110].

States bound by the Hague Protocol

11.81 All EU Member States apart from the UK and Denmark are bound by the 2007 Hague Protocol. A decision originating in those States[111]:

> 'Shall be recognised in another Member State without any special procedure being required and without any possibility of opposing its recognition.'

AND

> 'Shall be enforceable in another Member State without the need for a declaration of enforceability.'

11.82 That automatic recognition and enforcement is made subject only to the very limited circumstances in which the Member State of enforcement may refuse to enforce or suspend enforcement contained in Article 21. The following is a summary of that provision:

When must / may the court of E&W refuse to enforce (either in whole or in part)?

- **MUST** refuse if the limitation period for making an enforcement application has expired
- **MAY** refuse if enforcement is irreconcilable with a decision given in:
  - another Member State
  - E&W
  - a third state (which has fulfilled recognition requirements)
  - NB. a variation of maintenance based on a change of circumstances is not an irreconcilable decision
- **MAY** refuse / suspend if the Member State of origin is seised of an application for a review of the decision under Art. 19

Procedure to enforce

11.83 As discussed above[112], assuming the maintenance order originates in a country other than Denmark, it is capable of direct enforcement without any

109 Maintenance Regulation, Art 30.
110 Maintenance Regulation, Art 24.
111 Maintenance Regulation, Art 17(1)-(2).
112 At para 11.81.

special procedure. There are two options for a payee seeking to enforce an order in England:

Through the Central Authority

OR

Private application to the Family Court

11.84 The route via the Central Authority is what might be termed the traditional route. The process is very similar to that of registration and enforcement under other instruments (discussed above) and to that of *exequatur* (described above at **11.78**). The process is administrative and relatively straightforward. The steps are these[113]:

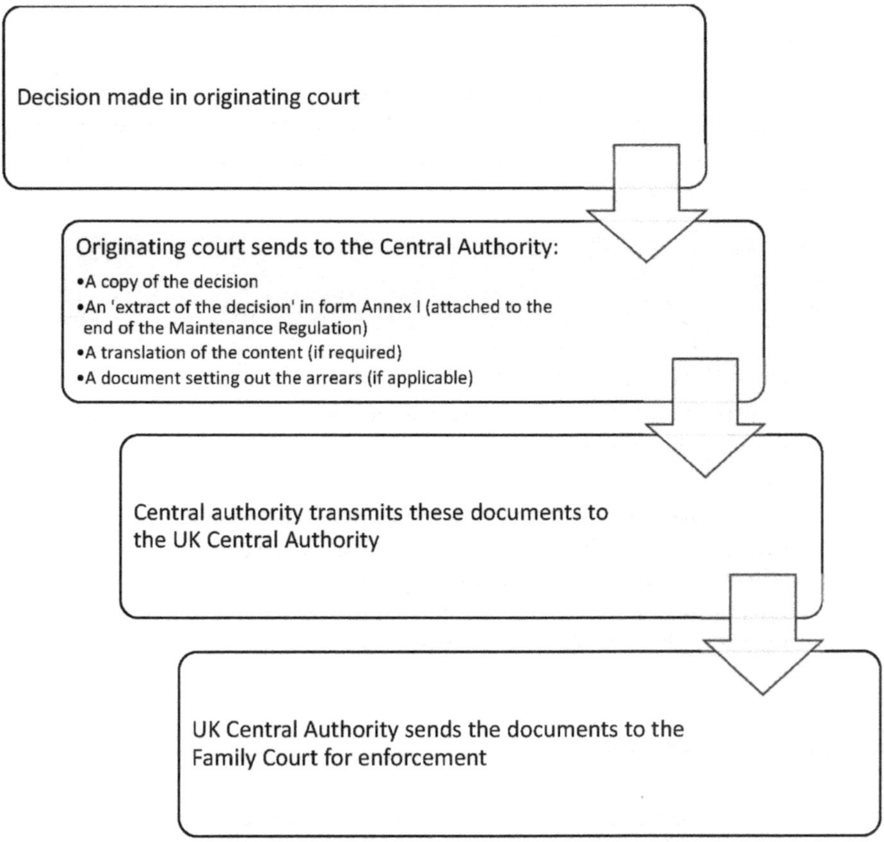

113 The documents required to accompany the application are set out in Article 20 Maintenance Regulation. Articles 49 to 63 of the Maintenance Regulation (Chapter VII) deal with the co-operation between Central Authorities of Member States.

A key factor in choosing to enforce via this route is the entitlement of an applicant to Legal Aid under Chapter V of the Maintenance Regulation[114].

11.85 There is an alternative and more direct route to that described above: a **private application** by the payee in the Family Court. However, an applicant by this method (ie outside of the procedure provided for in the Maintenance Regulation itself) is *not* entitled to legal aid.

This application is made in precisely the same way as an application would be made to enforce an English maintenance order[115].

Case summary: *MS v PS*[116]

Facts:

The German court made a child maintenance order in favour of M against F. M and the children lived in Germany, but F moved to the UK and refused to satisfy the maintenance order, alleging that M was obstructing his contact with the children.

M issued an application to enforce the order in the High Court in England.

The High Court made a reference to the Court of Justice of the European Union to determine as a preliminary issue whether an application for enforcement of an order imposing maintenance obligations may be issued directly in the court with jurisdiction (in this instance the Family Court in England) or whether the application must, in all cases, first be lodged with the Central Authority for forward transmission to the Family Court.

CJEU Decision:

> '[44] The answer … is therefore that Chapter IV of [the Maintenance Regulation], in particular Article 41(1) thereof, must be interpreted as meaning that **a maintenance creditor who has obtained an order in one Member State and wishes to enforce it in another Member State may make an application directly to the competent authority of the latter Member State, such as a specialised court, and cannot be required to submit the application to that court through the Central Authority of the Member State of enforcement**.'

114 See Maintenance Regulation, Arts 44 to 47.
115 For general enforcement see **Chapter 2**.
116 (2017) Case C-283/16, CJEU.

Variation applications

11.86 The court in which enforcement is sought has no power to review as to its substance a decision given in another Member State[117]. However, it is possible for a payer or a payee to make an application for the 'modification' of a decision given in another Member State[118].

However, such an application to vary must be made pursuant to a procedure prescribed by the Maintenance Regulation[119], which mandates an application to the relevant Central Authority. In contrast to an application to enforce, it is therefore not possible to make an application directly to the Family Court to vary an order made in another EU Member State[120].

Once the Family Court is seised of a variation application, it will be determined under the laws of England and Wales (ie not the Member State of origin)[121].

G 2007 HAGUE CONVENTION: EU (POST-BREXIT), USA AND OTHERS

The EU

11.87 On 1 August 2014 the 2007 Hague Convention 2007[122] came into force in the UK alongside all other Member States of the EU. On 28 September 2020 the UK ratified the Convention independently, in advance of the end of the transition period relating to its exit from the EU.

11.88 As between Member States of the EU, the Maintenance Regulation (see Section F above) takes precedence over the 2007 Hague Convention. Thus, if the substantive proceedings leading to the maintenance order were initiated *prior to* the end of the transition period[123], the EU Maintenance Regulation applies. If the substantive proceedings were issued *after* the end of the transition period, the 2007 Hague Convention applies:

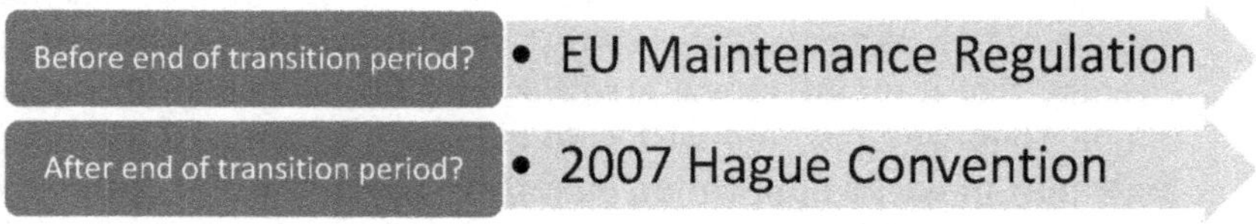

117 Maintenance Regulation, Art 42.
118 Maintenance Regulation, Art 56.
119 Maintenance Regulation, Arts 57-58 and Annexes VI and VII.
120 See *AB v JJB* [2015] EWHC 192 (Fam), [2015] 2 FLR 1143.
121 Maintenance Regulation, Art 56(4).
122 The Hague Convention on the International Recovery of Child Support and Other Forms of Family Maintenance dated 23 October 2007.
123 11.59pm on 31 December 2020.

Contracting States

11.89 The following is a list of the countries which are 'Contracting States' [124] to the 2007 Hague Convention[125]

Albania	Montenegro
Belarus	New Zealand
Bosnia and Herzegovina	Nicaragua
Brazil	Norway
Guyana	Serbia
Honduras	Turkey
Kazakhstan	Ukraine
Member States of the EU[126]	United States of America

Aim of the 2007 Convention

11.90 Article 1 of the 2007 Hague Convention sets out the object of the Convention:

> 'To ensure the effective international recovery of child support and other forms of family maintenance.' How?
>
> (a) Establish a comprehensive system of co-operation between states;[127]
>
> (b) Enable applications for the establishment of maintenance decisions;
>
> (c) Provide for recognition and enforcement of maintenance decisions;
>
> (d) Require effective measures for prompt enforcement of maintenance decisions.

Scope of the 2007 Hague Convention

11.91 Article 2 of the 2007 Hague Convention provides that it shall apply to three categories of case:

124 International Recovery of Maintenance (Hague Convention 2007 etc) Regulations 2012. SI 2012/2814, as amended. In this Chapter, references to 'Contracting States' are to each of these countries.

125 For an up-to-date list of Contracting States, see the HCCH Status Table.

126 Subject to what is said above as to the priority given to the EU Maintenance Regulation (if applicable).

127 This is achieved by reference to each Contracting State's designated 'Central Authority'. In England & Wales this is the Lord Chancellor (as with all the other instruments discussed in this Chapter). Chapter II of the 2007 Hague Convention (Articles 4 to 8) sets out the specific functions and responsibilities of a Central Authority.

(A) **Parent-child** maintenance obligations towards a person under the age of 21[128]

(B) Recognition and enforcement (or simply enforcement) of a decision for **spousal support, when the application is made alongside a claim under (A)**

(C) **Spousal support** in general (although the applications via a Central Authority available in Chapter III of the 2007 Convention do **not** apply to this category)

The text of the 2007 Hague Convention refers to 'creditor' (payee) and 'debtor' (payer)[129].

Structure of the 2007 Hague Convention

11.92 The structure of the 2007 Hague Convention is not particularly easy to follow. It is divided into several Chapters:

Chapter I - Object, Scope and Definitions •Arts 1 to 3	Chapter II - Administrative Co-Operation •Arts 4 to 8	Chapter III - Applications through Central Authorities •Arts 9 to 17
Chapter IV - Restrictions on Bringing Proceedings •Art 18	Chapter V - Recognition and Enforcement •Arts 19 to 31	Chapter VI - Enforcement by the State Addressed •Arts 32 to 35
Chapter VII - Public Bodies •Art 36	Chapter VIII - General Provisions •Art 37 to 57	Chapter IX - Final Provisions •Arts 58 to 65

The key Chapters for the purposes of enforcement are Chapters III and V, discussed below.

11.93 Chapter IV comprises solely of Article 18 which limits the availability of an application (i) to vary (modify) an existing maintenance decision, or (ii) for a new maintenance decision, depending on the creditor's habitual residence:

128 Subject to the right of Contracting States to issue a reservation limiting the application of the Convention under Art 2(1)(a) to persons under the age of 18 (see Arts 2(2) and 62).

129 Definitions are contained in Article 3 of the 2007 Hague Convention.

> Where a decision is made in a Contracting State where the **creditor is habitually resident**, proceedings to modify the decision or to make a new decision **cannot be brought by the debtor** in any other Contracting State **as long as the creditor remains habitually resident in the state where the decision was made**.

This limitation is subject to several exceptions[130]:

- Where the parties otherwise agree in writing (only child maintenance)
- Creditor submits to the jurisdiction of the other State
- The State of origin cannot or refuses to exercise its jurisdiction
- Original decision cannot be recognised / declared enforceable in the other State

Chapter III – applications through the Central Authorities

11.94 The potential applications in Chapter III of the 2007 Hague Convention – applications made via a Central Authority – are *not* available as regards 'spousal support', unless an application for recognition and enforcement of spousal support is made alongside an application regarding child maintenance obligations[131]. An application for recognition and enforcement of spousal support that falls outside this exception will need to be made by the maintenance creditor directly, a course permitted by Article 37[132].

Article 9 provides that an application made under Chapter III:

> **Shall be made** through the Central Authority of the **Contracting State in which the applicant resides** to the Central Authority of the requested State. For the purpose of this provision, **residence excludes mere presence**.

130 Hague Convention 2007, Art 18(2).
131 Hague Convention 2007, Art 2(1).
132 Article 37(2) provides that: '*Articles 14(5) and 17 b) and the provisions of Chapters V, VI, VII and this Chapter, with the exception of Articles 40(2), 42, 43(3), 44(3), 45 and 55, shall apply in relation to a request for recognition and enforcement made directly to a competent authority in a Contracting State.*' The provisions for recognition and enforcement thus apply to direct applications in the same way that they apply to applications made via a Central Authority. Article 17(b) entitles an applicant pursuing a direct application for recognition and enforcement to seek free legal assistance if they enjoyed free legal assistance in the state of origin.

11.95 Article 10 lists the categories of application available to a creditor[133] and a debtor[134] under Chapter III

Applications available to a creditor?

- recognition, or recognition & enforcement, of a decision
- enforcement of a decision made/recognised in requested State
- establishment of a decision where no existing decision
- establishment of a decision where recognition and enforcement is not possible under Article 20 & 22 (Chapter V)
- modification of a decision made in the requested State or another State

Applications available to a debtor?

- recognition of a decision leading to suspension or limiting enforcement of a previous decision
- modification of a decision made in the requested State or another State.

11.96 If one of the applications listed above is to be made, reference must be had to Articles 11 to 17 in Chapter III. These provisions can be summarised as follows:

Art 11
- Requisite contents of an application "as a minimum"

Art 12
- Process by which application is transmitted, received and processed by Central Authorities

Art 14
- applicants must have effective access to the procedure

Arts15 & 16
- applicants entitled to legal aid for all child-support applications
- means-testing permissible

133 Hague Convention, Art 10(1). A creditor can include '*a public body acting in place of an individual to whom maintenance is owed or one to which reimbursement is owed for benefits provided in place of maintenance*' (Art 36).

134 Hague Convention, Art 10(2).

Chapter V – recognition and enforcement

General

11.97 Chapter V of the Hague Convention 2007 contains the provisions relating to the recognition and enforcement. It applies to the following[135]:

> A **decision** rendered by a judicial or administrative authority **in respect of a maintenance obligation**
>
> This includes:
>
> - A settlement agreement
> - Automatic adjustment by indexation
> - A requirement to pay arrears
> - Retroactive maintenance
> - Interest
> - Determination of costs or expenses.
>
> If a decision is only **partly** related to a maintenance obligation:
>
> - Chapter V is limited to the part(s) of the decision relating to maintenance obligations.

AND

> A '**maintenance arrangement**', which is defined by Article 3[136] as
>
> 'an agreement in writing relating to the payment of maintenance, which
>
> i) Has been formally drawn up or registered as an authentic instrument by a competent authority; or
>
> ii) Has been authenticated by, or concluded, registered or filed with a competent authority, and may be the subject of review and modification by a competent authority.'
>
> The grounds for recognition and enforcement of a maintenance agreement are covered in a self-contained Article 30.

The provisions of Chapter V apply to all categories of maintenance within the scope of the Regulation including spousal support and are not subject to the restrictions in Chapter III on applications which can be pursued through a Central Authority. They apply to any application which is made by a maintenance creditor directly (not through a Central Authority) in accordance with Article 37[137].

135 Hague Convention 2007, Art 19.
136 Hague Convention 2007, Arts 3, 19(4) and 30.
137 Hague Convention 2007, Art 19(5).

Grounds for recognition and enforcement

11.98 In order for a maintenance decision made in one Contracting State to be recognised and enforced in another Contracting State, one of *six* criteria set out in Article 20 **must** be fulfilled[138]:

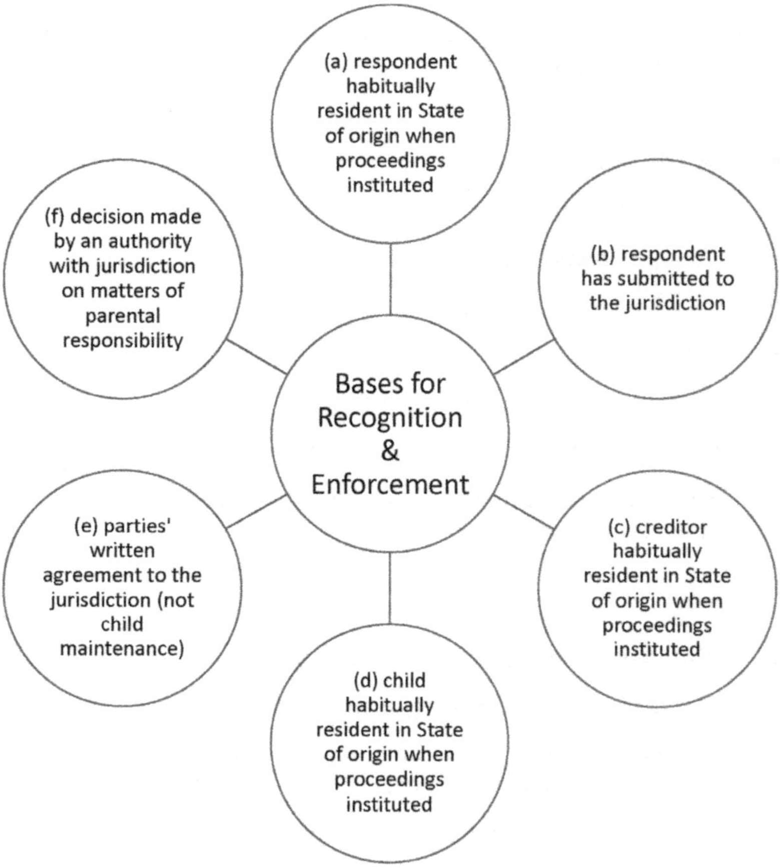

Grounds for refusal to recognise and/or enforce

11.99 Once one of those criteria is fulfilled, the grounds for refusing to recognise and enforce a decision are very limited and are set out in Article 22[139]:

138 Hague Convention 2007, Art 20(1). The following graphic is a summary only, and practitioners should refer to the full text of the Article 20 and its sub-paragraphs.

139 Hague Convention 2007, Art 22. This graphic is a summary only, and practitioners should refer to the full text of the Article 22.

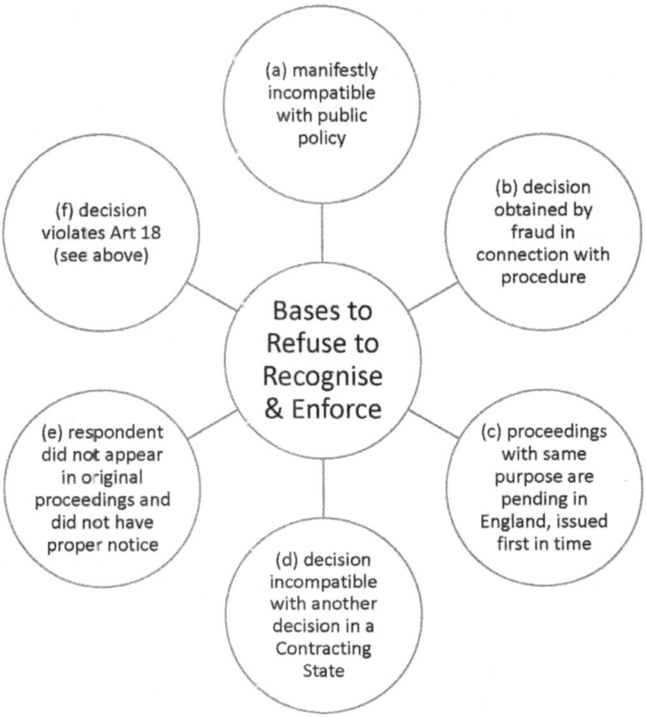

Jurisdiction in England & Wales

11.100 The International Recovery of Maintenance (Hague Convention 2007 Etc) Regulations 2012[140] incorporated the Hague Convention 2007 into national law in Sch 1. They have been amended following the UK's exit from the EU.

In order for the Family Court in England and Wales to have jurisdiction to register and enforce a maintenance decision, there are two jurisdictional criteria[141]:

> Either:
>
> The person against whom enforcement is sought is resident in England and Wales.
>
> Or:
>
> Assets belonging to that person, and which are susceptible to enforcement, are situated or held in England and Wales.

140 SI 2012/2814, as amended.

141 The International Recovery of Maintenance (Hague Convention 2007 etc) Regulations 2012, Sch 1 para 2(3). These are identical to the jurisdictional criteria for registration and enforcement of maintenance orders for reciprocating countries under the Maintenance Orders (Reciprocal Enforcement) Act 1972, discussed above.

Procedure on an application for recognition and enforcement

11.101 The procedure for recognition and enforcement in the Family Court of a maintenance decision made in a Contracting State is governed by the Hague Convention 2007, Arts 23 and 25, as supplemented by the FPR 2010, Part 34, Chapter III[142].

11.102 There are two procedural routes available to an applicant:

An application through the Central Authority (pursuant to Chapter III[143]) of the originating state, to be transmitted to the Family Court via the Lord Chancellor.

OR

Make a request directly to the Family Court[144]

11.103 An application for recognition and enforcement **must** be accompanied by the following documentation **from the State of Origin**[145]:

Complete text of maintenance decision	Document stating the decision is enforceable	Evidence respondent had proper notice of proceedings*
Dated calculation of the arrears**	Evidence re any automatic inflationary adjustment**	Evidence applicant received free legal assistance**

* If the respondent was not present or represented at the hearing at which the decision was made

** If appropriate

11.104 Once an application by either method has been received by the court officer in the Family Court the process is as follows[146]:

142 FPR 2010, rr 34.28A-34.40 (as amended) and PD 34E.

143 Hague Convention 2007, Art 23(2).

144 Hague Convention 2007, Arts 19(5), 23(3) and 37. The International Recovery of Maintenance (Hague Convention 2007 etc) Regulations 2012, Sch.1 para.2(1) provides that an application for registration is to be made to the Family Court.

145 Hague Convention 2007, Art 25.

146 All requirements in the graphic below are contained in the Hague Convention 2007, Art 25(1) unless otherwise specified.

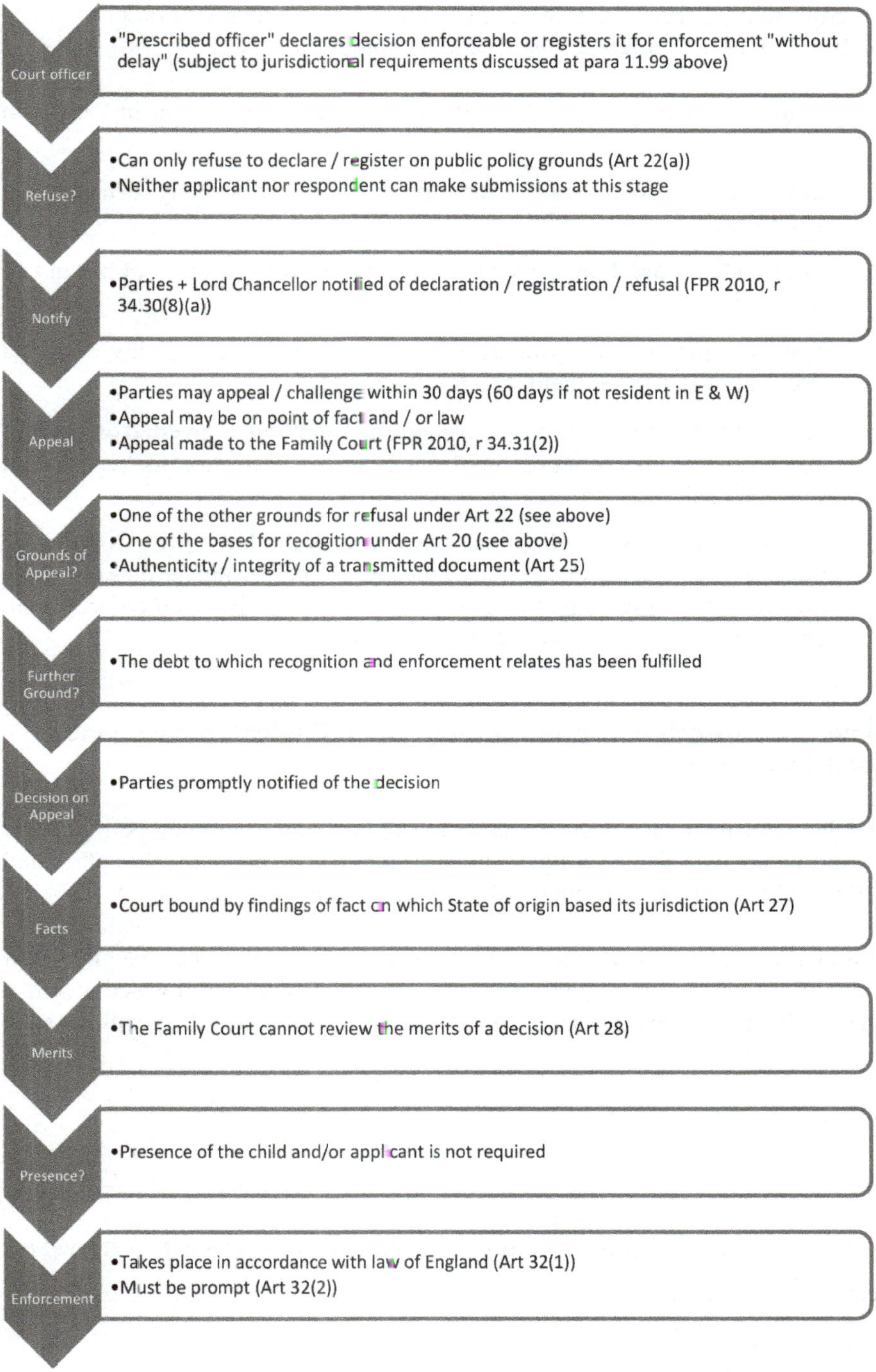

11.105 Once an order is registered for enforcement, or declared enforceable, enforcement takes place in accordance with the laws of England and Wales and the order will be enforced in the same manner as a maintenance order made by the Family Court[147]. A few things should be noted:

Court officer **may** proceed to recover sums under the order in their own name[148].

Court officer **must** recover sums under the order in their own name if arrears are 4+ weeks' old[149].

Court officer **must** take reasonable steps to notify payee of means of enforcement available to the court[150].

The court **may** order payments to be made direct to court ('may' suggests that it may also order them direct to the payee)[151].

Sums and any arrears are payable in **pounds sterling** (converted on basis of exchange rate prevailing on the date on which application for registration was received)[152].

If **interest is recoverable**, in accordance with the law of the Contracting State of origin, on the maintenance, the rate of interest and the date on which it started should form part of the application for registration/enforcement. Once registered, the interest can be enforced[153].

Onward transmission: enforcement of an English maintenance decision abroad

11.106 A maintenance decision made in England and Wales can be registered and enforced in a Contracting State by reference to the same Chapters and Articles of the Hague Convention 2007 discussed above.

FPR 2010, r 34.39 provides that, if an applicant wishes to enforce a Family Court maintenance order, they must apply for a **certified copy of the order** and **a certificate giving particulars**[154]. PD 34A provides more detail, specific to such an application[155]:

147 International Recovery of Maintenance (Hague Convention 2007 etc) Regulations 2012, SI 2012/2814, as amended (Sch.1, para.2(8)).
148 FPR 2010, r 34.33(4)(a).
149 FPR 2010, r 34.33(4)(b).
150 FPR 2010, r 34.33(2).
151 FPR 2010, r 34.32.
152 International Recovery of Maintenance (Hague Convention 2007 etc) Regulations 2012, SI 2012/2814, Sch 1 para 4 (as amended).
153 International Recovery of Maintenance (Hague Convention 2007 etc) Regulations 2012, SI 2012/2814, Sch 1 para 3 (as amended).
154 FPR 2010, r 34.39(1).
155 FPR 2010, PD34A, paras 7.1, 7.6 and 7.7.

Certified Copy of the Order =

- A sealed copy of the order
- With a certificate signed by the court officer

Certificate must include the forms required under Art 11 Hague Convention 2007 (completed by Court Officer):

- Abstract of a Decision
- Statement of Enforceability
- Statement of Proper Notice

Certificate also states:

- The jurisdictional basis on which the order was made
- With reference to the grounds for recognition / enforcement in Hague Convention 2007, Art 20(1) - see above

Index

[All references are to paragraph numbers.]